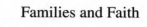

Families and Faith

Families and Faith

How Religion is Passed Down Across Generations

VERN L. BENGTSON
WITH
NORELLA M. PUTNEY
AND SUSAN C. HARRIS

OXFORD
UNIVERSITY PRESS

OXFORD
UNIVERSITY PRESS

Oxford University Press is a department of the University of
Oxford. It furthers the University's objective of excellence in research,
scholarship, and education by publishing worldwide.

Oxford   New York
Auckland   Cape Town   Dar es Salaam   Hong Kong   Karachi
Kuala Lumpur   Madrid   Melbourne   Mexico City   Nairobi
New Delhi   Shanghai   Taipei   Toronto

With offices in
Argentina   Austria   Brazil   Chile   Czech Republic   France   Greece
Guatemala   Hungary   Italy   Japan   Poland   Portugal   Singapore
South Korea   Switzerland   Thailand   Turkey   Ukraine   Vietnam

Oxford is a registered trade mark of Oxford University Press
in the UK and certain other countries.

Published in the United States of America by
Oxford University Press
198 Madison Avenue, New York, NY 10016

Library of Congress Cataloging-in-Publication Data
Bengtson, Vern L.
Families and faith : how religion is passed down across generations / Vern L. Bengtson, with
Norella Putney and Susan C. Harris.
pages cm
Includes bibliographical references and index.
ISBN 978-0-19-994865-9
1. Christian education of children.   2. Intergenerational communication—Religious aspects—
Christianity.   3. Intergenerational relations—Religious aspects—Christianity.   I. Title.
BV1475.3.B46 2013
249—dc23
2013005949

9 8 7 6 5 4 3 2
Printed in the United States of America
on acid-free paper

CONTENTS

PREFACE

Make [my way] known to your children and your children's
children... Keep these words that I am commanding you today in your
heart. Recite them to your children and talk about them when you are
at home and when you are away, when you lie down and when you
rise. (Deuteronomy 4:9, 6:6–7, New Revised Standard Version)

For more than 3,000 years, these words from the Hebrew Bible have
guided Jewish parents seeking to bring up their children in the faith.
For over 150 generations these admonitions have worked. The Jewish religion has survived despite persecution, dispersion, dispossession, prejudice, and intermarriage. This is a remarkable story of families maintaining
religious continuity across generations.

Today, however, many Jewish families today worry about whether and
how they will pass on their faith to their children in the context of contemporary American culture. They are not alone in their concerns. Parents
of all religious traditions, from Catholics to Evangelicals, Mormons to
Muslims are questioning how to effectively transmit their faith to the next
generation in today's religious pluralism.

This book is about families and how, or whether, they pass down their
faith in changing cultural circumstances. It's a very personal book, compared to most social science research reports, since it represents for me

a culmination of events that began over fifty years ago. In 1963 I was a first-year graduate student at the University of Chicago and was given a research assignment to observe a three-generation inner-city family over the year. It was the most interesting assignment I'd ever had. I was fascinated by the interactions across the generations, the family members' similarities and differences in values and behaviors, and the way their fervent religious beliefs and practices bonded the three generations together.

I too had grown up in a highly religious family. My father was a minister in a small Evangelical denomination. I remember his joking that we Bengtsons had inherited a "religion gene" from many generations back. It seems that in the 1640s, my great-great-great-great grandfather was bishop of Skara Cathedral in central Sweden. In the late 1800s, my great-grandfather was a leader in the missionary Pietistic movement that broke away from the liberal Lutheran State Church in Sweden. When I was growing up it seemed natural that all of my dad's brothers and sisters—all nine of them, and their spouses—were born-again Christians, and so were all their children, my thirty-three cousins. My family's commitment to Jesus and His teachings had stayed much the same for generations, despite the difficulties brought on by an unyielding Swedish soil, a hasty immigration to America, crop failures and losing the family farm during the depression, and then the moral challenges posed by Elvis, rock and roll, and the coming of bikinis to church summer camps in rural Minnesota. Still the family faith survived.

But at the University of Chicago, I discovered that my family's story of religious continuity across generations was quite different than the experience of my fellow students. One classmate had been a Catholic altar boy considering the priesthood but was now a confirmed atheist. A rabbi's daughter had become a Unitarian; a former Baptist was now keeping a kosher kitchen. Most of my classmates were not religious and said their parents were nonreligious too. With all this religious diversity around me, I began to wonder if my family, with our history of continuity across so many generations, wasn't sort of "weird," as one classmate not very helpfully put it.

In the years that followed, it seemed that I was to become the weak link in chain that had connected generations through faith. God didn't speak to me in the ways he spoke to my father and mother. Over the years I went from being a fundamentalist Evangelical to a moderate Presbyterian to a skeptical nonbeliever. It was a progression that increasingly distressed my family.

Religious differences in families can create profound distress. As I moved away from the Christian fundamentalism that characterized my childhood, my widowed mother became more and more distraught. When I told her I had joined a church different from the tradition in which I had been raised, she wrote me saying that I was "breaking her heart." In another letter she said this: "Vern, if I have to choose between you and my Jesus, I will choose Jesus." I couldn't understand. Why such a choice? What had I done? "You have turned your back on Jesus," she said. For the remaining twenty-six years of her life, my mother and I lived in a sort of uneasy truce. We had to avoid talking about religion—which was difficult, considering her faith and her church were the very focus of her life. To my everlasting regret, my mother died with sorrow and anger, believing that because of my "hardness of heart" she would never be able to see her only child and her grandchildren in heaven. Each of us loved the other so much, but we were formal and uneasy together because of the religious gulf between us.

My own family's story kindled a professional interest: As a social scientist, I decided I wanted to do research on the dynamics of intergenerational relationships. What is it, I wondered, that sustains religious continuity across generations in some families, and what leads to a break in that continuity in other families? In the late 1960s I began planning a research project to address these questions. Today, almost fifty years later, it has culminated in a multidecade study of four-generation families involving data from more than 3,500 grandparents, parents, grandchildren, and now great-grandchildren. The project became my academic career, helping me produce some 250 research articles and 16 books and leading to stimulating collaborations with many talented students and colleagues.[1] It provided the data on which this study is based, and this volume represents a sort of a capstone on my career.

This book addresses three major questions: (a) To what extent are parents passing on their faith in today's rapidly changing society? (b) Have the many social and cultural changes of the last half-century eroded the ability of families to transmit religion from one generation to the next? (c) Why are some parents successful at passing on their faith while other parents are not?

When my colleagues and I[1] began this project several years ago, we were starting from a hypothesis something like the following: "In the context of the profound cultural, familial, and religious changes in American society recently, intergenerational *differences* in values and religion will be more evident than intergenerational *continuities*." In other words, we expected that we would find less family transmission of religion in 2005 than was evident in 1970 This hypothesis was based on materials in both the scholarly and popular literature about the new religious directions being taken by young adults and about the growing numbers who identified themselves as not religious at all.

Now, however, as we look back on the data from this thirty-five-year research project, we see a quite different picture than we expected. Many of the results surprised us, and many appeared contrary to what could be regarded as "common knowledge" about religion and families today. For example, it is likely that a majority of Americans believe that families are not as important in influencing the values and life choices of children today as families were in the past or that today's parents and young adults are less similar in religious beliefs and practices than parents and youth were several decades ago. To these people it might seem evident that the enormous social and cultural changes over the past fifty years have decreased the likelihood of continuity across generations and that the religious diversity of today's youth represents a "generation gap" that is wider today than it was in the past.

But none of this "common knowledge" about the decline of family influence appears to be true, and the results from this thirty-five-year study show why. Our findings tell us how religious transmission occurs and why some families interested in passing on their faith succeed and others fail. However, we find the reasons for nontransmission to be different than what most churches, clergy, and youth ministers assume in designing their religious education programs. We looked at instances where parents did not pass on their faith, and discovered "Religious Rebels" and "Prodigals." We examined the unappreciated roles of grandparents (and great-grandparents) in religious influence. And we uncovered some new evidence that helps answer the question "Where are the fast-growing numbers of nonreligious youth coming from?"

We wrote this book with a variety of audiences in mind, and we think the findings from this study can have applications that are relevant to each of them. First are parents and grandparents who are interested in the religious future of their children and grandchildren. Second are the pastors, priests, rabbis, and youth leaders in churches and synagogues who are concerned about transmitting their faith to a younger generation. Religious education programs are intended to foster religious transmission, as evident in Sunday school classes, catechesis, youth groups, mothers' groups—but, as we point out in chapter 10, most congregations are missing a crucial point. If they really want to help families encourage religious continuity across generations, they will have to do something additional. Third, scholars and researchers in religion will find the results of this study important too, because some of the longitudinal data presented in this book challenge previous claims about families, religion, and trends over time. The results also contribute to sociological theory about families, socialization, and the life course. In the final chapter we discuss the concept of "intergenerational religious momentum," which ties together many of these findings, and present a theoretical model that can help to identify family and non-family influences on youths' religious practices and beliefs.

Because we wrote the book with a variety of audiences in mind—researchers, family members, clergy, religious education directors, the general public—we have tried to keep it nontechnical with statistics and figures as uncomplicated as possible. Readers interested in knowing more about the research methods and procedures in this thirty-five year study will find details in the Appendix.

To conclude: As for me personally, something unexpected happened on my way toward finishing this project on families and religion. On Easter Sunday three years ago, I wandered into a church service. Suddenly I was overwhelmed by the music and beauty, and bowled over by recollections and revelations—utterly "surprised by joy," as C.S. Lewis described his own later-life religious experience.[2] I came back. So these days I'm in church every Sunday, singing away in the choir. Every Thursday I'm there at a noon Bible study, and on Monday nights there's a theology study group. They put me on the Vestry, the church governing body, so I'm spending even more time there. In looking back over how things have turned out for me religiously, I think my father and grandfather would be pleased. I hope my mom would too.

ACKNOWLEDGEMENTS

This project has benefited greatly from the help and support of many individuals over the years. Thanks first to The John Templeton Foundation whose grant enabled the collection of interview data for this project and in particular to Dr. Kimon Sargeant, Vice-President for Human Sciences, for his encouragement, support, and advice. The survey data collection over thirty-five years has been supported by the National Institute on Aging and the National Institute of Mental Health; these two federal agencies provided almost continuous funding over four decades and eight waves of surveys for the Longitudinal Study of Generations (LSOG) on which this study is based. Thanks to Dr. Merril Silverstein, now at Syracuse University, who was the principal investigator of the LSOG during the final years of this project and a collaborator in the data analysis. Thanks also to Dr. Don Miller, director of the Center for Civic and Religious Culture (CCRC) and professor of religion at the University of Southern California (USC), who was co-principal investigator of the Templeton grant and whose suggestions for the project have always been right on. Thanks to Brie Loskota, also of CCRC, for her imaginative advice and support during the life of this project, and to Linda Hall, administrative manager in the Leonard Davis School of Gerontology at USC, who worked with me on the LSOG for many years.

A number of talented people helped to develop the research on which this book is based. I first want to acknowledge my enormous debt to Dr. Norella Putney and Dr. Susan Harris, who collaborated with me in the data collection, analysis, and writing on this project and whose names are therefore listed on the title page. Norella Putney was the central administrator of the project, serving as project director for more than five years. In addition to conducting many of the interviews, she led the analyses on marriage, divorce, and religious transmission. Susan Harris was the project's qualitative data director. In addition to coordinating the interview component and developing the coding system using the Atlas.ti computerized system, she developed the analysis of trends across age cohorts presented in chapter 2.

We worked with a creative group of doctoral and postdoctoral students on this project. In addition to conducting interviews, developing family case studies, and contributing to data analyses over the five years of the project, they each contributed to topics that became chapters. Dr. Frances Nedjat-Haiem assisted in the interviewing and data analyses for the chapters on religious "nones" (chapter 8) and Mormons, Jews, and Evangelicals (chapter 9). Joy Lam assisted in analyses on marriage, divorce, and remarriage (chapter 6), Thien-Huong Ninh on "nones" (chapter 8), and Petrice Oyama on parent–child relations (chapter 4) and grandparents (chapter 5). Other graduate students who conducted interviews were Postdoctoral Fellow Dr. Gary Horlacher, who worked with Merril Silverstein and me on some innovative multivariate analyses examining trends over time at both individual and cohort levels of analysis and assisted with chapters 3, 4, and 9. Ernie Horstmanshoff conducted interviews in Utah and wrote some of the most interesting family case studies; he also assisted in the analyses for chapter 9. Other graduate students who conducted interviews were Casey Copen, Betty Oswald, Julia Garami, Dr. Kara Lemma, Cecilia Poon, and Dr. Margaret Sallee. Dr. Roseann Giarrusso, LSOG project director, and Danielle Zucker of the LSOG staff also provided invaluable assistance in managing the LSOG database.

I was privileged to work with a wonderful editor, Jana Riess, whose skill enabled reducing a manuscript of 130,000 words down to 90,000 without losing the family stories it needed to get its message across. She is also the author of an engaging book, *Flunking Sainthood: A Year of Breaking the Sabbath, Forgetting to Pray, and Still Loving My Neighbor,* which is a useful companion to the discussion of Mormon, Jewish, and Evangelical families in chapter 10. I am very grateful to her.

Professors Mark Regnerus and Rhys Williams, two of today's powerhouses in the sociology of religion, provided insightful comments and suggestions on an earlier draft of this manuscript, as did Professors Malcolm Johnson and Victor Marshall, leaders in the sociology of the life course and aging, and Dr. Richard Flory. I also am grateful to my graduate students at USC for their critiques and suggestions on chapters: Matthew Bressette, Alexis Coulourides, Sandra Florian, Danielle Hall, Shoshana Hindin, Jeff Laguna, Sara McCleskey, Joohong Min, Brad Nabors, Samantha Rasnake, and Sara Bonnell.

Several other people helped to bring this project to fruition in ways of which they were probably not aware. They include Dr. Michael Polo; Dr. Keith Witt; Dr. Grey Brothers; The Rev. Mark Asman; Dr. Maria Schmeeckle; Dr. Keith Witt; the Trinity Episcopal Church Choir; Irene, Joyce, Anne, Yvonne, Anne, and Bill of the EfM group; Pris, Laura, Sue, and Barbara of the Pasadena Mission: the Renaissance art class; Linda, Gary, Danielle, George, Peggy, and others of the Santa Barbara Friday Morning Happy group.

Thanks also to the priests, ministers, rabbis, Mormon bishops, and campus religious life leaders who gave their time to discuss with me the implications of our findings and the ways families in their congregations might find them useful. They also provided the interviews that are summarized in chapter 10. Their names are, in alphabetical order (except for two who requested that their names not be used): The Rev. Mark Asman, Carrie Brothers, Dr. Peter Buehler (with Susan Croshaw), Dr. James Burklo, Rabbi Stephen Cohen, Father Paul Devot, Monsignor Stephen Downes, Dr. James Heft, Dr. Hilary Chrisley (with Teresa Pietch), The Rev. Don Johnson, Dr. Glen Libby, Dr. Aaron McEmerys, Dr. E.R. Mitchell, Pastor Troy Spilman, Ft. Varum Soni, LDS Bishop Paul Sorensen, The Rev. Dennis Wadley, and Vanessa Woods.

In looking back over the process of writing this book, my greatest debt concerns the amazing help and support of my family—my wife, Hannah; my daughters, Julie, Erin, and Kristina; and my grandchildren Zoe, Zadin, and Tyler. Their love and support enabled me to weather some challenging times in my life and to relish the good times too. Hannah is the wisest woman I have ever met, and her years of teaching writing skills to sixth-graders came in handy as she edited each and every chapter in this volume. My daughter Kristina helped me by retyping many of the chapters and correcting my errors.

Vern L. Bengtson
University of Southern California

Families and Faith

PART I | Families, Religion, and a Century of Change

CHAPTER 1 | Families of Faith
Challenges to Continuity

Generation (G) 3 Irene Turner was seventeen in 1970 when she first
participated in the thirty-five-year Longitudinal Study of Generations
(LSOG) surveys. She identified herself then as a "born-again
Christian," reported attending a Southern Baptist church three times
a week, and described herself as "very religious." In this she was
following the Evangelical tradition of her mother, G2 Eleanor, as well
as her grandmother, G1 Grace. All were participants in the first LSOG
survey, and all reported being "very religious" members of the Baptist
church. In 2006 we interviewed Irene again, when she was fifty-three.
She said she was still active in a Baptist church and added, "God is
the center of my life."

In 2005 we interviewed Irene's G4 daughter Sarah, born in 1980.
When we asked about her religious affiliation, she stated, "I don't
have any right now." She said that when growing up she went to
church often and participated in youth groups, following in her
family's Baptist tradition. But when she went to college, she began
to think that what her church defined as "sin" was quite arbitrary and
that the church members were hypocrites because their actions were
not consistent with what they professed. Much to the dismay of her
parents and grandparents, she stopped going to church. Now twenty-
seven, she says she has no intention of going back. But both her
mother and father, in their interviews, say that they pray every day for
her return to the faith.

IN THIS FAMILY'S STORY, we see a recent departure from a tradition of religious continuity across several generations. Sarah's great-grandmother Grace had transmitted her Evangelical faith to her daughter Eleanor, who in turn had successfully passed it on her daughter Irene. But with Irene's daughter Sarah, a member of the Millennial generation, there has been a break in this Evangelical Christian family's several-generation continuity in religion, at least for the present.

Why? How did this break happen? This is an important question, but one for which we have had few answers based on solid data. It is important to religious parents, whose faith forms the core of what is most valuable to them in life, what has meant the most to them, and what they would like to pass on to their children. For these parents, the child's acceptance or rejection of their religious faith is a source of joy or sadness. It is important for churches and religious leaders, because the vitality of their community depends on parents in their congregations transmitting their faith across generations. It is also important to religious scholars and researchers, since the question of how and why religious continuity occurs, or does not occur, in the context of rapid social and cultural change, is a puzzle yet to be solved.

An Era of Remarkable Change

The oldest of the Baby Boomers in our study were, like Irene, just entering adulthood in 1970 when we first surveyed them, their parents, and their grandparents. Today these Early boomers are parents of the Generation Xers like Sarah, whom we interviewed in 2006–2008.

How have the dynamics of intergenerational relationships about religion changed over the thirty-five years since the beginning of this study? In the context of the many demographic and cultural changes that have occurred during that time—increases in marital instability and single parenting, a growing cultural emphasis on individualism, declining adherence to religious traditions, media-driven youth cultures—has there been a significant change in the degree to which families exert influence in the religious orientations of younger generation members?

Changes in Ameri`can Society

During the 117 years represented by the birth dates of family members in this study, many events have combined to change the nature of American

society. Wars, disruptive economic trends, globalization and technologi-
cal innovations, changes in culture and political values—these and more
have altered the lives of successive generations of study participants.
Many of the oldest immigrated to the United States at the beginning of
the twentieth century; subsequently, they experienced the massive cultural and economic ups and downs of World War I, the Roaring Twenties
era of prosperity, and the subsequent economic devastation of the Great
Depression.

Then came World War II and the dislocations it created for everyone
involved in the war effort, including most young men and women. The
economic prosperity and stability of the postwar period provided an era of
seemingly inexhaustible growth and expansion. This soon gave way to the
political and cultural changes of the 1960s when the first wave of Baby-
Boomer youth launched protests challenging the politics, values, and life-
styles of their elders. The term "generation gap" became a byword for the
social unrest during this decade, since it appeared that American society
was becoming divided along lines that separated the younger generation
from their parents and grandparents.[1]

About this time, in the 1960s, social commentators began calling attention to the growing secularization of American society, prompting heated
public debates about the role of religion in education, politics, and mass
communication. In the decades to follow, collective and humanistic values
appeared to give way to an ethos of individualism and self-fulfillment and
a devaluation of community.[2] This was a trend that seemed to be leading to
what Robert Putnam famously called "bowling alone"[3]—from collective,
community-based activities to those pursued by solitary individuals acting almost in relative isolation compared to their peers in earlier decades.
In the years following 2000, it appeared that stock market and real estate
speculation, predatory lending, political polarization, and a growing
gap between the very wealthy and the middle and working classes were
symptoms of a decline in communal values and the rise of self-interest to
new heights. Because of this, many people today assume that the value
accorded in the past to intergenerational continuity has eroded, a casualty of cultural changes involving greater individualism. But is this the
case? Throughout Western history, during times of rapid social change,
two social institutions have often served to buffer individuals from the
uncertainties resulting from unanticipated events: the family and religion.
Does this hold true today?

Changes in American Families

Since World War II, there has been unprecedented change at the most intimate level of American society: family life. The rate of divorce increased slowly through the first half of the twentieth century and then rose dramatically over the next few decades. By 1990, one out of every two marriages ended in divorce,[4] and by the end of the century, almost as many children lived in single-parent households—most headed by mothers—as in dual-parent households. Of those children in two-parent households, one-quarter lived in "blended" families with stepparents and stepsiblings.

Statistics like these led to a chorus of public concern in the late 1980s about the "decline of the American family."[5] Particularly vocal were conservative politicians and religious leaders who saw moral decline related to a decrease in traditional family functions. Among sociologists, the most articulate proponent of this view was sociologist David Popenoe.[6] Most dismaying to Popenoe was the negative effects of high divorce rates on effective family functioning with respect to children, such as providing them with emotional, educational, and moral foundations. All this, he argued, fragmented family effectiveness and dissipated the positive influence of parents on the young.

The message of declining family influence continues to this day. Psychologist Jeffery Arnett finds little evidence for family influences in the lives of young adults, emphasizing "how little relationship there is between the religious training they received [from parents] through childhood and the religious beliefs they hold by the time they reach emerging adulthood."[7] Paul Vitz, a psychologist with the Catholic Youth Council, says, "When one puts the big picture together, the decline of the American family is obvious."[8]

The "family decline" argument has, however, been rebutted by other scholars. Family historian Stephanie Coontz[9] has pointed to the fallacy of romanticizing families of the past, noting that high maternal mortality rates left even more children in single-parent or blended family households in the nineteenth century than is the case with children from divorced families today. Scott Myers, in a longitudinal study comparing young adults with their parents twelve years earlier, concluded that "parents' religiosity is the primary influence on the religiosity of their adult offspring."[10] Christian Smith and Melinda Denton, on the basis of their groundbreaking National Study of Youth and Religion data, say, "Contrary to misguided cultural stereotypes and frequent parental misperceptions, we believe that the evidence clearly shows that the single most important social influence on the religious and spiritual lives of adolescents is their parents."[11]

Changes in American Religion

While in many families the religious practices and beliefs of parents greatly affects those of their children, in the broader society American religion itself has changed over the past few decades. Involvement in churches increased sharply following World War II, hitting a peak in 1950–1959. Then starting in the 1960s church attendance gradually declined, with the sharpest decrease occurring in the period from 1970 to 1980. Attendance then increased until 1986 but made a sharp downturn in the 1990s, followed by participation creeping up and then down in the 2000s.[12] Membership in both mainline Protestant and Roman Catholic churches reflected these trends, growing through World War II but seeing sharp declines in the 1970s and 1980s, though with the influx of Hispanic immigrants the number of Catholics has remained stable in the past two decades, offsetting losses among non-Hispanic whites. Evangelical Protestant churches experienced significant growth during this time, growing considerably from 1974 to 1993, but then their numbers declined slightly until 2004, followed by a small increase, and then began declining again.[13] Mormons emerged in the 1990s as the fastest-growing Christian community in America, although there are signs the rate of Mormon growth may be softening.[14]

But what seems most remarkable is the increase in the numbers of "nones" in American society—those who say they are "none of the above," who claim no traditional religious affiliation. By 2012 the unaffiliated represented almost 20% of the U.S. adult population, having doubled in just one decade.[15] The religiously unaffiliated are a varied group, as we discuss in chapter 8. Some are explicitly antireligious, articulate in their discomfort with any institutional form of religion such as churches, creeds, priests, ministers, or rabbis. Others are skeptical about God or have only vague beliefs about religion, while some define themselves as "spiritual but not religious." Many of the unaffiliated think of themselves as being religious, but they just don't go to religious services. Still others say they are still looking to find a religion they feel meets their needs.

In analyzing these trends, a number of religious researchers have described a rapid diversification of faith in our society, what Wade Clark Roof terms a growing "religious pluralism."[16] Others suggest that American religion has become culturally individualistic and subjectivist or point to the growth of religious "seekers" who have consumer mentalities about faith.[17] Related to this is the observation that a religion of "place," located in church traditions and creeds that characterized much of the twentieth century, has been supplanted by a religion of seekers who shop around for those elements of religious experience deemed more promising or fulfilling.[18] Still others argue that American religion is losing its meaning and coherence as individuals create their own personal belief systems by mixing and matching spiritual practices from diverse faiths.[19] Finally, many scholars see a growing separation between "spirituality" and "religion"[20] and increased individuation of religion, as linked to the increased diversity characterizing America's emerging adults, leading to what Jeffery Arnett and Lena Jensen have called "a congregation of one."[21]

Changes in American Youth

The nature and characteristics of the young adult population in American society have changed significantly over the past few decades. In 1970 when we began this study the Early Boomers, born between 1946 and 1954, represented a huge addition to the population, the product of the sharp increase in births following World War II. At the time of our first survey, these teenagers and young adults represented a larger proportion of the American population than those in their teens and twenties today. They also turned out to be an advantaged cohort in adult life, achieving higher levels of education and higher average incomes than any previous age group in American history.

There are a number of ways that the "emerging adults"[22] of today, ages 18 to 30, differ from the Early Boomers. Perhaps the greatest difference is that today's young adults, compared to earlier-born cohorts, are more likely to experience life course events, such as marriage and parenthood, later and outside of "traditional" family contexts. Comparing the demographic characteristics of youth in 1970 and youth in 2005—corresponding to the two bookends of data we report in this book—we can see that:

- In terms of marriage, in 1970, 38% of women age 20 to 24 had not married; in 2005 the figure was almost 40 percentage points higher at 76%.[23] Furthermore, the average age at which marriage occurred in 2005 had increased by about four years for men and five years for women.[24]

- Today's youth are staying in school longer and completing their education later by an average of almost three years compared to 1970.[25]
- For those who do marry, although the overall divorce rate has not changed much since the 1960s and 1970s, divorce rates have diverged by education level: They have increased for those without high school diplomas while decreasing for the college-educated, for whom the age at marriage is considerably higher.[26]
- While in 1950 only 5% of all births occurred outside marriage, in 2006, 38% of births did.[27]
- The percentage of children living in single-parent households was about 25% in 1970; it was 44% in 2005.[28]

Thus, there are striking differences in demographic characteristics between today's twenty-somethings and those of thirty-five years ago. Other contrasts between them have been drawn in terms of political involvement and what has been called "generational consciousness."[29] Then there is the issue of diversity. America's emerging adults today reflect a greater extent of within-age-group differences than did the youth of the 1960s and 1970s. There is greater diversity in age at marriage, numbers of children, years and timing of schooling, ethnic and gender identities, partnerships and living arrangements than perhaps any other cohort in American history. This diversity is reflected also in emerging adults' religion and spirituality.

The spiritual and religious orientations of emerging adults have been the focus of many recently published books—some based on social science surveys of youth and religion, others reflecting concerns of religious leaders and youth ministers, and still others analyzing more general aspects of "delayed" adulthood. The many ways in which these writers characterize the religious beliefs and practices of today's young adults is a study in diversity. Some describe how American youth, alienated from traditional religious expression, are constructing more authentic versions of spirituality for themselves—with many becoming part of the growing number of religious nones.[30] Several others see a trend in which youth are increasingly returning to religious tradition, orthodoxy, and conservative certainty.[31] Still others have identified a self-oriented, instrumental religious style emerging among contemporary American teenagers—what Christian Smith and his colleagues in their survey of youth and religion have named the "Moralistic Therapeutic Deism"[32] brand of religion that is based only loosely on Christian theology or church tradition.[33] Perhaps, as Robert Wuthnow has suggested, many twenty- and thirty-somethings today can best be labeled "spiritual shoppers."[34]

Awareness of such religious complexity among emerging adults has led to creative attempts to label this diverse generation in religious terms. Princeton Theological Seminary professor Kenda Creasy Dean developed a manual titled *OMG: A Youth Ministry Handbook* to help church youth leaders become more conversant about young people's spiritual growth.[35] In her book, *Almost Christian: What the Faith of our Teenagers Is Telling the American Church,* Dean describes teens as "worshipping at the church of benign whatever-ism."[36] In *Generation Ex-Christian: Why Young Adults Are Leaving the Faith...and How to Bring Them Back,* author Drew Dyck calls attention to what he calls the "postmodern leavers."[37] David Kinnaman, president of the Barna Group, an Evangelical polling and consulting group, looks at perceptions of what he calls the "outsiders"—the 24 million non-Christians in the United States who are sixteen-to twenty-nine-years-old—in his book, *unChristian: What a New Generation Really Thinks about Christianity...And Why it Matters.*[38] Richard Flory and Don Miller, two of the well-respected social scientists documenting the sweeping, worldwide Pentecostal movement, have also described the spiritual quest of the Post-Boomer generation.[39] Carol Howard Merritt writes about what she sees emerging in the *Tribal Church: Ministering to the Missing Generation.*[40] And in *Googling God: The Religious Landscape of People in Their 20s and 30s,* Catholic Youth Ministry director Mike Hayes discusses contemporary young adults' belief that "instant gratification is merely a click of a mouse away," a view they apply "to every area of their life, including religion."[41]

Some important studies have pointed to religious differences between age groups that have become pronounced since World War II. Wade Clark Roof, in his pioneering work on the role of Baby Boomers as religious trendsetters, calls them "a generation of seekers" because of their contrast to older Americans who held firmly to more traditional expressions of religiosity.[42] In a follow-up study, *Spiritual Marketplace: Baby Boomers and the Remaking of American Religion*, Roof describes how the Boomers created a market for diverse religious and spiritual practices that, he felt, represents the wave of the future in American religion.[43] In a similar vein, Robert Wuthnow, another giant in the sociology of religion, titled his 2007 best-seller *After the Baby Boomers: How Twenty- and Thirty-Somethings Are Shaping the Future of American Religion.*[44] His thesis is that "the religion and spirituality of young adults is a cultural *bricolage* [French for mosaic or patchwork constructed improvisationally from the increasingly diverse materials at hand."[45]

The Intertwining of Family and Religion

Given the tremendous changes that have occurred in American culture, families, and religion over the past half-century, one might reasonably conclude that these institutions have less and less influence on the religious outcomes of today's youth. In the eyes of many, families have lost a disturbing amount of their moral and religious influence, seemingly a consequence of parental divorce, excessive individualism, and a breakdown in traditional social structures. From this perspective, if parents are passing religion on to their children, they are not doing it very often or very well.

That is certainly the storyline of the mass media in discussing age groups and religion; it is also an unfortunate implication of some researchers in the field of religion. For example, the lack of intergenerational religious transmission is suggested in Robert Putnam and David Campbell's book, *American Grace: How Religion Divides and Unites Us*. In discussing their survey data showing that 40% to 45% of white Americans have switched from their childhood religion at some point in their lives, Putnam and Campbell conclude: "In short, it is misleading to think of religious identity in contemporary America as an inherited and stable characteristic."[46] Catholic Youth Ministry researcher David Dornan goes further, saying that "the research clearly shows that families are not passing on their religious values to children."[47] Developmental psychologist Jeffery Arnett agrees, arguing that this is because of emerging adults' rejection of parental values and beliefs. Emerging adults insist "on making their own choices about what to believe and what to value," he writes. "In their religious beliefs there is little relation between what they were exposed to by their parents in childhood and adolescence, and what they believe now, as emerging adults."[48]

Yet we are reminded that families and religion have been functionally connected as long as we have record of families or religion.[49] These are the two social institutions most directly concerned with passing on standards of moral behavior and the continuity of social order from one generation to the next.[50] Rather than concluding that there has been a decline in parental influence and religious inheritance in American society over recent decades,[51] we present this as the fundamental question for exploration in this book. The major questions of our research are:

1. To what extent are families able to pass on their religious faith to the next generation in today's rapidly changing society?

2. How has this changed over the past several decades, in the context of remarkable cultural, familial, and religious change in American society?
3. Why are some families able to achieve their goal of transmitting their faith to their children while others are not?

To answer such questions requires facts—reliable data collected according to the best standards of social science—and theory—testable explanations that provide understanding of the "why" behind what we find in our data. The theory we use in this book is called the "life course perspective."[52] We find this to be the most useful way to interpret and understand the intersection of families, religion, and time The life course perspective focuses on the influences represented by historical time ("period"), biographical time ("age"), and generational time ("cohort") and the way these intertwine to mold human behavior.[53]

An important concept of the life course perspective has to do with "linked lives"—the idea that, as individuals develop, their development is enmeshed with the developing lives of others in their social network, particularly parents and grandparents (or children and grandchildren). This is an important insight; our religious identities, for example, develop in ways that are linked to our parents' religious identities—which might change over time and might even be influenced by our evolving spirituality. This goes beyond the picture of a passive child receiving religious input from a parent. In addition, as life expectancy increases, one of the most obvious implications is that of "longer years of linked lives" than ever before in human history.[54] Today's young adults, for example, have experienced more contact with and influence by their grandparents than have any previous cohort of children and youth, a topic we discuss in chapter 5.

Surprisingly little research, however, has looked at the extent to which the linked lives of parents and children translates into enduring parental influences persisting into adulthood[55] or at the characteristics of religious transmission from the perspective of both parent and child.[56] We also do not know whether such influence can be seen across more than two generations—from grandparents to grandchildren, for example. These are issues we explore in various ways throughout this book, testing the common belief that there is diminishing religious inheritance in American society and that intergenerational religious transmission has weakened since the 1960s.

Moreover, we do not have research-based knowledge about *how* parental religious transmission occurs and *why* it doesn't. What we have are generalized exhortations from the pulpit about "train up a child in the way he should go, and when he is old he will not depart from it," and our churches and synagogues have a vast array of Sunday-school programs and a host of activities for children and youth, but these are based on often vague traditions and don't really focus on what *families* should, or should not, do to be effective in sustaining religious continuity. Church leaders and religious education directors have little in the way of science-based information to help them explain to parents what works and what doesn't in religious socialization. Religious leaders and parents need to know more about what we call "religious momentum across generations," how it can be encouraged, and why the momentum sometimes stops.

Before we turn to these issues, we want to illustrate what we mean by the intergenerational religious influences we will examine in the chapters to follow. To do this, we introduce the Pooles,[57] a four-generation family in our study with a mixed pattern of religious transmission across the thirty-five years of our research. The Poole family illustrates the similarities and differences in religion and spirituality that we find in our study, as well as some of the family processes that account for such transmission or nontransmission of faith.

The Pooles: "Religion Comes from Within the Heart"

G1 Edith Poole ("G1" refers to the first and oldest generation in our study) was ninety-seven at the time we interviewed her in 2007, still amazingly lively and articulate, though living in an extended care facility. In 1970 she participated in the first LSOG survey and provided us with data at each of the seven survey waves thereafter. She was born in 1910 and grew up on a poor share-cropper's farm in Arkansas, as did her husband Ben. During the Depression they migrated to California to escape the Dust Bowl. For several years they were migrant farm workers, picking any crop they could find and barely keeping their family alive. But when World War II began, their fortunes changed. Ben found work in southern California at a steel manufacturing plant, making parts for military planes. It turned out that he had found his niche in factory work, away from the fields. He began moving up the ranks, eventually becoming a supervisor. He and Edith formed a stable, blue-collar family. Ben was a member of a union, which provided medical benefits through a large southern California health care plan. It was from the membership rolls of this organization that, in 1969, we drew the original sample for the LSOG—and that is how Ben and Edith and their family came to be part of the study. The LSOG now involves more than (3,500) members of 357 multigenerational families. The Pooles were one of twenty-five such families whose members we later interviewed for the current study of families and faith.

At the time of Edith's interview in 2007, Ben had been deceased for six years. Their descendants numbered three children, fourteen grandchildren, and at least eleven great-grandchildren, as shown in the family genogram in Figure 1.1. Edith was not exactly sure about the number of great-grandchildren because there had been a rupture in family relations starting with one of her grand children, Bruce, a zealous Evangelical convert who had severed relations with the rest of the family.

There is considerable religious variation in the four generations of Edith and Ben's family, as we can see in Figure 1.1. Edith has been a dedicated member of the Methodist Church all her life, and only with advancing years has her attendance dwindled. Edith's husband Ben identified himself as a Methodist at the time of our first survey, in 1970; he also said he was "not very religious" and attended church only "once or twice a year." He gave similar responses in successive surveys up to 2000, shortly before he died—religion did not seem very important in his life. For Edith, religion

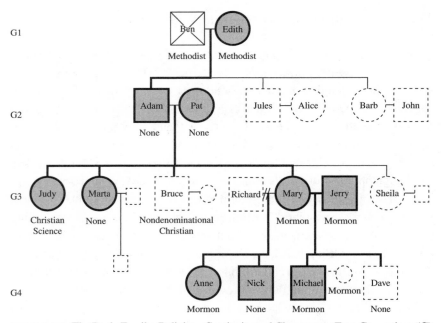

FIGURE 1.1 The Poole Family: Religious Continuity and Change over Four Generations (G)

was central. In 1970 she reported that she was "very religious" and ranked religious participation very high on her list of personal values. She said the same on each of the eight surveys over the next thirty-five years, although with advancing years her attendance at church services declined from "weekly" in 1970 to "several times a year" in 1988 and "never" in 2005.

Edith was highly devout and made every effort to raise her children in her Methodist faith. However, she emphasized that she wanted them to have the freedom to choose their own way to faith—even if that meant going outside her church. As she phrased it in her 2007 interview, "Religion comes from the heart I think everyone has to choose for himself." She says she had her children attend Sunday school and church with her until they were twelve or thirteen but then gave them the freedom to decide for themselves. "My minister didn't agree with that, but it's just the way I felt," she reported.

Edith's and Ben's three children, G2s Adam, Julius ("Jules"), and Barbara ("Barb"), were all raised Methodist. Two of them, Jules and Barbara (neither of whom we interviewed in 2007 but who had provided surveys since 1970), have followed in the path of their mother's religious devotion. Edith told us that they both have been leaders in their local church. She said that one of her grandsons, Barbara's son, is a minister in the Methodist church.

But Edith's other son Adam, age seventy-seven, is different. When we interviewed him in 2007 and asked about his religion he said, "I don't have any. I don't need it." He seems to have inherited his father's nonreligious views. In his 1970 survey, when he was forty-five, Adam identified his affiliation as Methodist (the same as his mother) but said he was "not at all" religious (like his father) and never attended church. In later surveys he reported having no affiliation and ranked religious participation last in a list of nine values in life. He is what we call "religiously indifferent"—it's not that he rejects religion; he just does not think about it very much.

Adam's wife, Pat, seventy-six, says they didn't press religion on their children; if they wanted to go to church or Sunday school, the parents would gladly give them a ride, but if they didn't wish to go, they didn't have to. "We wanted to support them in seeking their own paths. That's what my parents did for me," Pat says. "Then they turned out to be more religious than Adam and I are!"

Their four children (a fifth, Sheila, is deceased) indeed have turned out to be more religious than their parents but in quite different ways. The oldest is Judy, who at age fifty-seven said she is a very religious, "self-realized Christian" in the Christian Science tradition but attends church services only occasionally. She went on: "God and I are OK—Jesus and angels too. Love is the way." She feels that churches are unimportant and that people don't "need to be sitting in a building to be near to God." She joined the Christian Science church in college and reads Mary Baker Eddy's meditations frequently. Judy never married and has no children.

Judy's sister Marta, age fifty-five, identified herself as "moderately religious and very spiritual." Like Judy, Marta is a seeker who has studied other religions, including Catholicism, Mormonism, and Evangelical Protestantism. "I think, basically, I found that everybody wants to be good, do good, and as long as people behave that way, I'm happy." Marta had one child who died in infancy. She divorced and has not remarried. When asked about her religious affiliation, Marta stated that she had none. She says that several years ago she "backed away from the organized part, but I certainly haven't backed away from my spiritual or faith part." She attends church once in a while in a "multiple of different churches, if I'm invited." She emphasizes that she's "not affiliated, really, with any one [religious] organization. My spirituality is based on my beliefs in God and Jesus Christ and the way people live their lives. . . . [I pray] every morning and every night and a lot of times in between."

We don't know much about Judy and Marta's brother G3 Bruce because he has refused to participate in any of the LSOG surveys. From other family members we learned that he is a fervent Evangelical with a passion for "saving souls." We also heard that Bruce has precipitated a number of family conflicts over religion. Two of his sisters, Judy (Christian Science) and Mary (Mormon), told us Bruce had proclaimed that God would punish them for their lack of belief in the Christ of the Bible—*his* Bible. He has not had contact with the family for several years. Though he has been married and has children, Adam and Pat don't know how many children he has, and the Poole family has no contact with any of them.

Mary is the fourth of Adam and Pat's children, and she is very religious. As a nineteen-year-old in her 1970 survey, she identified herself as "having Methodist leanings" but said she was only "somewhat religious." After a short marriage that produced two children, she moved to a small community in eastern Oregon as a single mother. In her 1985 survey, she said she felt alone and very lost, and she worried about not finding someone to share her life with. In 1988 she reported she had converted to the Mormon faith after marrying Jerry, who was "from a long line of Mormons way back." In her 2007 interview Mary, then fifty-four, expressed absolute certainty about her beliefs and about the teachings of her church: "I have a strong testimony of the Church I belong to," she said. "I know my Heavenly Father lives. I know that Jesus Christ is my Savior and that He is my older brother and that I love Him and that He loves me." Mary was upset with her brother Bruce because of his intolerance and his beliefs about Mormons. Bruce had told her repeatedly that he was praying for her because Mormonism was a cult founded by a false prophet. Mary criticized Bruce's religion: "It's like going out and sitting on a rock in the woods."

Mary has four children who she has raised to be active, committed Mormons, with "Sundays, Family Home Evening on Mondays, Seminary before school, Wednesdays after school, missions—the whole bit," she says. She and her husband have made every effort to see that their children follow them in the Mormon faith. Their rigorous efforts in religious upbringing have turned out to be a partial success, since two of her young adult children are following the Mormon faith. But the other two are not.

Mary's oldest daughter, G4 Anne is still single at age thirty-four. She says she feels embarrassed about being an unmarried Mormon woman at her age. She talks about her wish to find a mate she can marry in a Mormon Temple wedding, a sacred rite reserved for Latter-Day Saints who adhere to certain standards of the church like tithing and keeping the "Word of Wisdom" (dietary laws that forbid alcohol and caffeine). She talked about moving to a community that is "99% Mormon—I can count on two hands the number of nonmembers" who live there, so, by her account, it is likely that she will marry a Mormon. She believes "in a God that blesses us and has given His son for us and given His law that we should live by, and the church and its teaching, and that's all you need in life." She feels "extremely close" to her mother and "very close" to her stepfather. She "prays constantly" for her brother Nick, who has left the Mormon faith.

On the other hand, G4 Nick, age thirty-two, says he is a "none" when it comes to religion, "maybe a Mormon, 'cause that's how I was raised. But I haven't gone to church in the last seventeen years." Raised by Mary and Jerry in a strict Mormon family context, he finds some aspects of the religion hypocritical: "There's some people around that I see doing things that I don't approve of, and then they're sitting in the front row in church every Sunday. That kind of pushes me away from it," he explains. "As I grew up I started drinking a little bit and I still enjoy some of that, some of the outside pleasures that the church doesn't approve of. So I don't want to be sitting in the front row every Sunday if I've been drinking on Saturday night."

Nick volunteers that his mother's father, G2 Adam, does not go to church either. "I must take after my grandfather and not my mom," he says. His mother, Mary, is concerned that Nick is not active in the Latter-Day Saints Church. Theirs is a complicated relationship. We have survey data from Nick starting in 1991, the year we began enrolling the great-grandchildren in the LSOG panel as soon as they turned age 16. In that survey and in subsequent ones, he said his relationship with his mother was "not at all close," that he was "not at all similar" to her, and yet that he felt he understood her "very well." He also reported that he felt "not close" to his stepfather Jerry.

With G4 Michael, twenty-three, the story is quite different. Mary says that he is the "most religious person in the family" and that she feels "very close" to him. In his 2007 interview, Michael said he had just returned from his two-year Mormon mission. He talked about how much he enjoyed sharing his testimony with non-Mormons every day during his mission and spoke with obvious enthusiasm about the Mormon faith:

> As I am getting older I am realizing for myself that I want the Church more in my life.... The Church is all around the little town that I grew up in. I mean, it's the reason that the town is there...Just like God is the reason that *we* are here. He created the heavens and the earth and sent us here to live with Him or to live in a body of flesh and blood, and he sent his only begotten Son so that we may go back to live with Him again (in heaven). So everything we do, everything around us has to do with Him.

In his interview, Michael talked with a great deal of warmth about his mother and his paternal grandparents, who are from a long line of Mormons.

Another son, G4 Dave, who is nineteen, was not interviewed for this study and has not participated in the LSOG surveys. According to his brother Nick, Dave was raised strictly Mormon like his siblings and like them began to attend the Mormon seminary classes every morning before his high school began. But after a few years, Dave quit and seems to have no intention of attending church again. He is not close to his parents, says Nick, "and they tried to push religion down his throat. He just rebelled. It was too much." But his parents have not given up hope. "They still pray for us and hope we will come back," Nick says.

Doing Research on Families and Faith

The story of the Poole family over four generations and across the thirty-five years of this study illustrates many of the issues and questions we address in this book. Why do some children stay on the path of their parents' religion while others take a different way? What are the circumstances under which continuity or discontinuity occurs across generations? How are religious and spiritual values transmitted—what are the processes and mechanisms of family religious socialization? What accounts for transmission and nontransmission, and what factors differentiate parents who are "successful" in their efforts from those who are not?

The data for this research are from the LSOG, a study of more than 3,500 respondents from 357 three- and four-generation families (for details about the sample and procedures, see Appendix A). The original 1970 sample of middle- and working-class multigenerational families was generally representative of the southern California area at the time, although minorities and low-income individuals were underrepresented. There were 2,044 respondents at Wave 1 in 1970. Subsequent surveys took place in 1985, 1988, 1991, 1994, 1997, 2000, and 2005. Beginning in 1991, the great-grandchildren (G4s) began participating in the survey as they reached age sixteen. At Wave 8 in 2005, the number of respondents was 1,766, ranging in age from 16 to 102. One thing we want to emphasize at the outset: This was not a nationally-representative sample. Therefore, the findings from this study should be regarded as valid for this sample and are not necessarily generalizable to the entire population of today's American families. An analysis of the generalizabiity of these findings is presented in the Appendix.

Because the LSOG provides four-generation panel data collected over a long period of time, we were able to construct family-linked grandparents, parents, and grandchildren in 1970 and 2005, when each generation was at about the same chronological age, and then compare these family-linked data at two different points in time (see chapter 3). Such a design allows us to consider the effects of social change such as cultural trends in American society on religious socialization and family influence.

The longitudinal survey data provide knowledge about the degree to which religious practices and beliefs are shared by family members and how these have changed over time. However, survey data are limited if we want to know about processes and patterns of intergenerational religious transmission. In 2005 we began a qualitative study to learn more about *how* parents and grandparents influence the religiosity of their children and grand-children. We selected twenty-five three- and four-generation families from the larger LSOG panel. We conducted 156 in-depth interviews focusing on respondents' perceptions of God, religion and spirituality, religious involve-ment, and family relationships and traditions. We then developed family case studies drawing from all survey and interview data, thereby allowing us to examine patterns and processes of religious transmission across generations.

These data allow us to examine pathways of religious continuity and change in families and how transmission may have changed over recent decades. To set the stage for these analyses of intergenerational dynamics, we begin, in chapter 2, by looking at how generations have changed over time in spirituality and religion.

CHAPTER 2 | Religion and Spirituality Across Generations

I believe He has a plan for me and we don't know what that is until He decides what to do with us. I know there's a lot of things I pray that He would change, but He does it during His time, not when I want it. (Nathaniel Knox, age eighty-one)

I'm a spiritual person, but I am not religious. I really don't like church. (Renee Walker, age fifty-one)

[E]verybody believes what they're going to believe and for the most part people have pretty wholesome intentions. And everybody's got their version of the truth that makes them who they are and that is why they behave the way they do. (Lauren Walker, age twenty-one)

NATHANIEL, RENEE, AND LAUREN, quoted above, differ in the ways they express their perspectives on God, spirituality, and religion. They also differ in their age and, as a result, in the historical and cultural experiences that have shaped their lives. It's important in our examination of religion and the family to explore the specific time periods within which the individuals in our study developed their orientations toward religion. Unlike other chapters, which describe the experiences of family generations—the generation (G) 1s, G2s, G3s, and G4s—in this chapter we focus on family participants as members of historically defined age groups—what sociologists call *age cohorts* and what are popularly known as "genera-tions." We consider the question of whether individuals born within a common period of history share common perceptions of religion, spirituality, and God. We ask whether and how the perceptions of one generation differ from those born earlier or later in time. This is especially important for a multigenerational study of religion, since religion in America has changed significantly in conjunction with the significant historical events and social transformations over the past century.

We identify these generations[1] using names often seen in the popular press—for example, Baby Boomers to refer to individuals born in the two decades following World War II (1946–1964)—and which often are tied to important historical events, such as the Great Depression. We split the interview sample into seven distinct age groups that roughly correspond with the family generations of the Longitudinal Study of Generations (LSOG).[2] They are as follows:

1. The World War I (WWI) generation, born 1890–1915 (those in the interview sample were born between 1909 and 1915)
2. The Depression Era generation, born 1916–1931
3. The Silent Generation, born 1932–1945
4. Early Baby Boomers, born 1946–1954
5. Later Baby Boomers, born 1955–1964
6. Generation X, born 1965–1979
7. The Millennial Generation, born 1980–1988

Although these broad categorizations can lead to interpretive problems—differences within the Baby Boom generation, for example, may be as great as differences between Baby Boomers and Generation Xers (or Gen Xers)—they are nevertheless useful for organizing data in order to identify patterns associated with age, cohort effects, and historical time. We look first at the experiences of the oldest generation: those who were born in the years leading up to WWI.

The WWI Generation (Born 1890–1915)

In order to learn about generational perspectives on religion and spiri-tuality, we left these concepts undefined during our interviews so that individuals could describe them in their own way. We asked each person, for example, "What role does religion play in your life today?"; "Do you believe in God or a higher power?"; "Do you consider yourself a spiritual person?"; and "What values would you like to pass on to your children?"

Difficulties in Describing Faith

Each of the elderly members of the WWI generation we interviewed expressed a firm belief in God or a higher power, yet many struggled to articulate their beliefs. This may reflect a decline in cognitive functioning in some cases, but we consistently heard members of the WWI group struggle to put their religious perspectives into words. For example, when asked about the role of God in her life, Fanny Wagner, a ninety-two-year-old woman who said she believes in God, replied:

> Well, I think *[pause]*. I don't know that any other way. *[Pause]* I'd say it's just that you're thinking there's a higher power than you.... I wouldn't know how to describe it.... Surely most people believe there's—... Everything didn't get here by just appearing.

Similarly, Myrna Jackson, a ninety-five-year-old nondenominational Christian, replies, "I still pray. But I don't... I don't know. I still believe in it, so I guess that's all I can say."

The nonagenarians also struggle with terms such as "spirituality." For example, ninety-six-year-old Viola Walker, who has been a member of the same Church of Christ congregation for eighty years, notes that religion is "still very important" to her. But when asked if she is a "spiritual person," she replies, "I haven't given it a thought. What do you mean when you say 'spiritual'?"

"God Is in Nature"

Despite such difficulties in articulating their beliefs, several members of the WWI cohort described their faith in God as being strengthened by evidence they find in everyday life, especially in the natural world. Notes Myrna Jackson, "I know that there's another power above us. All I have to do is look out in the morning and see the sunshine and the birds singing and all that.... I don't know how to express it. It's just there."

The ninety-seven-year-old matriarch Edith Poole, whose family we met in the last chapter, describes her faith in God in similar terms as "the beauty all around us.... I really don't know how to describe it. You look at everything outside, with all the beauty around, and everything as it progresses, and you know that there has to be *[pause]* someone who's regulating all of it. I don't know how to answer that."

Religious Participation—and Substitutes for It

Most of the WWI generation members interviewed can no longer attend church because of frailty or limited access. But many, including Viola Walker, pray at home on a daily basis, and some have created a religious space in their households in which to pray. Gladys Sanchez, at ninety-five, describes her home-based Catholic religious practices: "I [have] big saints in my room. I have two. It's Saint Anthony and Jesus....I can't go to church. I can't kneel down. My knees are bad. Once in a while, I go and put money or light a candle. Or else, I light it here. In the morning, I pray before I come to the kitchen. Because I [am] always falling down."

For Viola, attending church connects her with God, her friends, and the past. "I have wonderful friends there," she says. "And they're always available if [I] have any problems.... The health of the friends and neighbors, and that all goes back to where it's the things you believe.... I think about them in the mornings, so we've got the telephone. We can talk." Like Viola, other members of her generation who still attend church seem to benefit from the fellowship and interaction with others. Myrna Jackson says she enjoys religious services because of the camaraderie. "That's why I go on Sunday," she adds, "because that's the worst day of the week. That's the most lonesome day of the week." For these women, church provides an important social outlet that may, in some cases, be lacking other days.

Beyond social value, it was difficult for members of this generation to articulate the role of religion in their lives. As Florence Poole explains: "We would go to church. It was just there, and we went." Fanny Wagner concurs: "That was just our life, you know, and so [my parents] didn't say anything about it." As we will see, this vagueness about religion is a sharp contrast to the expressive clarity of some later generations, perhaps because the WWI generation took religion more for granted, as part of the landscape, in a way that successive generations could not.

The Depression Era Generation (Born 1916–1931)

The Depression Era respondents in our sample spoke more clearly and confidently about their religious beliefs than those in the WWI group. While a few question their belief in God, the majority say they are religious.

God as My Copilot and Protector

For some in this generation, God can be described as a guide and ultimate protector. Many attribute their successes—and even their very lives—to God, who watches over them and keeps them out of harm's way. This image appears regardless of their affiliation or degree of faith. Kenneth Brigham, an eighty-eight-year-old nondenominational Christian who has a strong faith in God, credits God with keeping him alive when he served in the military as a pilot:

> I've had times flying when the engine is cutting out, and the automatic direction finder tells you which way you're going...and so forth, and I'll say, "God, please help me make the right decision." I've got eight or ten stories where I know if I had not had Him sitting beside me, I would have been killed.

Others tell stories of divine intervention and say that God helped them avoid peril or certain death. George Lieberman, seventy-eight, is Jewish and questions his faith in God. Yet he believes God intervened to keep him from joining a military unit with high casualty rates in the Korean War. "There was a plan, or an angel was sitting on my shoulder and telling me to say no," he says, then pauses. "That's the only time I really felt like somebody was looking out for me."

Stan Sabelli, a seventy-nine-year-old former engineer and amateur race car driver, also attributes his longevity to God:

> I mean, I know that there's somebody up there that has watched out for me for a lot of years. I mean, I should have been dead so many, many, many times....I really do believe there is somebody up there that makes every-thing right....And, you know, but to me, I'm not a religious zealot, okay? But I don't mind telling people, I think I'm here doing something that the

guy up there wants me to do [*laughs*]. I don't know what name he goes by, but he wants me to do it, and I'm getting it done.

One thing that comes through clearly in our conversations with members of the Depression-born generation is their assumption that God is watching out for them in a very personal way.

"I'm not Religious, but I Believe in God"

Despite a relatively strong belief in God, many of the members of the Depression Era generation (nearly half of those we interviewed) do not regard themselves as "religious." Edna Sabelli, the wife of Stan mentioned above, is a seventy-seven-year-old Catholic. She explains that she is not religious because "I don't talk religion. . . . I'm not a religious person, although I do pray." Similarly, Harriett Holmes, a seventy-eight-year-old Episcopalian, explains that she is not a "religious person," despite her belief in God. "I would say I was trying to be a Christian person, but not necessarily religious in that I don't necessarily feel that I can quote from any ideology or scripture or anything." She adds that she would like to be known as a person who lived what she believed.

Some reject this designation in order to distance themselves from those they perceive as self-rightous and sanctimonious. Seventy-six-year-old Ruth Lieberman, for example, expresses her frustration with "religious Jews" at her temple:

> Well, from what I've seen from a lot of people that go to temple, they're not honest, and I've seen them behave differently to what they do when they're in temple, which . . . makes me angry. And I'm very honest, and I say what I feel, and I have very high morals, and I don't think I need [to be] religious to be that way.

Kay Adams, a seventy-nine-year-old who has attended mainline Christian churches over the course of her life, agrees with this sentiment. Most religious people, she says, "go to church, and they do all the things, they believe in what the church says, and they don't necessarily carry it over into their life, but they think they're religious." For many in the Depression Era cohort, belief should make itself apparent in ethical behavior. With the exception of highly religious Mormons, the

Depression Era respondents in our sample mostly discounted the importance of religious attendance, a reliance on Scripture, and other traditional markers of "religiosity."

A Focus on Action

In lieu of strict attendance at services, what seems to be most important to this group is action. They emphasize *doing*, not just believing. More specifically, they focus on the importance of putting their principles into practice, especially with regard to how they treat other people. Kenneth Brigham, who describes himself as a nondenominational Christian, argues that "actions speak louder than words." He explains:

> I believe there is a higher entity, sort of bird-dogging you, watching you, and you've got to be a good person. I just think that to me is my idea of being a helpful, responsible, good person to help others in life. That's maybe not "religion," but that's what I try to practice.

Nathaniel Knox, an eighty-one-year-old Lutheran, explains that what is important to him about being religious is "[his] moral values and the way [he] treat[s] people." For him, this includes "honesty, fairness to people, trying to help people when you can," like with charity programs at his church.

Those we spoke to place greater value on concrete actions than on an abstract "spirituality," a term with relatively little meaning to this group. Norman Bernstein, an eighty-six-year-old religious Jew, is not interested in reflecting on the meaning behind his religious practice. When asked about the role of spirituality in his life, he responds:

> The term "spiritual" is something that I find hard to put into words; I don't quite understand what it means. I don't sit and meditate. I don't sit and try to discover why I'm doing what I'm doing. I accepted it years back, and I hardly ever review it. I know that it was good then, and it's good now.

A Protective, Benevolent God

Members of the Depression Era generation came of age during the Great Depression and World War II. Nearly all of those we interviewed reflected on the impact of one or both of these events on their lives, noting the great sacrifices made by their families and the resulting ethic of hard work, patriotism, practicality, and thrift. Yet some also noted the horizon-expanding effects of the war through the exposure to worlds far removed from the limited geographies of their childhoods. These experiences may explain, in part, the tendency of members of this group to describe their religiosity in both down-to-earth yet awestruck terms.

These individuals experienced circumstances caused by the Depression or the war that were beyond their individual control. They credit a protective, benevolent God with seeing them through these difficult and sometimes life-threatening times. Through sheer determination and a strong faith in God, they persevered and even thrived. An emphasis on hard work, beginning in childhood, is reflected in their religious beliefs as well, where "actions speak louder than words." Being faithful and committed to God is important and is evident in what a person does but not necessarily what one says or thinks.

While the WWI generation members we interviewed appeared to have difficulty articulating their religious beliefs, those in the Depression Era offered clear, straightforward descriptions of the directive role God played in their lives, as well as the connection between being a good person and being rewarded by one's Heavenly Father.

The Silent Generation (Born 1932–1945)

Whereas the members of the Depression Era cohort that we spoke to described God as a powerful being that provides guidance from on high, beginning with the silent generation—a relatively small group that was born during the lean times of the Great Depression and World War II but too young to experience the full extent of the Depression or to serve in the war—we see increasing discussion of the accessibility of God and of His "embeddedness" in every aspect of life. Taking this a step further than the WWI cohort, whose members offered descriptions of God in nature, many in the silent generation expressed the belief that a higher power dwells within the human spirit. This sentiment is especially common among those who have no religious affiliation or who question their faith in God.

The Internalization of God

Bernadine Wagner, age seventy-three, who attended many different churches before settling on a New Age type of spirituality, describes what God means to her:

> I feel I have a connection. I feel that I have a force within me that connects to a force, to the higher self.... I just, well, sitting here in my living room right now, I just feel that He's there in everything. That sounds silly, I guess, but I mean, whether it's the fan that's going, whether it's a painting on the wall, a knick-knack on a shelf, I just feel that I am surrounded by God all the time. And I don't mean that He's here watching every single move that I make, but I just feel that there is, that everything I say and do and think, and all, is connected.

Rather than an angel on one's shoulder, a copilot, or the "guy up there," as noted by those in the Depression Era generation, God for the silent generation is a *part of us*. Charles Jensen, a seventy-four-year-old unaffiliated believer in God, explains the role of "the Almighty" in his life as "a steadying thing. I think sometimes the general circumstances are such that nothing is there that can really help you." So Charles looks for "support from within."

Frank Baker, who is sixty-four and Jewish, says he does not have faith in God, but he believes in the "essence" of people. "I tend to think of people's essence rather than their beings," he says. "I guess I feel like there are other things happening in the world besides the pragmatic everyday plane that we exist on. And I guess I feel that that's inside every person and they can project that spirituality or project that essence even outside of themselves."

Communicating Directly with God

Another common theme in the interviews of silent generation respondents is that individuals have the ability to communicate directly with God or a higher power, regardless of where He resides. Yvette Walker, seventy-four and an Episcopalian, says, "I've always known there was something there, and that something guides me. And it tells me things. So of course I believe that. It's a little voice that you listen to and you know."

Carol West, a seventy-two-year-old Methodist, feels she obtains that divine guidance directly from God through prayer. "I just feel like He's always there with me," she says. "If I need Him, I can call on Him." Similarly, seventy-four-year-old Al Wagner, who identifies himself as a member of a Methodist church, notes, "I am a religious person. I don't pray every day. But I do try to maintain a contact and that sort of thing with a higher power."

For some, this relationship is facilitated by religious institutions; for others, the relationship is unmediated. For Bernadine Wagner, it is the latter. When asked about the role of religion in her life, she describes it as

> None, so far as an organized religion. So far as me communicating with my God or my maker or a supreme being, a lot, a great deal. I think it helps me stay focused on who I am, and how I need to react with others, for the [benefit] of myself and them. So I ask for guidance in that, and to please lead me to the correct path. I just communicate every day.

"If You're Spiritual, You're Religious"

As noted earlier, the WWI generation found little meaning in the word "spiritual." Those born in the Depression Era tended to be unsure about the term as well. In contrast, the members of the silent generation with whom we spoke are more likely to embrace a "spiritual" identity, although for most of them spirituality is indistinguishable from religion. As Carol West explains, "I don't know what the difference would be. If you're spiritual, you're religious, really."

Indeed, even the question is puzzling for some. Charles Jensen, seventy-four, says he has no religion. When asked how he would distinguish "spirituality" from "religion," he replies,

> Hmmm, that's a good question. I'm afraid you've got me at a loss. To me, one is almost as, I want to say, tied to the other. I suppose not necessarily, but my feelings about it are the same.

While others more easily describe how spirituality and religion function in their lives, they often use the same words to do so. For example, when asked to describe God and the role of religion in her life, Carolyn Wilson, a seventy-six-year-old evangelical Christian, replied, "Well, He's who we worship and believe in and Jesus is the Holy Spirit, we believe, that guides and directs us. And we pray every day and have faith." When asked about the role of "spirituality," her response mirrored that for religion: "I would say my deep spiritual faith, my belief in God, my belief in Jesus."

A great number of silent generation members equated spirituality with religion. Yet many beliefs professed by the Silent Generation are not unique to this group; we interviewed many Baby Boomers, gen Xers, and Millennials who also spoke cogently about spirituality and having a personal connection to God. What is significant is that the Silent Generation is the *oldest* group to describe religion and spirituality in this way. This suggests, at least for our sample, that the Silent Generation could mark the beginning of an important transition in generational perspectives about religion and spirituality. The Silent Generation's beliefs signify a distinct shift from an older group that defines religion in relatively limited or concrete terms to a younger group that places greater emphasis on the intangible and deeply personal aspects of spirituality. This transition may reflect the dramatic social changes that began during the 1960s when the silent generation entered adulthood—changes that had profound effects on the Baby Boomers as well.

Early Boomers (Born 1946–1954)

As noted above, many members of the silent generation do not distinguish between "spirituality" and "religion." Many of the early Baby Boomers in our sample, however, see clear differences between the two.

Religion as Institutional Practice; Spirituality as Feeling of Connection

Like many in the silent generation, the Early Boomers we spoke with described their lives as having both "religious" and "spiritual" dimensions. However, many went on to describe these as two separate and distinct concepts. As Nicholas Bernstein, a fifty-seven-year-old Jewish man, puts it: "I think ... you don't have to be religious to be spiritual and I don't think you have to be spiritual to be religious."

Early Boomers frequently talk about religion as something one *does* and spirituality as something one *feels* through one's relationship with God. Karl Brigham, a sixty-two-year-old Mormon, describes this distinction:

To me, being religious is doing the services that you [do] for other people and things like that. And then spiritual, to me, is being able to receive. You feel the love from the good coming to you and it makes you feel better. That's spiritual to me. Religious is doing those services and things. . . . Yeah, spiritual is more about feeling.

Some Early Boomers take this distinction a step further, describing religious practice as being determined or scripted by a religious institution and spirituality as "personal" and emerging from within an individual. Sandy West, fifty-three, who attends services at the Unity Church and the Church of Religious Science, explains religion as

more of an institutionalized practice, where you go to church and you believe certain things that have to do with the Christian faith. Spirituality, being a spiritual person, means you're in connection. You're in communication and connection with God on an ongoing basis, every day; not just once a week when you go to church.

These Early Boomers describe religion and spirituality as discrete practices that take place in physically distinct contexts. Yet both are considered integral dimensions of life and one feeds the other; one is not necessarily "better" than the other. Through religious practice, one may develop a deeper spirituality and stronger connection to God. For Regina Shepherd, who is fifty-two and Mormon, spirituality and religion are inextricably linked:

The more faith you have, and the more you try to obey the Commandments, the more spirituality you are blessed with. [T]rue spirituality comes from how you feel inside, how you treat other people, how you feel about God and the Savior. You know, if you're going to be spiritual, then it's got to be a part of your life, you know. It's not a Sunday thing.

Other comments point to the relationship between religion, spirituality, and emotion. For many, faith is the "feeling" one gets through religious and spiritual practice:

- "[It's] more like a feeling."—Robert West (fifty-five, Methodist)
- "It's just a feeling that, you know, that transcends."—Beatrice West (fifty-three, Methodist)

- "It's feeling something real good, something warm inside."—Luis Garcia (fifty-eight, Catholic)

This feeling can be quite profound. Sandy West describes her experience with meditation:

> When I was in the Yogananada, the Ananda Church, when I would go to the meditation classes, I felt just extreme bliss that I have never felt before in my life. And that was a pivotal experience for me, understanding the connection between meditating and going inside and feeling God. I mean, I just felt like I was connected to spirit and I never had been in that way before.

Ken Wilson, a fifty-five-year-old Evangelical, experienced powerful emotions when he became a born-again Christian at the age of eight. "At that particular point in time, I actually felt the Holy Spirit—you actually feel it come into your being. It's a miracle. I mean, I don't know how to explain it."

Faith as a Coping Mechanism

The notion of religious and spiritual practices as regulators of emotion—and ultimately of behavior—is important for many of the Early Boomers we interviewed and is less dominant in the discourse of other generations, especially older ones, who rarely describe their faith in these terms. A related idea is that religion and especially spirituality provide a way to cope with life's challenges, sustaining individuals through difficult times.

For example, Nicholas Bernstein notes that spirituality "[is] what helps you when you're depressed. It's sometimes what you share with your mate or your friends or your family, a feeling of goodness that's a core inside and it's not something that's learned." Beatrice West explains how her faith helped her cope with several serious health crises in her family and with the death of her father:

> There's been a lot of things, a lot of challenges that have happened in my family. And if it hadn't been for the faith of our—not necessarily our religion—but faith in God or in our belief and in our family support system, I don't know how I would have been strong enough to have survived....But it's there inside of me. I guess I can feel the peace of it, or the peace of

someone there that says okay, you can do this. It's not that bad. You know, you can get [through] this.

Denise Sanchez, an evangelical Christian who describes experiencing the Holy Spirit as "electricity," claims her faith gave her the strength to survive the abrupt break-up of her marriage and the challenges that ensued. "I would've never made it" without God, she explains. "Because I got to know God, and to know what it feels to know Him, He has helped me so much in my daily living to cope with everything."

Knowing that "God has a plan" helps some deal with crises. When Charlotte Jensen's family experienced multiple devastations within a matter of just a few weeks, for example, her religion was her life support. "So we've had just a lot of crazy things happening this year and I just can't imagine going through all that and not knowing that somebody was there watching over them and everything happened for a reason," she explains. She is comforted knowing that "He's got a plan for this" and "God knows why" difficult challenges arise in her life.

The Early Boomers' dependence on God as a coping mechanism presents an interesting generational observation. As we discussed in chapter 1, Christian Smith described the spiritual outlook of teenagers and emerging adults as Moralistic Therapeutic Deism.[3] The Millennials, Smith notes, are quick to rely on God when they have a problem to resolve; they believe God wants them to be happy, feel good, and treat others fairly. But given the Early Boomers' similar approach to many questions, it's worth asking how new moralistic therapeutic deism actually is. Its antecedents seem to be present in a much earlier generation.

Why Do Bad Things Happen to Good People?

For many Early Boomers, life's challenges help to build character and spiritual strength, thereby deepening their feelings of connectedness to God. Some of the individuals we interviewed—much like Job in the Old Testament—have had to cope with enormous difficulties that put their faith to the test. Marjorie Brigham, a Mormon, came through a difficult period with a renewed faith in God. She explains:

For example, when I was getting divorced and I was separated, it was a very lonely time.... So this is a time when people could commit suicide, right? But I never had those thoughts because I knew God loved me and he understood. And so that thought in my heart has always been comforting....I think that my relationship with my Heavenly Father has just been a wonderful thing, and I'm so grateful every day for everything around me. I mean through my religion I have learned that my life is a period to be tried and tested, and the real test is to see if I will love my Heavenly Father and follow what He wants me to do.

Yet for some Early Boomer respondents, life's tragedies have served to erode rather than strengthen their faith in God. As Cheryl Smith, fifty-one, who is "agnostic at best," explains: "When bad events happen, it seems even less likely that there's the God that they put in with the organized religions—seems more like He isn't there than He is."

For some, like Nicholas Bernstein, when bad things happen to good people, it leads to questioning God's intentions: "[W]hen something or someone that is harmless that does nothing bad in the world gets ill or becomes incapacitated or dies for no good reason, it's tough to say that there's a God," he observes. This sentiment appears to be especially true among the Jews we interviewed, whose religious tradition encourages questioning. As Howard Rosenberg, a fifty-five-year-old Jewish man, explains: "There's this school of thought [that developed] after the Holocaust that God didn't exist. [A] school of Jewish thought."

Fifty-six-year-old Esther Bernstein, who is Jewish, declares that she questions her faith nearly on a daily basis and especially "when bad things happen to good people," the title of a bestselling 1978 book by Rabbi Harold Kushner. The death of a loved one seems especially likely to prompt this kind of questioning. For example, after a friend's son died at the age of twenty-five, Vicki Lieberman found little comfort in her Jewish tradition. She explains: "In going to the temple, or listening to what they had to say, because I didn't think, you know, it had anything to do with it. And, you know, why would God take away somebody like that, you know? It just doesn't make sense."

Some atrocities prompt a crisis of faith that is simply too great to overcome. After fifty-five-year-old Dawn Adams's daughter was molested by a relative, she rejected her Christian religious tradition, although she continues to pray. She explains:

I stopped going to church and I was really mad at God, but every day I prayed that He would strike [the molester] dead. I prayed that every day for a year. And then I decided, after a year, that that just must not be something that should happen, because otherwise it would have. I think God just didn't want it to happen, and so I stopped praying it. *[Pause]* But I didn't go to church anymore. I just couldn't do it...I was just like this, I was going to church, and I was trying to do everything right, and this happens, and like, forget it.

From these interviews we see that the leading edge of Early Boomers was born in the wake of World War II's carnage and came of age during a period of extensive social change in the United States. Political unrest, rising divorce rates, changing mores about gender and sexuality, and the increasingly influential role of the mass media in the 1960s and early 1970s coalesced to destabilize the relatively conservative social conventions of the 1950s.

Perhaps because of this, Early Boomers often mentioned that they relied jointly on religious institutions and spiritual practice as coping mechanisms and sources of emotional support; they emphasized the healing qualities of religion *and* spirituality. However, for some in our sample—Jews in particular—the impact of the war and other tragedies proved too much to cope with, prompting them to question their faith in God.

Later Baby Boomers (Born 1955–1964)

As a group, the Later Boomers in our sample displayed perhaps the most consistent religious and spiritual characteristics of all of the generations we interviewed. This is not to suggest that the group is homogeneous or stable: The Later Boomers we interviewed hailed from more than a dozen different religious traditions, and their religious affiliations have changed relatively frequently over time. While one-third of our interview sample had changed religious affiliation during adulthood, nearly half of the Later Boomers had switched affiliation at least once. Thus, part of what defines this age group is a constantly changing set of definitions.

Favoring the Personal over the Institutional

Whereas the Early Boomers we spoke with seem to value both the religious and the spiritual realms, the Later Boomers are less comfortable with "Religion" with a capital R. Many reject what they perceive as the institutional nature of religion in favor of a more personal spirituality. Whereas all but one of those we interviewed believed in God and nearly all identified as "spiritual," only one-third claimed to be "religious." As detailed earlier in this chapter, the concept of spirituality generally emerged in the silent generation and was distinguished from religion by the Early Boomers. The Later Boomers we interviewed not only discriminated between religion and spirituality, they clearly rejected the former in favor of the latter.

As Stephanie Holmes, a forty-nine-year-old Episcopalian puts it, "I don't really consider myself religious, because I'm not. I'm less inclined to...read about having to do all the ritualistic parts of church than I am in knowing that I have my communication line with God." When asked if she considers herself a "religious person," Elizabeth Goldman, a fifty-two-year-old "nondenominational Christian" with a strong professed faith in God, did not hesitate to give a response: "Religious? No." When asked to explain why not, she added, "Well, to me, in my mind, religion would be a practice of like, oh, you know, like religious ceremonies and things like that...could have meaning to some people, but wouldn't to me." She is clear about one thing, however: "Now I have a relationship with God....I need advice, I go to Him."

For many Later Boomers, religious practices such as going to religious services detract from, rather than encourage, a deepening spirituality. Fifty-one-year-old Mary Adams, who identifies herself as "just Christian," says she gains far more from her personal spiritual practices than from institutionalized ones. "To me religion is about what building you go to, what day you go, what time you go, and who's telling you what to believe," she says.

> And spirituality is your connection you feel with God. But when they tell me that certain people aren't going to heaven, or you have to be such and such or you'll go to hell, then I feel that religion is too invested in perpetuating its own lies. So I don't feel religious in that way, because I don't feel like—I don't think God looks at how often people go to church.

"I'm Not Religious—But I Believe in God"

Some of the Later Boomers appear somewhat defensive about not being religious. Catholic and forty-five years old, Brad Sanchez hesitates to define himself as "religious" since he is divorced, which is inconsistent with Catholic doctrine. Harold West, a fifty-two-year-old nonpracticing Catholic, fears he may be "hypocritical" since he doesn't "go to quote 'the house of the Lord' unquote and pray and spend my hour there, whatever, and go to confession, and things of this nature." He continues:

I'm not a practicing religious person. I don't go to church. I haven't gone to church in a long, long, long time, but I still believe in my beliefs, right, wrong, or indifferent. But I figure, when it comes time, the guy upstairs, he'll make the final choice.

Marta Poole, fifty-two, who says she is "a member of the Methodist Church," admits that she rarely attends church. But as if to compensate for this she quickly offers a list of her other "religious" activities, such as praying every morning and night "and a lot of times in between." She also reads a great many books on faith. However, she's not active in any one religious organization. "My spirituality is faith—based on my beliefs in God and Jesus Christ and, frankly, the way people live their lives."

Marta is not alone in this. Much like our Depression Era respondents, Later Boomers disassociate themselves with the "religious," despite a professed faith in God. The reasons for this differ between the two cohorts. Depression Era respondents seem to avoid the term "religious" because they feel they are not knowledgeable about religion or they associate the label with putting on a pious, yet hollow, display. Later Boomers, in contrast, associate being religious with going to church and participating in other organized and institutional religious practices—practices they reject in favor of a personal and spiritual connection to God.[4]

Reflecting the increasing individualism and anti-institutional sentiments of the era of their youth (i.e., the 1960s and 1970s), the Later Boomers express a greater distrust of religious institutions than do those in the Depression Era and the early wave of Baby Boomers, perhaps also because of an increasing tendency to look inward to find God. This rejection of institutional religion may explain the relatively high rates of movement from one religious affiliation to another that we see in this group of Later Boomers as well.

Generation X (Born 1965–1979)

In comparison to other generations, the Generation X members in our study are far more difficult to characterize. As a group, they have virtually identical rates of believing in God as the overall interview sample (both 80%) and are the least likely of all the groups in our study—with the exception of the WWI generation—to describe themselves as "spiritual" (61% compared to the total LSOG sample average of 69%). This is remarkable, because it reverses the trend of increasing use of the term "spiritual" across cohorts, and because Generation X is sandwiched between the two cohorts with the highest rates of self-identified spirituality: the Later Boomers at 86% and the Millennials at 84%. Despite this, Gen Xers are unique in their tendency to describe a communion with God through nontraditional practices (from a Western perspective), such as dancing or yoga.

Viewed as a group, and when looking for common religious themes, Generation X appears rife with contradiction. Yet when broken down into two groups—specifically, the believers and the nonbelievers—some clearer patterns emerge.

Those Who Believe: Religion as a Way of Life

Among the 75% of Gen Xers in our sample who believe in God, many make religion the central organizing principle of their lives. As Daniel West, a thirty-two-year-old nondenominational Christian, explains, "[God] is the foremost part of [my life]. Everything we do is by His design." Nathan Brigham, thirty-nine and Mormon, agrees: "[God] is everything. And what I mean by that is everything that I have, we have been blessed with, comes from Him."

For some Gen Xers, religion infuses every aspect of their day-to-day lives. Catholicism is such a fundamental part of Richard Jackson's life that it is difficult for the twenty-eight-year-old to describe how it operates independently:

> You know, it really has a fulfillment characteristic to my life. *[Pause]* I'm struggling for words, here. It's really...It's hard to put words to it, something that's so into our life....I think of myself as a free-thinker, but I do think of myself as a religious person, because I *[pause]*...and I think that's a part that I have of my life in order to be happy, because there was always something missing before.

Deborah Brigham, Nathan Brigham's thirty-four-year-old wife, has less difficulty describing how her Mormon religion works for her. It is "my driving purpose," she says. "I think it's the reason and, you know, the purpose for all things, and so for me it's very important. It's the

explanation for why is it important for me to do laundry all day today."
She laughs. "And, you know, it shapes every decision. When it doesn't,
I regret it."

Religion as a Tool in Raising Children

Religion informs many of the decisions religious Gen Xers make,
including those related to raising children. Indeed, many we interviewed described how helpful religion is for raising children in today's
complicated world.

Eduardo Garcia, a thirty-six-year-old Catholic, suggests that *the* most
important aspect of religion is how it helps him as a father. In response to
the question "How would you characterize the role of God in your life?"
Eduardo responded simply, "It's an important part in that my faith helps
me raise my children and helps me teach them how to act." Regarding
the Bible, Denise Smith, who is also Catholic, responds similarly: "I feel
comfortable with what it says, and how ... it applies to my life, personally.
And it's something that I want in [the] education of, you know, as far as
the foundation for my children."

Deborah Brigham explains in greater detail how religion assists her in
parenting:

> It makes a difference because it gives me answers to my children's ques-
> tions. It gives them purpose and a reason for things: "Why can't I do that?"
> you know? And they see things on TV that are against our values and they
> see things in the world that are against our values and, well, it answers the
> questions for them, "why?" And so, not just as a resource and a comfort for
> me, but also as a source of reference for them to learn. I don't know how
> I would raise kids without religion.

Putting Religion on Hold for a Time

Despite their belief in the importance of making religion a central part of
their lives, many of those we interviewed find it difficult to actually do
so. Now in their 30s and 40s, most Gen Xers in our sample are spending
long hours at work, raising young children, caring for aging parents, and/
or going to school. Juggling the demands of daily life requires some to

put religion on hold for a while. Ella Goldman, twenty-nine, describes her struggle to incorporate the Jewish community into her life:

> Like I feel like [Judaism] is, you know, definitely a part of who I am. . . . I know it's something I want to get back [to], like more involved in, but right now, it's kind of on the back burner, a little bit, because I'm so kind of overwhelmed with, you know, having a young child and managing everything else right now. . . . But you know, it's something that I think we want to make more of an effort to get involved in later on.

For Anne Poole, a thirty-four-year-old Mormon, work has limited her ability to participate in religious life as fully as she would like. When she was in college, she had spare time, but since then she's always had a job where she sometimes has to work on Sundays. "I haven't been able to come as often as I did growing up to church or to church activities," she says.

Similarly, Noah Shepherd, thirty-three, who is descended from Mormons but was raised in an observant Jewish family, struggles to balance religious practice with the rigors of graduate school. He explains that he "would like to get more spiritual. I feel that graduate school is sort of forcing me out of my religious awareness and my sort of spiritual centeredness. And I hope that I can, through Buddhism and what you gain in Judaism, to sort of get that back." He hopes that when he starts his doctoral research, he'll have "the time and the sort of peace of mind to be able to get back into some kind of religious tradition."

The "Independent Thinking" of Believers

Noah Shepherd's comments suggest another theme that emerged in our interviews with Gen Xers: religiously independent thinking. Many take temporary breaks from religious practice and feel free to selectively adopt doctrinal beliefs in order to make religion work for them.

For thirty-five-year-old Marisol Garcia, graduating from a Catholic high school and leaving home to attend a nonreligious university put her in the position of having to actively choose to incorporate religion into her life, rather than simply relying on her parents' or teachers' prodding to do so. She says that moving away from home "required [her] to be more independent about it. If I wanted to continue to grow in my faith and to practice, I had to go to church. And not going to church with Mom on Sunday, that's a big change. That's making a decision to go on my own."

Marisol's decision to take a break from religion was prompted not by school or work but rather by her discomfort with some of the Catholic Church's teachings. She explains:

> Every once in a while there's trouble if we have a disagreement with a teaching or we're just not feeling comfortable in the parish. We might stop going for a while, but it's still there and we always pick it back up and we have to show our kids that this is the way we want them to be, and in order to do that, we have to go to church and we have to practice it and we have to pray, we have to read the Bible. We have to show them how or they're just going to think we're pushing it on them, and that's not what we want.

For Marisol, ensuring that her life centers on religious beliefs and practices—for her sake and for the sake of her children—is more important than agreeing with every aspect of the religion. Thirty-two-year-old Erika Johnson is also skeptical about Catholic Church doctrine. "It's just that I don't necessarily subscribe to everything that the church teaches," she says. "Just because the Pope, or just because even the priest at my church says 'this is how we...should be doing as Good Catholics,' or 'This is how we should view this issue, or this particular situation.' I may not agree with that.... So I guess I'm a little independent, too." She says that while religion plays a role in her life, she is "open to other ideas."

This focus on "independence" and choice may also relate to Gen Xers' perceptions of God; those who say they believe in God are more likely than the other cohorts in our sample to describe Him as a grantor of free will. As Kimberly Knox, thirty-two, who identifies herself as a "Christian," explains: "[God] is all-knowing, and He is everywhere, and He can do everything, but He also gives you your free will, which is very important." Adds Kristin Wilson: "How much He must love us to give us the free will to choose not to be with Him."

Those Who Do Not Believe: Self-Determination and Skepticism

In fact, "independence" is one of the few themes that bridge the gap between the believing and nonbelieving members of Generation X. For the believers we interviewed, freely choosing a more flexible approach to religion ultimately allows them to remain committed to their faith. For the nonbelievers in our sample, however, "independent thinking" about religious beliefs and practices translates into a rejection of God altogether. For example, thirty-one-year-old Eric Baker, who defines himself as an atheist, declares, "I believe very much in self-determination and not following, you know, the status quo....I think religion is a quest for people that can't deal with reality."

For some, a rejection of religion and faith in God happened as they got older and began to question their religious upbringing. Thirty-six-year-old Ivan Shepherd accepted the "cult-like" beliefs and practices of his "born-again" Christian mother until he became a teenager. At that point, he began to think her beliefs were "pretty freakin' weird." He continues:

> And then when I started learning that certain things about it were flawed, or I thought they were flawed, it seemed to me more and more that it was flawed. And the more I wanted to ask questions and the less I got answers, I kind of got bitter towards the whole thing.

Despite being raised in a different religious tradition (Judaism), Luke Shepherd, Ivan's thirty-three-year-old cousin, had a similar experience as he grew up. "I don't really think I've thought that much about what the religious meaning was. I just thought that was what I was supposed to do," he explains. "And at the point where I started to actually think about all that, I started to think, 'well, this is just kind of silly.' Like I don't understand why people would believe this or anything in particular....So I guess at that point, I became agnostic."

And then there is skepticism about religious people. Gina Adams, a thirty-six-year-old atheist, says that religion sometimes brings out the worst in people: "Well, I mean, I don't hate people that are religious or anything," she begins, "but...I think religion is...not based on reason and it doesn't make any sense and I don't think it helps people be better people. I think a lot of times it makes people worse people." She would rather put her faith in science as "a better way for us to learn the truth about the universe than religion."

Faith in Science

Gina Adam's comments tap into one of the reasons for the nonbelieving Gen Xers' lack of belief in God: They can't take the leap of faith required to believe in something that isn't empirically verifiable. As Tracy Smith, a thirty-year-old unaffiliated agnostic, puts it: "Seeing is believing." In part because faith is intangible and cannot be seen, Tracy and other Gen Xers like her have fundamental doubts about the existence of God.

Thirty-one-year-old Brianna Shepherd, who like her brother Ivan has no religious affiliation, captures this perspective quite well: "I mean there could be something, but I don't know. I really don't know. And so I don't really choose to put all my energy into something that I don't know, and that can't be scientifically proven."

For Eric Baker, an atheist, those who are religious in today's society represent something of an intellectual curiosity. "I'm very interested in how people can convince themselves," he says. Religion seems "very cult-ish" to him, and he is interested in it from a sociological standpoint. "And the cultural stuff is amazing to me. I mean, it's amazing the amount that we've created sort of out of our heads, as a human race." But for Ivan Shepherd, religious faith, and spirituality in particular, is just plain weird. When someone thinks that he or she is in touch with spirits or "another world that's not earthly," it makes him uncomfortable. "You know, I'm a physical world person," he says.

The members of Generation X whom we interviewed share few common characteristics in their experiences with religion. They also seem to reverse some of the trends that grew with each preceding generation, such as an increasing identification with spirituality. Upon closer examination, however, there is a pragmatism that underlies and guides the religious perspectives of both the believing and nonbelieving Gen Xers we interviewed. Many Gen Xers, juggling the demands of work, school, and caregiving, find themselves forced to set aside religion—particularly organized religion—in order to achieve more balance in their lives. While faithful Gen Xers may temporarily stop going to church or synagogue, they still rely on assistance from God to get them through the day. One wonders, though, if this pragmatism is due more to the stage of life Gen Xers find themselves in, rather than something that uniquely defines the generation.

For the nonbelieving Gen Xers we interviewed, we find a similar pragmatic sensibility that leads them to doubt that God exists. While agnosticism and atheism are by no means unique to Generation X—there are those who question the existence of God in every age group—the Gen Xers we interviewed were more likely to reject religion in general and God in particular because they are "illogical" or otherwise counterproductive to civil society. In other generations, most notably the Early Boomers, a personal tragedy or some unspeakably terrible event, such as the Holocaust, is more likely to be named as the source of individual doubt. For the Gen Xers it may be the absence of clear evidence for the existence of God that leads to lack of belief.

Millennials (Born 1980–1988)

If the religious orientations of Gen Xers in our study are difficult to capture, the Millennials—called "Generation Y" by some—almost defy characterization. Among those we interviewed, more than half said they were affiliated with a conservative denomination or congregation, such as Orthodox Judaism, Mormonism, Pentecostalism, or Evangelical Protestantism. From this, one might assume high rates of religiosity in this group. However, 22% of Millennials define themselves as "not at all" religious—more than any other cohort in the LSOG—and another 33% report they are "not very" religious. Only 16% report that they are "very religious"—the lowest rate of all cohorts—despite their high rates of affiliation with "very religious" denominations. The interview data also suggest high rates of interest in spirituality among Millennials, nearly all of whom describe themselves as "spiritual."

Findings such as these might suggest a twist on the "I'm not religious—I'm spiritual" stance we found among the Later Boomers—something like "I'm religious, but I'm not *Religious*." But the story of the Millennials in our sample is more complicated. Unlike many of the Later Boomers who, regardless of affiliation, actively reject organized religion in favor of spirituality, most of the Millennials we spoke with do not demonstrate the same level of antipathy to institutionalized religion. Those who profess belief often do not attend church regularly. Many commented favorably on the sense of community provided by a church or synagogue, and still others suggested they are shopping around in order to find a congregation with the right "fit." Furthermore, some Millennials, like many Early Boomers, describe the complementary nature of religious practice and spirituality.

Part of what makes the Millennials so difficult to characterize is that they seem to offer few truly distinctive perspectives on religion that stand out from other generations. Millennials seem far less coherent as a group and espouse a much wider range of religious perspectives than their predecessors. Furthermore, our analyses indicate that the religious and spiritual concerns expressed by some members can be found in greater concentration in older groups, although perhaps with a slightly different emphasis. As twenty-five-year-old Isaac Walker suggests, "A lot of times our generation likes to think that we know everything, [but] we don't know anything. But if you look at the overall, you know, we're, kind of, following the same things. We just do it in a different way or by different means." Kelly Goldman, a recovering addict and Adam Goldman's sister, also relies on God to lead the way, although less by the threat of punishment than as a reassuring guide:

> He's in my life every day. When I don't know what to do, I ask Him and hopefully He'll show me what to do. And usually something does show up and I'm like, "Okay, this is what I'm supposed to do." He doesn't tell me or anything but something will pop up, like, "Oh, okay, this is like"— basically a door will open or whatever.... When I start to freak out, like, "What am I supposed to do?" or whatever, I just know He's there, all the time.

Religious Ambiguity and Doubt

Millennials' perspectives on religion are difficult to characterize because many of these young adults actively question their own perspectives. Many of the Millennials who doubt the existence of God appear uncertain even about their doubts. Whereas the nonbelieving Gen Xers are relatively firm in their rejection of religion and spirituality—as are the Later Boomers in their judgment of organized religion—the Millennials we talked to seem more tentative. Twenty-six-year-old Sarah Turner, who was raised as a Baptist but says she no longer has any religious affiliation, struggles with her uncertainty. "I'm really torn because I grew up with the religious beliefs that I did and I was really, at one time, a very faithful person," she confides. But that has changed. "I have a lot of doubt. I don't have faith right now. I haven't really found somebody in my life who I could talk about these things to." She can't open up to her parents or grandparents because they would just try to "talk [her] into" religious faith. But in her mind, "the thing [that] is unfortunate about faith is that you either have it or you don't. You don't 'kind of' have it. So I'm kind of in that, 'I don't really know' part."

Samantha Rosenberg, a twenty-year-old who calls herself a "Conservadox" Jew, also wrestles with the "leap of faith" one must take in order to believe in God. "It's hard to sort of grasp onto something that you really just cannot understand," she says. "I think it's already a leap of faith to follow any religion." She says she doesn't think she's ready to believe that God is all good and "will do the best for you if you just pray to God....Like, I see so much bad in the world with what's going on now, like Darfur....I see just so much evil in this world and I can't imagine why—how, if God was good and God was just, if He did exist, how He could be letting this stuff go on. He or She."

Lindsay Lieberman, a twenty-seven-year-old nonobservant Jew, questions the usefulness of religion in the modern world. She says that a part of her believes that if "there were no religion, the world would be better....I don't think it's as useful anymore, because of all the things that science has taught us. I mean, I understand that it gives people like something to, like a feeling of belonging somewhere, and *[pause]* why it's important to believe in the higher power, because it's a source of comfort." However, she also thinks "that's just the easy way out."

Similarly, Josephine Smith, a twenty-five-year-old unaffiliated agnostic, is skeptical about Biblical stories, which she used to hear as a kid when she went to church or Bible study. "Listening to them talk for two hours or being in their little Bible group, it just seemed like stories to exemplify how you should be living, rather than stories that actually happened," she says. "I'm not sure if they've been embellished over the years or not. I kind of think that they were....It makes more sense to me than saying that God created us in seven days, when there were dinosaurs and so much that went on before humans came in the picture. I don't believe it."

But at the same time, Josephine finds herself leaning toward God and the spiritual. "I'd like to believe in karma. I'd like to believe that if you keep yourself intact, that things won't get too bad for you," she says."I know that when I'm really in a bind, I go towards the spiritual and I've prayed to God quite a few times. I'm never sure if anybody can hear it, but I have used that as a way, if anything, for meditation just to get out my own feelings....Hopefully, I'm not just talking to myself."

Even some Millennials with a firm belief in God seem unable to express their thoughts and feelings about their spiritual and religious perspectives.

This may be due, for some, to a lack of familiarity with the theological foundations of their particular faith. Natasha Sanchez, who is now a Pentecostal but was raised in a Catholic family, is disconnected from her Christian roots:

> I believe that there's a heaven, I believe that there's hell. I believe that there is a God, and I believe that certain things happen for a reason. A lot of the things that the Bible says, you know, we see happening. I do believe, I fear Him, I fear God. So I know that—I just believe what I feel. I don't know if it's just what I was taught or just, you know. Because, I mean, I went to a Catholic [Church] for my communion for three years. But none of that stuff really stuck.

Many of these comments seem to mirror what Christian Smith and Melinda Denton describe in the National Survey of Youth and Religion as "Moralistic Therapeutic Deism."[5]

Those Millennials who grew up in a family that emphasized religious education seem to have a much more solid grasp of the history and theology of their faith. Keith West, who was raised as a Methodist and is now a highly involved Baptist, studied Christianity throughout college and graduate school and has worked for Evangelical Christian ministries in a variety of capacities. His education had a major impact on his understanding of religion:

> I understood and I made my faith my own, which was something new. You know, it had always been something that was pretty formulaic that had been handed down from people above me in the church and my parents. So, I started to understand why I believe some of the things I always took for granted.

Lauren Walker, a twenty-one-year-old Episcopalian who has attended Episcopal or Catholic schools from kindergarten through college, also has reflected on the insight and appreciation of her faith that comes from a religious education. Her high school had a mandatory religion class every year, and she also took classes in college. "So it's been such a big part of my education. Having a pretty solid understanding of what religion does historically and what it is meant to do, I think that it's something that I have a lot of respect for."

Both Keith's and Lauren's experiences reflect a historical and experiential foundation that comes from broad religious study. Those with more extensive religious socialization in a specific faith also spoke with great clarity about their beliefs. Yet with some exceptions, including Keith West, Lauren Walker, and some Jews and Mormons we spoke with, most Millennials in our sample report limited experience with formal religious education. This may explain their lack of connection to the core beliefs that make up religious organizations and faith traditions today.

Embracing Religious Diversity

Nearly one in five of the Millennials we interviewed identify themselves as "just Christian" or "nondenominational Christian"—more than any other cohort and almost twice the sample average.[6] This may reflect a lack of denomination-based religious education or simply a lack of concern about the sectarian roots of their beliefs. Alternatively, it may be a more intentional attempt to draw from a variety of "Christian" principles, pulling ideas together into a unique set of beliefs that work for them as individuals.

Deidra Johnson, a twenty-seven-year old whose parents are devout Catholics but who has not been to church since leaving home, questions the value of putting all of her eggs in one religious basket:

> Like, just because I believe in the Bible does not mean that it's right or wrong, or that the—some other saying is wrong, or Buddhism is wrong. Or even though, like, I believe in God and I do believe that He created—But I don't know if it's necessarily the Christian perspective, or the Buddhist perspective, or the Muslim perspective, or the Jewish perspective. I don't know that is the actual thing. I think there's truth in all of it.

Many Millennials hesitate to adopt a single religion uncritically and in its totality, preferring a flexible belief system that draws from religion but is not entirely dictated by it. A tendency to draw from a range of religious perspectives or to selectively choose from the tenets of a particular religion reflects the nonjudgmental attitude of many Millennials. An open-mindedness and appreciation for diversity was one clear theme that frequently emerged in the Millennials' interviews, whether they were speaking about religious or nonreligious ideas. For example, Sarah Turner has "an awareness of appreciating other people" and "believe[s] in treating people with respect"—values she inherited from her mother and maternal grandfather, each of whom "embraced diversity" and excelled at "communicating with people of different religions, different ethnicities and backgrounds."

Even Millennials who are committed to a single religious tradition appreciate the value of religious diversity. Twenty-year-old Nicole Young, who is firmly rooted in her Mormon faith, remarks, "I like to learn about other people's religions. When I was younger, I was just like, 'Oh no, there's no other religion but being Mormon.' And, you know, so I kind of wasn't shown what other religions were out there when I was younger. But as I got older, I got to see that and it was really interesting. I think it's really great that other people believe, you know, other things too."

Overall, the Millennials we spoke with expressed such a wide range of perspectives on religion that it is very difficult to categorize them as group. This is undoubtedly due to their relative youth—they were between twenty- and twenty-seven-years-old at the time they were interviewed—compared to the other generations in our sample. As they age, the Millennials' defining characteristics may become more apparent. On the other hand, and as Christian Smith and Melissa Denton suggest, any "generation gap" that exists between Millennials and their parents, grandparents, and great-grandparents may be outweighed by their similarities.[7] This seems to be the case for the most of Millennials we interviewed, whose perspectives are shared by members of older generations. In the subsequent chapters of this volume, we examine in considerable detail the degree to which there is generational continuity within families in religious beliefs and behaviors, similarities between generations that are the result of transmission processes involving religious socialization.

Yet one characteristic of the Millennials stands out. As they espouse a wide range of viewpoints, many of the Millennials lack confidence in their beliefs and clarity about the theological roots of their religious affiliations, perhaps in part because of relatively limited experience with formal religious education. This is similar to what Christian Smith reports from the National Survey of Youth and Religion: an inability of many teenagers to articulate their religious beliefs or to identify the specific attributes of their church or congregation's doctrines, practices, and symbols.[8] But this lack of religious specificity may also stem from the Millennials' appreciation for diversity. Many noted their interest in learning about other religions and their appreciation of the heterogeneity of contemporary American society. This, too, may drive them to create Robert Wuthnow's religious "bricolage," or "construction improvised from multiple sources,"[9] rather than adopting a well-defined religious tradition in its entirety—a sort of religious ambiguity and appreciation of diversity that seems to characterize many of our Millennial respondents.

Generational Change and Religion: Trends over a Century

In this chapter we have sampled the vast array of perspectives on religion and spirituality that characterize contemporary American society. We have organized these to show similarities and differences across age groups. In the following chapter, we'll explore how—and whether—religion is imparted from one generation in a family to the next, looking at snapshots of religious transmission in 1970 and 2005. Before that, however, we conclude by reviewing the results of our analysis and describing some unexpected generational trends.

Figure 2.1 summarizes the characteristic generational expressions of religion and spirituality of all seven age groups. It further identifies three emergent trends in religion and spirituality across all generations. The first cross-cohort trend addresses the question "What and where is God?" (see the top row in Figure 2.1). Our interview data suggest that there is an increasing tendency over successive generations to internalize and deobjectify God or a Higher Power. Older generations describe an all-powerful Heavenly Father who is evident in nature and observed through everyday miracles. Beginning with the silent generation, respondents describe a more personal, accessible God that resides within the human spirit.

A second trend (summarized in the middle row of Figure 2.1) addresses the "location of religious and spiritual practice." This reflects the increasing separation of religious practice from religious institutional contexts such as traditional church worship and participation. While some WWI generation respondents have set up household shrines to compensate for their increasingly limited access to church due to advancing age, for them, religion and church are synonymous. However, starting with those in the Depression Era we see a tendency to differentiate between going to church and leading a religious life. Later generations also separate these two concepts, particularly distinguishing institutional religious practice from non- or even anti-institutional spirituality, which is practiced in increasingly diverse contexts. The growing emphasis on spirituality, first described by Early Boomers, served to further separate religious

	WWI 1900–1915	Depression Era 1916–31	Silent Generation 1932–45	Older Boomers 1946–54	Younger Boomers 1955–64	Generation X 1965–79	Millennials 1980–88
What and where is God?	External and universal		Internal and universal				
	God is an awesome Higher Power, evident in nature	God is an benevolent Higher Power, knowable through His actions	God is inside me and everything around me	God is a healing spirit	God is a personal relationship	God is a state of mind	God is whatever you want it to be
Location of religious and spiritual practice	Dependent on the institution; rooted in a particular theology			Not dependent on the institution, rooted in a particular theology	Not dependent on the institution; not rooted in a particular theology		
	Religious practice = Church	Religion and spirituality = Church; Belief in God ≠ Church	Religious and Spiritual practice = Church	Religious practice = Church; Spiritual practice = anywhere	Spiritual practice = NOT in a church	Believers: Religion and spirituality in church and everyday life; nonbelievers: Religion and spirituality are irrational	Religion and spirituality can be in or outside of Church
Religion vs. Spirituality	Limited concept of spirituality	Spirituality indistinct from religion		Spirituality distinct from religion			Limited concepts of religious traditions
	Spirituality? What's that?	Religion = Spirituality	Religion = Spirituality	Religion = Church; Spirituality = A Feeling	Religion = Church (=bad); Spirituality = A Feeling (=good)	Religion = Church; Spirituality = A Relationship with God	Religion? What's that?

FIGURE 2.1 Spirituality and Religion: Themes by Age Cohort

devotional practices from religious institutions such as churches and to provide a framework for understanding the personal and highly individualized "relationships with God" described by Later Boomers and the cohorts following them.

A third and closely related trend concerns "religion versus spirituality" (bottom row of Figure 2.1). Here we see an increasing differentiation between "religion" and "spirituality" and a growing appreciation for the latter. While "spirituality" had little significance for the oldest generations, as either a meaningless term or indistinguishable from "religion," starting with the Baby Boomers we see clear distinctions between religion and spirituality and ways in which individuals incorporate them into their lives.

The trends seen across generations provide persuasive evidence of historical events interacting with time of birth to influence religious and spiritual experiences. We see increasing complexity of religious and spiritual experience today in ways that do not conform to the more clearly demarcated institutional boundaries of the past. As the accounts of the Millennials in particular suggest, religious formulations from prior eras do not seem to work for many younger people today. Time will tell how these age cohorts, and younger ones to follow, will continue to modify the religious practices and institutions of American religion. In light of the profound social and cultural changes over the past several decades reviewed in chapter 1, as well as the distinctions between age groups in expressions of spirituality described in this chapter, how much similarity is there between parents and young adults in religion today, and how can religious momentum across generations be maintained in families of faith? We turn to these issues in the next chapters.

CHAPTER 3 | Has Family Influence Declined?[1]

A devout Catholic, Generation (G) 2 Estella Garcia, age seventy-five, remembers how her mother frequently reminded her to go to church. Her son, fifty-two-year-old G3 Manuel, says that it was his mother's "faith and belief in the Lord" that instilled in him the belief "that the church cannot be second to anything." Twenty-seven-year-old G4 Marisol, also a devout Catholic, speaks warmly about her father and says: "We [she and her husband] have to show our kids that this is the way we want them to be, and in order to do that, we have to go to church and we have to practice it."

G4 Erik Lieberman, twenty-four and an observant Jew, says: "I see that I'm Jewish, and I see my parents are Jewish, [and] my grandparents are Jewish...This is just the way I'm supposed to do it."

HOW SIMILAR OR DIFFERENT are young adults and their parents in religious orientation? How similar or different are they compared to parents and young adults in the 1970s, and how does this correspond to the changing social landscape of families and religion since then?

Most people would probably assume, as we did at the beginning of this study, that the religious influence of parents on their children has weakened over the past four decades. This prediction would seem consistent with information about recent cultural trends. More Americans than in the past appear to be switching religious affiliations, leaving the faith in which they were raised, and moving to another affiliation or to no faith at all. In a recent national survey 44% of Americans said they did not have the same religious affiliation today that they had when they were growing up.[2] Yet parents who value their own faith invest considerable effort to educate their children in that faith, by both word and example. In so doing, they hope to enhance the likelihood of transmitting their religious faith to their children. We use the term "transmission" to refer to long-term efforts by parents to teach something they feel is highly desirable to their child, such as religious values, beliefs, and practices.

Continuity and Contrast: Religious Transmission in 1970 and 2005

To assess the intergenerational transmission of religion over time, we examined the degree of religious similarity between parents and their young adult children in 1970 with that of young adults and parents three and a half decades later, in 2005. We first compared these over dimensions of religiosity that we had been measuring over thirty-five years in our longitudinal data collection: religious affiliation; religious intensity ("How religious would you say you are?"); religious participation (frequency of religious service attendance); agreement with a literal or conservative interpretation of the Bible; and agreement with the importance of religion in civic or public life. Results are shown in Figure 3.1.

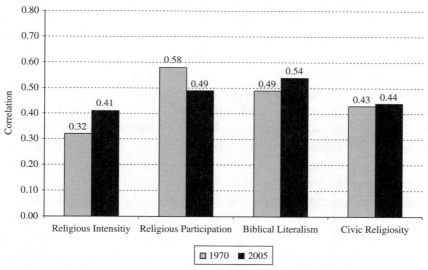

FIGURE 3.1 Similarity Between Parents and Young Adult Children on Four Dimensions of Religiosity, 1970 (G2–G3) and 2006 (G3–G4)

At each time period, 1970 and 2005, there is statistically significant similarity between parents and their young adult children in all four aspects of religiosity.[3] This is strong evidence for religious transmission. Equally striking is the similarity between the 1970 and 2005 rates of similarity. We expected that correlations between parents and their young adult children would be significantly lower in 2005 than they were in 1970, but these data indicate otherwise: Parent–youth similarity in religiosity has not declined over thirty-five years.[4] From viewing Figure 3.1 it might appear that religious participation is an exception to this trend, since the correlation between parents and children was slightly lower in 2005 than in 1970; however, this difference is not statistically significant. Moreover, in Figure 3.1 it might appear that parent–child similarity was even *greater* in both religious intensity and Biblical literalism in 2005 than in 1970; but again, these differences were not statistically significant.

That we found so little change in rates of parent–child religious similarity is particularly noteworthy given the many social and historical changes that occurred over this period (see chapter 1). For example, it was a surprise that so many of the young adults had a religious affiliation in the same faith tradition as their parents. These results suggest that family influences on the religiosity of the younger generation have not weakened to the degree that has been widely reported.[5]

Several reasons can be given for the widespread but mistaken assumption of a decline in family intergenerational influence in religion. Most of the evidence that has led to this interpretation is from surveys consisting of one-time interviews with one individual; such surveys often ask about only one or two aspects of religiosity, usually religious affiliation (e.g., "To what religious group do you belong?") and participation (e.g., "How often do you attend religious services?"). However, religious affiliation today appears less central to core aspects of religiosity than, say, an individual's feeling of the importance of religion or spirituality to his or her personal life.[6] Moreover, affiliation with a particular church or religious organization can be dependent on characteristics that are somewhat peripheral to religious tradition: the personality of the minister or rabbi, the music or format of the service, the stance of the denomination on social issues such as the ordination of women, abortion, or homosexuality. This is one explanation for the high rate of religious switching in America; denominational loyalty is lower today than in the past.[7] Finally, salience of faith (religious intensity) may be more relevant for parents to transmit to children than a particular religious affiliation.

Religious Affiliation: Catholic, Protestant, Jew, and Others

G3 Miriam Bernstein says she is a "Modern Orthodox" Jew. She talks about the meaning of being Jewish and why it is so important that her children marry someone Jewish and what would be lost if they did not: "What would be lost would be the feeling of being Jewish, following the laws of Judaism, the traditions of being Jewish, celebrating the holidays and the Jewish festivals. Being Jewish is not simply a religion, being Jewish is a way of life. And that is what would be lost—the Jewish way of life." The Bernsteins transmit Jewish values through holiday rituals and celebrations. G4 Rachel describes her family as being traditional and "very food-centric" with all the holidays: "[W]e always get together for a meal and talk about the historical significance behind each of the different holidays and we retell the story every year so that it could be taught to the younger kids as well as kind of just remembering. I identify family as being Jewish—to me, being Jewish is very connected with being family-oriented."

Religious affiliation is perhaps the most obvious aspect of religiosity, and the extent to which young adults affiliate with the same religious tradition as their parents is the most visible aspect of intergenerational transmission. To assess parent–child similarity, we took the dozens of specific religious affiliations reported by the family members in our sample—for example, American Baptist, Southern Baptist, Holiness Baptist, Free Will Baptist—and grouped similar denominations[8] into the five religious traditions most highly represented in our sample: Evangelical Protestant, Mainline Protestant, Catholic, Jewish, and Mormon, plus a group of who wrote "none": nonreligious, unaffiliated, atheist, or agnostic respondents (see the Appendix for details). We assessed how similar parents and their young adult children were in 1970 and compared this a generation later, in 2005.

In the 2005 survey, six in ten parents had young adult children who reported their religious affiliation was in the same faith tradition as their parents. In 1970 the percentage was somewhat higher, almost seven in ten. Some readers might be surprised, as we were, by the extent of this similarity in faith tradition between generations, given the trends of America's increasingly individualistic cultural climate, declining authority of religious institutions, and increase in religious switching. However, as we will discuss later, within-family patterns over time do not necessarily follow cultural trends over time.

There is considerable variation across religious traditions in rates of intergenerational transmission, as can be seen in Figure 3.2. For

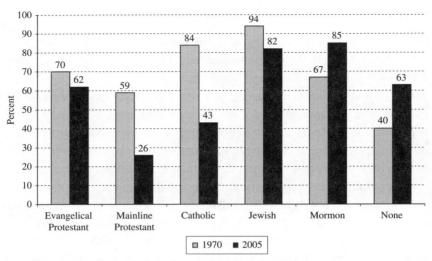

FIGURE 3.2 Percentage of Parents Whose Young Adult Children Have the Same Religious Tradition, 1970 (G2-G3) and 2005 (G3-G4)

Evangelical Protestants, the transmission rate has been high; in 2005, 62% of parents in our sample had young adult children who were following in their Evangelical tradition, down slightly from 70% in 1970. On the other hand, both Mainline Protestants and Catholics showed low levels of parent–child similarity in 2005, and both reflected considerable declines from 1970 similarity rates. Mainline Protestants declined by 27 percentage points, and Catholics dropped an eye-opening 41 percentage points.

According to national statistics, Mainline Protestants and Catholics (excluding recent immigrants) were the two religious traditions that showed the greatest overall decreases in overall membership since 1970, just as they had been the ones whose membership showed a surge in the years following World War II.[9] The total number of Catholics in America has remained stable since 1990, however, because recent waves of immigrants from Catholic countries have offset the large decline in U.S.-born non-Hispanic Catholics.

For the Jewish parents in our sample, there has been very high intergenerational similarity in religious affiliation (82% in the 2005 survey). But we must be cautious in treating this as indicating high *religious* transmission across generations, since Jewish identification can reflect a *cultural* Judaism that is not necessarily religious. That is, when children of Jewish parents answered the question "What is your religion?" by saying "Jewish," like their parents, they may have been referring to a cultural identity, since their responses to other questions indicated they had no belief in God or any affiliation with a temple.[10] We discuss this more fully in chapter 9.

In Figure 3.2 we see a very high rate of parent–child similarity in religious affiliation among Mormons in our sample compared to the other religious traditions. But we should not make too much of this for two reasons. First is the relatively small number of Mormons in our sample compared to Protestants and Catholics, so percentage comparisons may not be appropriate. Second, like many cultural Jews, some Mormons identify with a long familial identity even when they are no longer practicing members in good standing with the Church.

The final bar in Figure 3.2 reflects the percentage of parent–child pairs who together indicate "none," or no religious affiliation. In the 2005 survey we were surprised to see that a remarkable 63% of nonaffiliated parents had children who were also nonaffiliated, an intergenerational similarity rate eclipsed only by Jews and Mormons. How to understand and interpret a "no religion" response is a challenge for religious surveyors today, as we discuss in chapter 8. Here we are concerned only with the similarity in responses between parents and children in religious identification; if both identify themselves as "none" it makes little difference for our purpose whether they are antireligious, religiously indifferent, or skeptical of organized religion. In our sample, however, the parent–child similarity rate among the nonreligious has increased by more than half from 1970, when it was 40%. The magnitude of this increase suggests support for an observation in the 2008 Pew Forum report[11] that in the 1960s and 1970s many young adults switched to "no religious tradition" because they were influenced by changes in the larger religious and cultural environment, particularly the declining legitimacy of formal religious organizations. Years later, when these religiously nonaffiliated youth had children of their own, they passed on their nonreligious orientation to their offspring.

The high degree of parent–child similarity in the nonaffiliated category deserves discussion, since this has not received much attention in the religious research literature. As we see in chapter 8, many of these parents and children are simply "religiously indifferent," individuals who do not care about religion and perhaps never have. Others may be "spiritual but not religious," rejecting any organized church but deeply committed to their relationship with a personally defined supreme being. Others (and these categories are not mutually exclusive) are overtly antireligious, what one minister we interviewed called "religious refugees," resulting from a wounding experience with a priest, minister, rabbi, or overzealous missionary. Then there are those who identify with and call themselves "atheists," some of whom belong to organized groups, the numbers of which are growing, particularly on college campuses.[12]

Some might argue that when parents and children resemble one another on nonreligious indicators this does not signify "transmission," because there is nothing to transmit. In a religiously indifferent parent–child dyad, according to this argument, similarity exists simply in the absence of any religious training. However, the results we present in chapter 8 show a quite different picture. Many of the "nones" speak about the efforts they have made to teach their children values that are not tied to a traditional religious organization. They speak about this as determinedly as some of the most active churchgoing parents in our sample. It seems clear that there is intergenerational transmission of nonreligiosity as well as religiosity.

In sum, as we look at trends in parent–child similarity in religious tradition over the past thirty-five years, we see declines in transmission rates among the traditionally mainstream denominations and increases among Mormons and the unaffiliated, with Evangelicals' transmission levels decreasing slightly. Nevertheless, for a surprisingly large number of families in our study, similarity between parents and children in their religious tradition across generations remains relatively high. Sixty percent of Baby Boomer parents and their children share the same religious affiliation (or nonreligion) at a time when most Americans perceive that cultural and historical forces have been eroding family influence. In subsequent chapters we explore the processes and contexts of intergenerational religious transmission to examine how and why these transmission patterns are occurring.

Religious Intensity: Self-Reported Religiousness

Religious affiliation is a relatively objective, external aspect of religiosity. A more internal, subjective dimension is what we call religious intensity. We asked respondents, "Regardless of whether you attend religious services, do you consider yourself to be … very religious; moderately religious; somewhat religious; not at all religious?" The level of parent–child similarity in 2005 was, in statistical terms, no different from that in 1970. Overall, in the 2005 survey 40% of parents and their young adult children answered the question in the same way, about the same (41%) as parents and children in 1970.

We were interested to see whether there was higher parent–child agreement in the middle or at the extremes of the response categories in 2005 compared to 1970. Higher parent–child agreement at the extremes ("very religious," for example) would be much stronger evidence of a transmission effect than high similarity in the "somewhat religious" category. As can be seen in Figure 3.3, the data do show higher agreement in the "very" and "not at all" religious categories. What is perhaps most interesting is that they indicate a trend toward polarization in religious intensity over time. Parent–child congruence in the "very religious" response category increased by 10 percentage points between 1970 and 2005 (from 33% to 43%), and the "not at all religious" category increased by 17 percentage points (from 36% to 54%). By contrast, the degree of congruence between parents and children who said they were "moderately religious" declined, decreasing by a remarkable 25 percentage points. Both as individuals and as parent–child dyads, the Longitudinal Study of Generations (LSOG) study panel members were moving away from the more moderate response categories over these thirty-five years. Such polarization is consistent with nationwide trends[13] and bolsters, for example, Robert Wuthnow's observations about the increasing divisions within American religion during the latter decades of the twentieth century.[14]

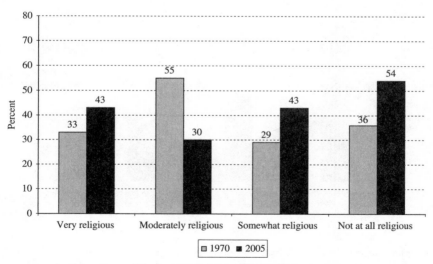

FIGURE 3.3 Percentage of Parents Whose Young Adult Children Report the Same Level of Religious Intensity, 1970 (G2–G3) and 2005 (G3–G4)

Religious Participation: Frequency of Service Attendance

Over several waves of the LSOG survey, members of the Knox family consistently ranked "religious participation" as one of their most important values. G2 Diane, a Lutheran, says she "love[s her] church" and reports attending services at least once a week. Her husband, Nathaniel, adds that he and his wife have gone to church on Sundays "for fifty-seven years, since we got married." Their daughter, G3 Ellen, also attends church once a week and says, "I just feel better when I go to church.... I guess it kind of calms me, renews me and it just makes me feel better." But Diane and Nathaniel's son, Todd, does not attend church, nor do their G4 grandchildren. This is a source of sadness for Diane, who wants to "make sure my great-grandchild goes to church." Her daughter, Ellen, conspires in this effort to encourage church attendance among the younger generation: "Even though my daughter doesn't go to church, I take her son to church with me."

When we look at the degree of parent–child similarity in frequency of religious service attendance (see Figure 3.4), we find that this declined very slightly between 1970 and 2005 (53% to 47%). It is interesting that parent–child similarity is highest for those who report attending religious

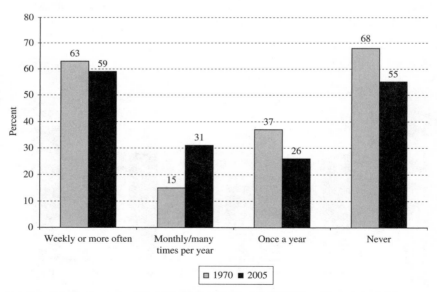

FIGURE 3.4 Percentage of Parents Whose Young Adult Children Report the Same Frequency of Religious Service Attendance, 1970 (G2–G3) and 2005 (G3–G4)

services frequently (weekly or more often); in 2005, 59% of parents in this group had children who also attend very frequently (see Figure 3.4). Also, in 2005 we see high parent–child congruence, 55%, for those who report that they "never" attend religious services. In the intermediate participation categories, parent–child similarity is much less.

In frequency of church attendance therefore children seem to model themselves after the behavior of parents who attend church frequently—or who don't attend at all. What's intriguing is that we see relatively little decline over the past thirty-five years in the similarity of parents and their adult children in *frequent* church attendance—weekly or more often—even as overall rates of church attendance in the United States have declined during the same period.[15] On the other hand, the pattern of parent–child similarity across all response categories suggests a greater polarization—moving toward the extremes—of service attendance frequency in 1970 than in 2005.

Religious Beliefs: Literal Interpretation of the Bible

For families in conservative and Orthodox religious traditions, passing on a reverence for the sacred words of Scriptures was very important. For example, G3 Marjorie Bingham, a Mormon, describes her efforts to do this for her four children. "We went to church on Sundays and we had a Family Home Evening. [Every Monday night] we would have a lesson and use the Scriptures [to teach] about being Godlike and being kind to each other. [Then we would] ask the children questions about how they would be involved."

In each of the LSOG survey waves, we asked respondents to indicate their agreement or disagreement with a number of statements about attitudes and values. Two of these items reflect orthodox or conservative religious Judeo-Christian beliefs reflected in Biblical inerrancy, that is, the view that the Bible is the Word of God, literally: "God exists in the form as described in the Bible" and "All people alive today are descendants of Adam and Eve."[16] Family members who say they "strongly agree" with these items support the view that the Bible is the literal Word of God, a view held by conservative groups within Jewish and some Christian (particularly Evangelical Protestant but also Catholic) faiths. For our research analysis, we combined the two items. In 2005 the level of congruence between parents and their adult children on Biblical literalism beliefs was 42%; it was about the same in 1970.

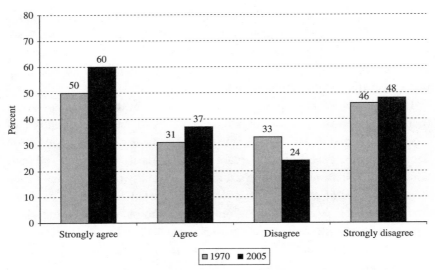

FIGURE 3.5 Percentage of Parents Whose Young Adult Children Report the Same Beliefs Reflecting Biblical Literalism, 1970 (G2–G3) and 2005 (G3–G4)

We saw some interesting patterns in the response categories when we examined individually to see where the greatest parent–child agreement occurred. We find this at the extremes (see Figure 3.5): Among those who "strongly believe" in the literal accuracy of the Bible, there was a much higher degree of congruence between parents and children—six of ten. In fact, parent–child congruence in the "strongly agree" category increased over the thirty-five years by 10 percentage points, from 50% to 60%. The same is true at the other extreme, those who "strongly disagree": Here we also see high parent–child congruence. That is, we see higher parent–child similarity among those whose beliefs are on one end of the spectrum or the other—those who strongly endorse or strongly reject a literal interpretation of the Bible—than for the more moderate positions in between. This is a polarization, and it is somewhat stronger in 2005 than in 1970.

Beliefs: Civic Religiosity

Regardless of whether individuals believe that the Bible should be taken literally as the inerrant word of God, they may feel that religious values

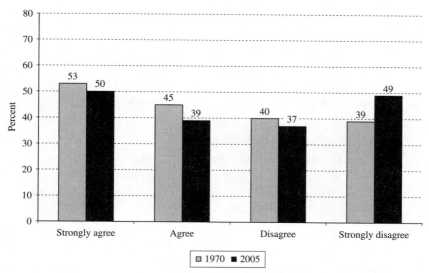

FIGURE 3.6 Percentage of Parents Whose Young Adult Children Report the Same Beliefs About Civic Religiosity, 1970 (G2–G3) and 2005 (G3–G4)

are important to teach children or that they should guide behavior in society. We asked respondents to agree or disagree with two statements that reflect such beliefs in civic religiosity—"Every child should have religious education" and "This country would be better off if religion had a greater influence on daily life"—and combined them for the purpose of this analysis.[17] There was no significant difference between parent–child similarity in 1970 and 2005. In 2005 slightly more than four out of ten parents and children were in agreement concerning their responses to the civil religiosity questions.

When we examine congruence on the separate response categories, we find the same pattern as in the other measures of religiosity (see Figure 3.6). In 2005, parent–child congruence was highest on the extreme responses: 50% on "strongly agree" and 49% on "strongly disagree."

In Religion, Parents Really Matter

To what extent are the parents and adult children in our study similar in religion? How does this compare to a generation ago? Is there significantly less religious continuity over two and three generations today than there was in the 1970s?

First, it appears that in 2005 a surprising number—well over half—of the parents and young adult children in our sample were similar across the five dimensions of religiosity we were able to assess in the course of this study. There was significant parent–child similarity in religious affiliation, participation, religious intensity, Biblical beliefs, and civic religiosity. We were surprised at the high rates of intergenerational religious transmission these figures indicate. In the context of cultural changes reflecting increased individualism and altered family forms and functions, we had anticipated considerably greater evidence of a weakening of parental influences on religiosity.

The surprises continued when we compared rates of transmission in 1970, when the study began, to those in 2005, the most recent survey. Our second finding is that religious transmission between parents and children does not appear to have declined over time in this sample. We had expected to see a significant decrease in indicators of overall transmission from 1970 to 2005 because of so much evidence, or at least opinion, indicating waning family influence and declining religious involvement on the part of youth.

Third, we identified significant contrasts in intergenerational transmission across the religious traditions represented in our study. Among Mainline Protestants and Catholics, parent–child similarities declined over the thirty-five years. Among Evangelical Protestants, the rate of similarity between parents and their young adult children remained essentially the same. For Mormons and Jews, the rates of similarity appear to be somewhat higher in 2005 than in 1970, although this may be an artifact of their relatively small numbers in our sample. Nevertheless, it is clear that there is high intergenerational transmission of religiosity among Evangelicals, Jews, and Mormons in our sample, for reasons we discuss in chapter 9.

In summary, despite sociohistorical changes in recent decades suggesting the decreased role of family and religion in society, we find considerable religious continuity between parents and children generations in our study. We examine some of the practical implications of these results in chapter 10. First, in the next part of this book, we examine different relationships within the family to determine what processes are the most important for passing religion down from one generation to the next. We open Part 2 with information from both survey and interview data. What do the respondents tell us in their own words about religion and spirituality? What do they say about the intergenerational influences that have affected them as they are nurtured religiously—or not—by their families of origin?

PART 2 | Family Patterns and
Religious Momentum
Across Generations

CHAPTER 4 | The Importance of Warmth
Parental Piety and the Distant Dad[1]

Fifty-four-year-old Nina Sabelli says she did not have a close relationship with her parents when growing up. They raised her in the Catholic faith, but she left the Church as a teenager and is now a fervent Evangelical. When asked to recall her childhood, she describes her father as distant and "very withholding of his affection towards me."

Twenty-five-year-old Brandon Young's relationship with his Mormon father has been one of conflict: "It was a lot of 'you need to be going to church, we raised you this way,' and just trying to be very forceful, and try[ing] to make me feel bad about it." In contrast, Brandon indicated in his surveys over time that he felt "very close" to his mother, also a devout Mormon: "When I was growing up she was always there. So I think a lot of who I am is a result of my mom." Nevertheless, as an adult Brandon has followed neither his father nor his mother in their Mormonism and is not involved in any church.

THE FIRST EMOTIONAL BONDS we form are with our parents, and the nature of these bonds influences us throughout our lives. For many young adults, parents have been the primary influence on their spiritual and religious development, and relations with parents are linked to their first conceptions of God.[2]

Sociologists and psychologists use the term "socialization" to refer to the process by which parents and other adults impart to children the knowledge, skills, and values that they feel are important in preparing them for adulthood.[3] For religious fathers and mothers, transmitting faith to offspring is an important part of that preparation. Their efforts at religious socialization in most cases are reinforced and amplified through religious organizations, most of which have extensive programs and activities directed toward training children and youth in practices and beliefs. Still, parents are the key to religious socialization. To religious parents, faith forms the core of what is most valuable to them in life, what has meant the most to them, and what they would like their children to live by. For these parents the child's acceptance or rejection of their religious faith is a source of joy or of sadness.

But what promotes—or hinders—religious socialization? To date, we have not developed theory-based explanations about religious socialization that are based on social science data. There are, however, theories of socialization and intergenerational transmission to provide the foundation for such models.[4] Certainly one factor is parental behavior, such as role modeling and consistency. If the parents are not themselves involved in religious activities, if their actions are not consistent with what they preach, children are rarely motivated to follow in their parents' religious footsteps. That parental influence on values is important few will argue. But are parents as influential today as in they were in the past? In an earlier book based on our research, *How Families Still Matter: A Longitudinal Study of Two Generations of Youth,*[5] we reported data from the Longitudinal Study of Generations (LSOG) panel of families showing that parental influence on youths' achievement orientations and values such as humanism and materialism has not declined. We saw in chapter 3 that there are higher rates of parent–child resemblance in religiosity than had been expected and that the degree of intergenerational transmission does not appear to have decreased over the past thirty-five years.

In this chapter we examine how the quality of the parent–child relationship affects whether children adopt the religion of their parents. Does the likelihood of parents successfully passing on their religious beliefs and practices vary by the degree of emotional closeness children feel toward their parents?

Intergenerational Solidarity and Transmission: Inheritance, Modeling, Affection

When our study began in 1970, a major objective was to explore the emotional and interactional complexities of intergenerational relationships over the life course, a topic neglected by previous research. To address this knowledge gap, we developed a conceptual framework that we called the "intergenerational solidarity model," defined as the degree of emotional closeness, contact, exchange of support and services, and feelings of family obligation that characterize the bonds across generations in the family.[6] What the model proposed, and what our subsequent data confirmed, is that there are six distinct but related dimensions of the intergenerational relationship, what we termed "intergenerational solidarity." (See Appendix A for a discussion of the solidarity dimensions and their measurement in survey research.). We have used the solidarity model to predict similarities and differences in value orientations between generations, such as individualism and materialism,[7] and to examine how the quality of intergenerational relationships corresponds to mental health and psychological well-being. In survey measurement, we found that the one best summary indicator of intergenerational solidarity is the question, "Taking everything together, how close do you feel is the relationship between you and your father (or mother) these days?" We use this item— affectual solidarity, referring to perceived intergenerational closeness—in the analyses that follow.

In the first part of this chapter, we examine our longitudinal survey data to assess linkages between the quality of parent–child relationships and religious transmission, focusing on whether the child's perception of that relationship is warm and affirming or distant and removed. In the second part, we analyze interview data to take a closer look at relationships between parenting styles, parental religious socialization processes, and religious transmission. Which types of parenting and styles of religious socialization—for example, religiously firm parenting or religiously open parenting—were most effective in raising children who would follow their parents in faith? Which parenting styles were least successful?

The Pivotal Factor in Successful Transmission: Warm, Affirming Parents

In studying religious transmission, we wanted to examine differences between children who feel close to their parents compared to those who do not. In each wave of the study, we asked questions assessing intergenerational solidarity of both parents and children.[8] Below we focus on young adults' perceptions of the quality of their relationship with their parents and how this varies with parent–child religious similarity.

Close or Distant Parents

In Figure 4.1 we see that, for each of the four dimensions of religiosity, there is a higher rate of parent–child similarity for those who perceive a close relationship compared to those who feel their relationship is not close. It is thus likely that when a child feels close to a parent, he or she is more likely to imitate or model that parent, for example being highly involved in church. Close parent–child bonds are more conducive to religious socialization,[9] and in the absence of close parent–child bonds, this transmission effect is less likely to occur.

The results depicted in these figures may actually be conservative estimates of the effects of parent–child closeness because children tend to rate the quality of their emotional bonds with parents lower than their parents do. This reflects what we have called the Intergenerational Stake hypothesis[10]: in describing their mutual relationship, youth tend to describe lower rates of closeness and higher rates of conflicts than

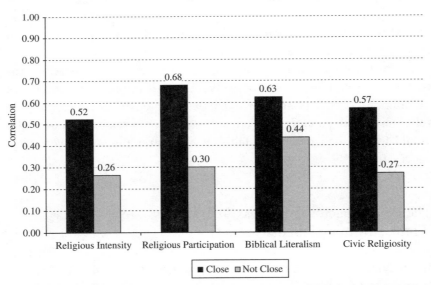

FIGURE 4.1 Similarity Between Parents and Young Adult Children Who Perceive Their Relationship as Close or Not Close for Four Dimensions of Religiosity, 2005 (G3–G4)

do their parents. The Intergenerational Stake theory explains this as follows: Parents expend huge amounts of time, energy, money, and love in raising a child; consequently, they are highly invested in the relationship and are more inclined to see continuity and cohesion—they have a high "stake" in the next generation. Their children, by contrast, have much less investment in their relationship with their parents. They are developing their independence and affirming their individuality; thus they tend to see greater differences with their parents, less cohesion, and more conflict.[11] Their "stake" will be invested in their own children, the generation to come.

Transmission effects might also be expected to vary in different religious traditions; we saw in chapter 3 that there were substantial differences in transmission across religious groups. However, when we look at the effects of parental closeness on the transmission of religious identity, we find a similar pattern across each of the different religious traditions (see Figure 4.2). Whether a family is Catholic, Jewish, or Mormon, there is greater similarity when there are close parent–child relations.[12]

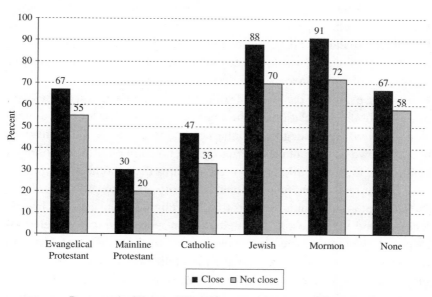

FIGURE 4.2 Percentage of Parents Whose Young Adult Children Have the Same Religious Tradition by the Closeness of the Parent–Child Relationship, 2005

There are intriguing differences from one religious tradition to another. Mormons show the greatest contrast: The percentage of children reporting a close relationship is 19 percentage points higher in religious resemblance than those not close to parents. Among Jews, almost the same degree of contrast is seen—an 18 percentage point difference. For Evangelicals, Catholics and Mainline Protestants, the difference between close and not-close parent–child relationships is somewhat less (10 to 14 percentage points). For "nones," atheists, and agnostics, interestingly, we see the same result: The degree of parent–child similarity for a nonreligion orientation is higher when children feel emotionally close to their parents, as compared to not being close to parents. We examine family transmission of "nones" and of nonreligion in chapter 8.

Gender Differences: Comparing Mothers' and Fathers' Religious Influence

We looked at adult children's perceptions of their relationships with mothers and fathers separately to determine the impact of gender on intergenerational transmission. First we looked to see if there were differences by the gender of the parent in the degree of parent–child religious similarity. While it might be expected that mothers are more influential than fathers in religious socialization, that turns out not to be the case. There is no significant difference between mother–child and father–child religious similarity (see Table A-4 in the Appendix).

Then we examined the effect of solidarity, or the perception by the child of a close or distant relationship. In Figure 4.3 we see that for each dimension of religiosity the degree of father–child and mother–child correspondence (shown as percentages) varies by parent–child emotional closeness or the lack thereof. Children who feel close to their mothers and fathers have higher rates of intergenerational similarity and vice versa.

But what is really interesting is that, for religious transmission, having a close bond with one's *father* matters even more than a close relationship with the mother. Clearly the quality of the child's relationship with his or her father is important for the internalization of the parent's religious tradition, beliefs, and practices.[13] Emotional closeness with mothers remains important for religious inheritance but not to the same degree as it is for fathers.[14]

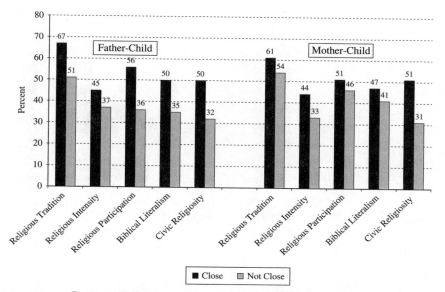

FIGURE 4.3 Percentage of Fathers and Mothers Whose Young Adult Children Are the Same on Five Dimensions of Religiosity by the Closeness of the Parent–Child Relationship, 2005 (G3–G4)

When we look at differences by the religious traditions in our sample, we find some interesting gender differences in influence (see Figure 4.4). First, consider the bars for Evangelicals, Mainline Protestants, and Catholics in the left half of this figure (father–child) and compare the same religious groups with the right half (mother–child). For each of these groups, closeness to father matters more than closeness to mother in religious transmission. Among Evangelical fathers, there is a 25-point difference in similarity for children who feel emotionally close to fathers compared to those who are not close; for Evangelical mothers the difference is just 1 percentage point. A similar pattern exists for Mainline Protestants and Catholics.

For Jews, on the other hand, mother–child relationships appear considerably more important than father–child relationship for passing on religious tradition. For mothers, the similarity rate is 30 percentage points higher when the relationship is emotionally close, while for fathers it is enhanced by only 6 percentage points.[15] In Jewish tradition, it is through the mother that a Jewish identity is imparted, and this might be a reason for this difference. Among Evangelicals it is the father–child

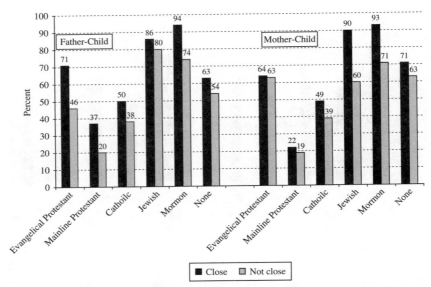

FIGURE 4.4 Percentage of Fathers and Mothers Whose Young Adult Children Have the Same Religious Tradition by the Closeness of the Parent–Child Relationship, 2005 (G3–G4)

relationship that is clearly more related to transmission: A 25-point difference separates those who feel close to those who feel distant from their father, while only 1 point separates those who feel close to or distant from their mother. Turning to Mormons, while there is a large gap in transmission between close and non-close parents, there is not much of a gender difference (fathers who are perceived as close are 20 percentage points higher than those in non-close relationships, about the same as for mothers).

Thus, within tightknit religious traditions such as Mormon, Jewish, and Evangelical, the chances of passing on faith are highly dependent on the quality of parent–child relationships. This may run counter to advice about effective religious socialization in these communities that emphasize parental piety as the crucial factor—setting a good example, teaching the right beliefs and practices, keeping strictly to the law. Without emotional bonding, this is not sufficient for transmission. Throughout the book we can see how a distant or nonaffirming parent–child relationship—particularly with a father—is often mentioned in our interviews as a catalyst for conversion to another faith or dropping out of religion altogether.

These data indicate how important the quality of parent–child relationships is in religious transmission. In addition, gender of the parent amplifies the effect of emotional closeness, and having close emotional bonds with the father is strongly associated with the transmission of religiosity. These are, however, conclusions drawn from our survey data.[16] While surveys are appropriate for describing the degree of intergenerational solidarity and the extent of religious transmission, they are not very helpful in understanding processes involved in gendered intergenerational transmission—pathways of influence that result in similarities or differences between parents and children in religious beliefs and practices. To explore such issues we look next to the stories of families in our interview sample and the words our respondents use to describe them.

Parenting Styles and Religious Transmission

To better understand the complex dimensions of religious socialization and the relationship between parents and young adult children, we turned to the in-depth interviews conducted with 157 members of 25 multigenerational families in our study described in chapter 2. In addition to asking respondents about their spiritual and religious orientations, we asked them about their relations with other generations in the family as well as about their religious and spiritual influences. We identified several patterns or themes in parent–child relationships that appeared relevant to religious transmission. From those patterns that seemed important to the dynamics of these relationships, we then conceptualized what sociologists call "ideal types," constructs that characterize the core features of a particular type of parent–child relationship[17]:

1. Warm, affirming parenting, perceived by the adult child as a consistently close relationship with one or usually both parents
2. Cold, distant, or authoritarian parenting
3. Ambivalent or mixed-message parenting, when either parent is perceived as sometimes warm, sometimes cold; or where one parent is perceived as warm, the other parent as cold or distant
4. Strained or preoccupied parenting, as when parents are distracted by marital, financial, health, or substance abuse problems

In the remainder of this chapter we present examples of families that illustrate the patterns of parenting noted above and describe associated religious socialization mechanisms that promote or discourage religious transmission across generations.

Warm, Affirming Parenting

Data from both the LSOG survey and our interviews indicate that parents who interact with their children during their formative years in a warm, affirming, and respectful manner are more likely to pass on their religious tradition, beliefs, and practices.

The Walker Family

Seventy-four-year-old generation (G) 2 Yvette Walker, an African American, raised her daughters as Baptists in the religious tradition of her family dating back many generations, perhaps to slave days. Because her husband was in the Air Force when their children were young they frequently moved, so Yvette carried the major childrearing responsibilities in their family. Close and supportive emotional bonds were forged between Yvette and her children that have only deepened over the years.

Yvette's eldest daughter, fifty-four-year-old G3 Dorothy, recognizes the powerful influence her mother had in shaping her values and beliefs: "I grew up in a military family, and . . . [fathers are] gone most of the time and the wife is the one that has to take care of the kids and do all this. So I guess she had a bigger influence over me." Dorothy's admiration of her mother is evident in her description of Yvette as "very strong. She's a very strong woman. And we were all raised that way." Yvette made sure her children were involved in their church. Dorothy recalls being taken to church and Sunday school "all the time." Her parents would talk with the children about religion and take an interest in their spiritual development.

For the Walkers, attending church every week had the effect of strengthening parent–child bonds while reinforcing their mutual religious orientations and values. It is not surprising that when asked who in her family had the greatest *religious* influence on her, Dorothy responded, "Probably my mother."

At the time of our first survey in 1970, Yvette reported that she had recently switched her religious affiliation from Baptist to Presbyterian.

This change occurred, she explained, when the family moved to a different city where Yvette was not able to find a Baptist congregation that was welcoming to African Americans. But the Presbyterian Church, which she describes as a mixed-race congregation, made them feel comfortable.

Dorothy recalls that when her family started going to the Presbyterian Church, religion became even more important for them: "It was a big deal for them, and they were really happy." In their surveys over time, both G2 Yvette and G3 Dorothy indicate that they are highly religious and are closely aligned in their religious beliefs and practices. Dorothy comments that religion played a central role in her childhood but that she always felt that she had a choice in her religious participation; it was voluntary and not forced on her by her mother. Consequently, she frames her religious upbringing and her mother's religious influence in a very positive light. "[My mother] didn't make a big deal about it," Dorothy says. "I don't think it was ever forced on [me]."

Yvette's religious parenting style—providing religious guidance that was both nurturing and respectful—was transmitted to Dorothy, who in the same manner influenced the religious orientation of her daughter, twenty-one-year-old G4 Lauren: "I don't push [her] any more. I figured [she's] adult now and can make decisions if [she] wants to go or doesn't want to go [to church]." Lauren says she is very religious, a Presbyterian, and attends services on her campus frequently. She reports that she has a very close relationship with her parents and feels that she was able to choose her own religious path without coercion from her parents:

> [My family] treat[s] children like they're adults in a really nurturing way. My mom always did tell us that we do what works for us. It's our church and we choose whatever we believe. I got to experience it and like it or dislike it [on] my own and I liked it, and I'm continuously practicing it.

The Walker family's story of religious transmission illustrates the influence of warm and affirming parent–child relationships on intergenerational religious continuity. The Walkers are a very close family of believers with a Mainline Protestant tradition that has continued across four decades now. The intergenerational continuity of their faith is very much a consequence of the close and affirming ties between mother and daughters across the generations.

The Wilson Family

The Wilsons are a devout Evangelical Protestant family that has been successful in passing on their religious faith across generations. When we look at this family's stories, what stands out is the combination of their religious continuity and strong emotional bonds. Close parent–child relationships across generations are at the heart of their religious socialization and transmission processes. The Wilsons are a tightknit family. They all live very close to one another in a semirural community, they see and talk to each other almost daily, and they help and support one another frequently. The whole family—grandparents, adult children, and grandchildren—attend the same church. Fifty-three-year-old G3 Elaine remarks, "Those are our traditions, going to church on Sunday. It feels like a family day. Generally we all go out to lunch afterwards." For the Wilsons, religious participation and family togetherness are intertwined.

As explained by Elaine, each individual's "relationship with God" as practiced within their Evangelical Christian faith is the foundation of their family life. She says she and her husband Ken felt that bringing up their children in the faith was "of utmost importance." They taught and modeled their religion in many family-centered activities—including family prayer before meals and at bedtime, daily Bible reading and discussions, and attending church together. When their daughter, G4 Kristin, age twenty-nine, was asked who had the greatest influence on her religious views, she replied, "My mom and dad. They're a team." Similarly, her sister, G4 Susan, age twenty-seven, talked about how her parents shaped her religious faith:

> My parents are very joyful people, very loving people, and it was always made known that it was because of their security in Christ and their love that they passed down to us, so it's always been that God has been a loving God and a protecting God, and I'm sure that I'm very blessed to be born into the family that I have.

Another daughter, thirty-year-old G4 Tina, says that among the values she learned from her parents are "being generous and giving to others who are less fortunate. Being joyful, laughing, smiling, even through difficult times." When other people remark on her attitude and ask her how she can still be smiling through any adversity, she credits her parents: "That's how they both are."

Elaine has been highly involved in the church, teaching Sunday school, singing in the choir, and participating with her children in summer church camps, while her husband Ken has been in church leadership positions and on boards. Interestingly, Elaine does not think of herself as overly strict religiously, even though she is very active in her church. She says that she and her husband "have never been sticklers that you have to go [to church] every Sunday," adding that they allowed their children choice in whether they would go to church or not.

Ken's and Elaine's interviews suggest some mechanisms of success- ful religious socialization, of how religious faith is modeled and rein- forced through everyday practices and thus passed down to the next generation. From their remarks we can see how religious socialization works in their family, particularly the central role played by close and respectful parent–child relationships. Elaine describes how she and her husband would talk to their children about religion and other issues, continually taking advantage of opportunities to communicate with and teach them:

> [I]f they have a question about something we go ahead and answer it as best we can. Maybe it starts like, "What should I do in this situation?" Their father has always been very [open]—I mean they've always been able to talk to their father about anything, especially [when they were] high school age.
>
> As a parent you have to be willing and able to catch those times, because [later] kids will just clam up, they don't want to talk. I always made a point of trying to go up to bed with them, pray, sing them a song. And then it's kind of a time to, you know, ask, "Do you want to talk about anything?" That's the time of the openness.

The Wilsons' hands-on style of parenting continued after their daugh- ters reached adolescence. Elaine describes her husband Ken as a night owl: "He would stay up late with them, kind of sitting there, having long talks about their day and about their faith and so forth. Sometimes these discussions about faith and how to live a Christian life would go on for hours."

Such dedication has paid off. The Wilsons have seen their children not only assimilate their Evangelical beliefs and practices but pass them on to their own children. Elaine, who made a point of saying prayers and singing Christian songs with her children most nights when she put them to bed, now sees the same tradition occurring with her grandchildren. "I know my kids are following in those steps with their children. They have little books that they read to them, or sing, even as they're taking naps and stuff."

The Wilsons reflect the warm, affirming parenting described earlier as well as a religious parenting style that is loving, supportive, and respectful. The methods they have used in socialization involve teaching, modeling, and living in a community that affirms their religious activity. Parenting has been the number-one priority for Ken and Elaine, and they have developed guidelines, based on religious principles, for effective parenting. Their efforts have been successful: all of their children have adopted their parents' evangelical faith.

Cold, Distant, or Authoritarian Parenting

In the Walker and Wilson families, we see that close, affirming parent–child relations are important for successful religious transmission. At the other extreme, a parenting pattern perceived by the child as cold, distant, or authoritarian can undo the most dedicated efforts by parents to pass on their religious tradition.

The Young Family

G3s Debbie and Chuck Young are members of a large family that has been highly successful in transmitting their Latter-Day Saints faith across many generations. In 1970, when our study began, they had just gotten married following Chuck's return from his Church mission. (Mormon young men give two years to the Church following their twentieth birthday, witnessing and proselytizing for their faith, often in another country.) Since then Debbie has described how involved their family has been in the church. In 1991 she spoke of her hopes for her son G4 Brandon, then only 7 years old, and how much she looked forward to "seeing my child's religious progress," an implicit expectation that he would take on their Mormon tradition and would in turn pass it on to his children.

G4 Brandon began participating in the longitudinal survey in 2000 when he was sixteen-years-old. At that time, his responses to questions about religion were very similar to those of his parents—participating in many Mormon activities, attending church several times a week, and agreeing with the statement that "religion is the most important influence" in his life. The surveys of Brandon and his two sisters portray their father Chuck as a strongly religious family patriarch with high spiritual standards and expectations that family members would live up to the teachings of their church. In his 2000 survey, Brandon said that religion was "very, very important" in his family and that it seemed to him like "everything revolved around church." His strong Mormon upbringing taught him to follow church teachings. Brandon noted that "serving a mission for my church" was something that he looked forward to but also worried about. He mentioned the pressures he felt from his family and church regarding his mission.

Three years later, in 2003, Brandon, went on his mission, assigned to Croatia. But he soon experienced serious episodes of depression. A doctor insisted that he return home. Brandon recalls the stress of coming home early from his mission, saying it was a "very difficult" experience. "It was supposed to be fun, and I guess a life experience, but unfortunately it wasn't a good life experience for me, so it kind of put a damper on things."

Brandon's father was highly critical of his son's failure to complete his mission: "You will regret this for the rest of your life." Brandon was devastated by his father's reaction to the situation. "I was upset," he says. "I felt like a child, really, like I was being lectured, even though here I was, twenty years old, supposedly old enough and responsible enough to go out on my own and live for two years, but yet when I didn't do what he wanted me to, [he was] still treating me like a child."

Brandon's religious life was disrupted by this experience. His church attendance dropped from "more than once a week" in his 2000 survey to "once a year" in 2005, when he reported that religion was "not at all important" in his life. When we interviewed him in 2007, he had stopped attending church altogether, creating additional tension in his relationship with his father. "It was a lot of, 'You need to be going to church, we raised you this way, you're not fulfilling your obligations and duties,' and [my father] was really just trying to be very forceful, and trying to make me feel bad about it." Brandon went a step further and married a non-Mormon— the first of the Young family to do so in many generations. This also was a great disappointment to his parents. As the only inactive Mormon in the Young family, and one that married a non-Mormon, Brandon says he is the family "outcast."

In this sequence of events, we can see the role of parent–child relation quality as it fosters or inhibits religious transmission. Even before Brandon's mission experience, his survey data indicated that his relationship with his father was distant and fraught with conflict. Looking back on his childhood, Brandon recalls not having a close relationship with his father. He felt Chuck was a stern parent who was absent a lot: "So especially when I was young, he really wasn't around that often." How did Chuck feel about this situation? Unfortunately, we don't know. Chuck refused to participate in our study except for one survey, so we don't have his point of view and don't know what he would have to say about his son Brandon.

About Brandon's mother Debbie we know a great deal, and we can see that she had a different parenting style than Chuck. In her 1997 survey, she said she disagreed with her husband's parenting of their young adult son: "I don't like it when [Chuck] becomes critical," she said. "He seems too negative at times. We differ somewhat on discipline, or what [a child] can or can't do. We differ somewhat on when does a parent become too controlling and when to exercise trust in a child."

In contrast to his conflicted relationship with his father, Brandon indicated in his surveys that he felt "very close" to his mother: "When I was growing up she was always there. A lot of who I am is a result of my mom." In his interview, when asked what values he learned from his mother, Brandon replied, "I guess from my mother I learned how to be kind, and how to love, and how to take care of somebody, and [to do] service." When we interviewed Debbie, she said she tried to be understanding and supportive of her son's decision to return home early from his mission. "Maybe I'm a little more accepting....Sometimes members of our church can get a little narrow-minded and short-sighted."

The Youngs' story reveals how negative parent–child interactions can stymie the parents' intent to transmit their faith. While Brandon's relationship with his mother was warm and affirming, this did not mitigate the negative effects of his strained relationship with a stern, unbending father who placed Brandon's duty to his Church ahead of his well-being.

The Jackson Family

If the Young family demonstrates how an authoritarian parent can disrupt the continuity of religious transmission for one family member,

the Jacksons exemplify a family where warmth and emotional closeness are largely absent and religious transmission is almost nonex-
istent across the generations. The interviews also reveal how easily
religious commitment can be undermined by family conflict. The
young adult family members we interviewed seemed to yearn for close
family relationships, which they did not experience consistently while
growing up.

G1s Myrna and Norbert Jackson were participants in our first survey
in 1970; Norbert died in 1987, but we interviewed Myrna in 2007 when
she was ninety-five. When asked about the role of religion in her family
when she was young, she replied, "We had no religion...Our family did
not even go to church on Christmas together." When Myrna had children
she sent them to Sunday school "until they were old enough" (their early
teens). What were her children learning there? "Oh, how to get along with
other people and how to be kind and generous to other people. Do unto
others." Other than this, there is nothing that she or her husband did to
promote religious socialization. Asked if religion had ever served to bring
family together in some way, she replied:

> No, not really. We got every kind [of religion in the family], but nobody
> pays any attention to the religion...I mean they don't make an issue of it.
> They don't pay attention to that part of it. Everybody can have his own. It's
> a free country. Everybody has a right to their own religion.

Her entire family fits the "religiously indifferent" category: "They just quit
one place, one church and went to a different one. But I don't think anybody has any...any impact on another person....Nobody cared."

Myrna's daughter, G2 Olivia, seventy-four, does not recall that religion played any role in her family as she was growing up. According to
Olivia, her parents took her to Sunday school only occasionally. She does
remember that there was a Bible in the house, but when asked whom it
belonged to, she struggled to recall: "[pause] I don't know. I really don't
know. Maybe my dad's father was Catholic." Olivia does not remember
any religious instruction or discussions about religion from her parents or
her grandparents.

Olivia has three adult children and describes her relationship with them
as "distant." All her children were baptized Catholic—the religious tradition of their father—but she does not think any go to church today, as

adults. Asked whether there are any religious values or spiritual traditions she would like to see continued in younger generations in her family, she responded, "Wow, they're so scattered. It's so hard. I would like to be together with more of the younger people, but like I said, they're so scattered, and I don't see them very often." When asked if she could think of a word or phrase to describe her family as a whole, she answered, "Loosely joined. We're joined, but we're not—you know, we're not in each other's pockets. When we need help, or need contact, we do. Otherwise we go on our own way."

Olivia's daughter, fifty-one-year-old G3 Karen, was baptized a Catholic, but she does not feel that any religious tradition was passed down to her. Asked about going to church when she was growing up, she noted that "It was just kind of a place where we just had to hang out for a while on Sunday and then we could go home. It wasn't a time to be with family—it wasn't something we went home and talked about afterwards. From what I remember of it, it wasn't like family time at all. It was an obligation." For Karen, religion was potentially a source of family conflict. "If I did believe something, it was best to just keep it quiet, keep it to yourself to avoid coming under attack for believing or not." She added that the person who was most critical of her beliefs was her grandmother, G1 Myrna. Much of Karen's interview focused on family dysfunctions, now and in the past: "It just didn't work." But she did not appear to be particularly distressed by this or by the lack of closeness in her family. As for religion, Karen is largely indifferent. Her daughter G4 Sheila, thirty-one, says she is not religious, though she is interested in learning more about religion. Sheila said that family members do not talk to each other or get together. She doesn't see her mom very often, and she has a limited relationship with her father, Curt.

The Jacksons' family story indicates a pattern of distant parenting that seems to have been replicated from one generation to the next. It is not surprising that there is little resemblance in religion across generations in this family.

Ambivalent or Mixed-Message Parenting

While the Jackson family is almost uniformly uninvolved and the Wilson family universally warm and close, some families display mixed messages about the emotional bonds between parent and child. Sometimes a parent, usually a father, appears to shift between criticism and nurturance, creating an ambiguous image in the child's eye. Sometimes a child perceives parents as occupying two extremes, with one parent nurturing and the other critical. In our research, we have found both of these types of "mixed-message parenting," often occurring in the same family. In these families we also discovered less intergenerational continuity in religion.

The Garcia Family

A large, five-generation Hispanic family, the Garcia elders have been very successful in maintaining their Catholic faith across generations. On the surface it would seem there is a connection between their religious beliefs and practices and their warm and mutually supportive intergenerational relationships. Their family rituals and activities appear intimately connected to their Catholic faith; they celebrate church holidays together and events such as first communion and confirmation.

But if we look more closely at the family's dynamics over time, we also notice an asymmetry in the religious influence of fathers and mothers. An example of what we call "mixed-message parenting," this is especially the case for the older generations. In their gender relations, the Garcias are a traditionally patriarchal Hispanic family. In enacting their separate gender roles, it falls to the women to be responsible for socialization of the children, including religious instruction and training. From interviews we see that mothers in the family are called upon to mediate between fathers and children; in the process the mothers solidify and extend their influence on the religious orientation of their children.

The Garcias' family stories indicate that for generations the men have been strong, dominating figures—but not particularly nurturing. Fifty-eight-year-old G3 Luis recalled his grandfather, G1 Ignacio, as being so domineering that he could command others with his eyes. "If we were doing something [wrong]...he talked to you with his eyes. With his eyes, he told you no. And with his eyes, he told you to go outside. His eyes would tell you to be quiet. And that's all we had to do was just look at him."

In the G2 generation, seventy-eight-year-old Estela described her husband, Bernardo, as a "macho" man from Mexico. Their son, G3 Manuel, fifty-four, commented on his father's authoritarian presence in the family: "He was really hard," but he also taught Manuel "values and morals" and "a lot of the work ethic." Another son, G3 Luis, has consistently reported in several surveys that he felt "very close" to both his parents and that they had very similar values. However, in his interview Luis provided a retrospective account of his childhood that contrasted his relationship with his mother, Estela, from that with his father, Bernardo. "My dad was the stern one," he recalls. "He was the one that told you, 'Okay, this is how it's going to be.' We went to tell Mom to talk to him, and then she, in turn, would talk to my dad," and things would change. The children received mixed messages from their parents.

Estela describes the situation in the same way. She talks about her husband Bernardo's stern fathering and says she tried to raise their sons differently, with greater affection as well as more support for their choices. When asked if her husband's attitude influenced their children she replied, "No, [not much], because they weren't brought up like that. They heard their dad but they knew that [his authoritarianism] was wrong."

The other son, G3 Luis, also recalls that his emotionally distant relationship with his father placed his mother, Estela, in the role of mediator in the father–son relationship. There were some benefits to this arrangement. Estela's mediating role provided greater opportunities for mother–son interaction while reinforcing her religious socialization efforts and enhancing transmission of her Catholic faith to her children. Luis' surveys indicate that they are "highly religious" like their mother. In his 2008 interview, Luis says his difficult relationship with his father influenced him to be the opposite. He wanted to be warm and supportive. "My dad was stern. He was hard. So I don't want that for my kids, his sternness."

Luis's different approach to parenting appears to be paying off in terms of religious transmission. His son, G4 Eduardo, joined the study in 1997 when he was in his twenties, and like his father before him, Eduardo is "highly religious." In his surveys, Eduardo reports feeling "extremely close" to both his parents. When G3 Luis was asked about the source of religious continuity with his son, he said that it is due to their loving father–son relationship: "Because of the love we show for each other. And I feel that you show that love, it grows and it makes it nice." Now thirty-six and a father of three young children, G4 Eduardo goes to mass weekly and remains committed to his Catholic faith. Eduardo's perceptions of religion and family are very similar to those expressed by his father, Luis:

My family is loving. We have a loving environment. You can talk at them, and you're not going to get nowhere. But if you talk with them, and talk to them, you're going to get someplace more. And to me that's about listening, and listening to God, and just being close to God, as far as I'm concerned... We can sit and talk, and we listen, we talk from our hearts, not just from our mouths.

The Garcias' family story suggests a mixed-message pattern of parenting—for example, the stern and the loving. Their religious continuity across generations was rooted in close mother–son relationships developing in contrast to the distant and perhaps harsh father–son relationship, as we saw for Estela and her son Luis. In the Garcias we also see the possibility of arresting dysfunctional family patterns from continuing across generations. Bernardo's harsh parenting style did not get passed down from generation to generation, because his son Luis decided on a different approach with his own children. But the major message is the importance of warm, affirming, and supportive parenting, particularly on the part of the mother, in enhancing religious continuity across generations.

The Sabellis

The Sabellis are a four-generation Italian-American family that has largely retained the Catholic identity of the first generation, though not its piety or devotion. Some younger generation family members are no longer Catholic, some never go to church and are Catholic in name only, and some who left the church years ago have since returned. Here we focus on the lineage of seventy-seven-year-old G2 Edna, her children, and her grandchildren. What we quickly noticed was the ambivalent nature of intergenerational relationships across these generations and the lack of religious influence by parents that seems to have resulted. We also noticed the larger-than-life presence of the family patriarch, G1 Leo, even though he passed away more than two decades ago. He is remembered as a warm, loving man whose devoted Catholicism set the standard for subsequent generations.

G2 Edna talked about her father Leo's strong support when she was growing up and how she had tried to replicate this with her children:

I always knew that my mom and dad were going to be there for me, and I think my [own] children grew up with that. They always say that "Mom, you know, we always knew you were going to be home when we got home from school." I think it's important to be there, you know, whenever your kids are always going to need you, even when they're married. I think that's one of the things I learned that, being from an Italian family. So I was raised like that—you have to help your family.

Asked who had the greatest influence on her values, Edna credits her Catholic parents, though she left the church for a time in her twenties. "I married a Protestant—so that's where I kind of parted from what my mom and dad, you know, their philosophy." Though she does not attend church these days, she says she is religious and will always remain a Catholic like her parents. "I realized, after a while, that I could not leave the church because I loved hearing about the Blessed Mother, and other religions don't recognize her that much," she says. "So I stayed with the Catholic faith, and I thought I'd just—I just won't go to church. I just won't go to communion. I just let it go." Edna tried to provide her four children with religious training when they were young: "They went to the classes so they'd make their first communion and confirmation." Today, her three sons are Catholic, and she mentioned how proud she is that one of them is a lay leader in the church. "Oh, he's just really so much like my dad [G1 Leo]. It's amazing how much he's like my father."

However, when we interviewed Edna's daughter, G3 Nina, fifty-four, it was clear that she did not regard the relationship with her mother as close, nor did she believe her mother had much influence on her religious life. Her relationship with her father also appears to have been ambivalent. Nina recalls:

My mom was not a stabilizing force as far as making me have a sense of responsibility, I guess you could say. So I can't look at her and say she was a role model. But Grandpa [her grandfather, G1 Leo] was that . . . My father, but my father was very withholding of his affection towards me. When I was born, he was in the Marines and he didn't really meet me for a year.

As a child Nina thought her father did not love her, but now that she is older she believes she is following in her father's footsteps "as far as getting out of bed in the morning and going to work; being responsible." While she can't remember having any discussions about religion with her parents in her childhood, she says, "I do now, especially with my father, but not with my mom."

Nina says that she is very religious, a born-again Christian and very devout in her Evangelical faith. But Nina has not succeeded in passing on her religious passion to her G4 son Lucas, and his relationship with her appears ambivalent, repeating the pattern of Nina's relationship with her own parents. When we interviewed Lucas, age twenty-seven, he observed, "Over time, I guess we for the most part went our separate ways." Lucas also had trouble remembering what traditions there were in his family while growing up. "We all just do our thing. I think we've always been kind of loosey-goosey." He talked about "the loss of family solidarity" when his great-grandfather, G1 Leo, died and his parents divorced. He said of his mother's role in the family, "Oh, she's the one that's always pushing everybody.... That's her role—she's the annoying one."

When we asked Lucas whether his values differ from those of his parents, he replied, "My mom's like, religious. And I'm definitely not religious.... She always sends me all these Bible CDs and DVDs, and then God books and this and that, 'til I'm— which, you know, is annoying." Lucas says that his mother talked to him constantly about religion when he was growing up. He knows his mother is Christian but doesn't know what denomination. "I think my mom is the only real radical, as far as going to church constantly." Today, Lucas has no religious affiliation but says he is "spiritual":

> Okay—I'm just not religious. That doesn't mean I'm not spiritual. It doesn't mean I don't believe in this and that, or faith and that—it's just that I just can't take all of the hard-core, you know, dos and don'ts as far as organized religion is concerned, and my own personal views of organized religion [are very negative].

Lucas has somewhat of an ambivalent relationship with his mother, and that has likely contributed to her lack of success in passing on her faith to him. On the one hand he talks of his mother's "pushing religion" on him as "annoying." On the other hand he loves her dearly, saying:

> Really, the only person in my life—the only family member in my life that would, that I interact with enough to get annoyed at, would be my mother. I'm not really close to my dad, or anybody else in our family, for

that matter.... I can't fault her in any way for what her beliefs are, so I can't really say I've had any issues with it....And I love her dearly.

Strained or Preoccupied Parenting

A fourth type of parent–child relationship is one we call "strained by preoccupation." Here we see parents who are distracted by marital, financial, or health problems, occasionally involving substance abuse. Not surprisingly, this kind of preoccupied parenting, in which the children are not near the center of their parents' attention, does not typically lead to successful transmission of the parents' religion.

The Sanchez Family

The Sanchezes are a large, traditional Hispanic family that had been Catholic for generations. But starting with the G3 Early Boomer generation members, their unquestioned loyalty to the Catholic Church changed, with an interesting gender-related twist. The men in this generation, as well as most of their sons and grandsons, have remained in the Catholic faith. But the G3 women have left the Catholic Church and become Evangelical Protestants, in turn passing on their new faith to their daughters and granddaughters. How did this happen?

What emerges from our interviews with Sanchez family members is a family pattern of strained relations between parents and children that loomed large in the daily lives of the younger generation when they were growing up. This repeated theme of strained interaction seems associated with a cultural value of *machismo,* with its traditional dominant roles for men, including marital infidelity, and the tension and conflict this has created. In the family's interviews we see this dynamic playing out in generation after generation, resulting in long-lasting effects on marriages and on the troubled quality of parent–child relationships. Yet these relationships also show much affection and closeness. The tension between these emotional extremes results in strained parenting and conflicted religious socialization.

As a consequence of persistent marital strains and the parents' preoccupation with their own relationship, the Sanchezes have not modeled their religion well or transmitted their faith to their children. In earlier generations, when the Sanchez family's self-identity as Catholics was unquestioned, the church itself performed the principal role in religious socialization, particularly through its Catholic schools. Catholicism was reinforced by the Sanchez family's embeddedness within the Hispanic community, where to be Hispanic was to be Catholic. But the authority and influence of the Catholic Church began to wane with the Early Boomer generation in the 1970s, as described in chapters 1 and 3. When we look closely at the religious commitment of the Sanchez family, with two exceptions (G1 Orval and his grandson, G3 Manuel), family members' identification with the Catholic Church appears nominal at best; most seem to know very little about their faith and do not attend church.

The efforts of the G1 great-grandparents, Orval and Gladys, to socialize their children into their Catholic faith were authoritarian on the part of the great-grandfather and indifferent on the part of the great-grandmother. Their surveys indicate that their marriage was often contentious. Orval attended church weekly and made sure his children did as well. According to Gladys, "My husband always makes them go to church. He was always after the kids" When asked if she went with them, she said no. By late adolescence all of their children had stopped attending church.

While Orval and Gladys (and their parents and grandparents before them) attended Catholic schools, their children and grandchildren went to public schools. Their religious education was limited to church catechism classes in preparation for first communion and then confirmation. G2 Roberta, age seventy-one, remarked, "I don't know what it means . . . we just [went]. Religion was not talked about in the home." In the next generation, Roberta's son Manuel said, "I don't remember going to church with my parents." This was seconded by his sister, fifty-one-year-old Denise: "My mother was raised Catholic. But I don't remember my mother [taking] us to church very often. My mom always spoke about being Catholic, but in reality it was really something we didn't do every Sunday."

G3 Denise talked about her parents' strained marriage and their anger at each other. She noted that she did not see her parents as religious models and that is why she turned away from the Catholic Church. She mentioned her parents' frequent arguments when she was a child. She feels that her mother was so preoccupied by her marital problems that she neglected her children. Denise describes this as an intergenerational pattern that predated her parents: "Well, my grandfather never showed his kids [any] love. Neither did my grandmother."

Denise wanted to do things differently in the way she raised her children—to be different from her mother and maternal grandparents:

> I wanted to be what my mother wasn't to me. Women have a tendency to— they're so in love with their husbands and what their husbands are doing that some women forget they have children. And that becomes a problem. Sure the mother's at home, which my mother was, but I think a lot of times my mother would take frustrations out on us or yell at us—a lot of her neglect toward us was because she was [preoccupied]—her mind was on my father throughout those years.

Following a divorce, Denise had a "born again" experience and became an Evangelical Christian. In the years that followed, she relied on her faith to help her through tough times. "[I] wanted to live right and bring up my children right. So that was my thing, and I think that rubbed off...on my kids as far as values." In fact, each of Denise's children has followed in their mother's Evangelical Christian footsteps. Today Denise thinks she may be influencing the religious orientation of her parents as well; in a case of reverse intergenerational socialization, she is encouraging them to follow her in her faith:

> My mother, I took her to church. She's learning, but I have a feeling by the time she learns, she's going to be too old....I think she questions the Catholic religion. She's questioning it a lot now...learning later in life, maybe, what [she] should've been like thirty years ago.

These changes have improved Denise's relationship with her mother, whom she now describes as her "best friend."

In the Sanchez family we find a strained husband–wife relationship in the first generation and preoccupied parenting that resulted in ambivalent parent–child relationships in later generations. We can see the negative effects of marital stress on religious socialization. On a more positive note, we also see the potential for parent–child relationships to change over time and for "reverse" child-to-parent socialization to occur.

In Families of Faith, Warmth Matters

Throughout this chapter we have seen that the quality of the parent–child relationship directly affects how much influence mothers and fathers have on their children's religious orientations in adulthood and on religious continuity or discontinuity across generations. The young adults in our study who felt particularly close to one or both parents were most likely to have inherited that parent's religious orientations. They explicitly mentioned feelings of closeness when describing intergenerational influences and positive experiences with religion. In contrast, having a relationship that was perceived as cold or ambivalent dampened the likelihood of cross-generational religious inheritance.

In the Mainline Protestant Walker family, for example, we see how close emotional bonds with one parent can successfully facilitate that parent's influence on a child's religious orientation. G3 Dorothy feels that in response to warm and understanding parenting, children perceive their relationship with parents as one of mutual respect, which affirms their feelings of closeness. Children understand that individual differences are accepted but remain committed to their parents' religious tradition and beliefs because they feel that the choice was theirs to make and would be respected. The parent–child relationship is able to adapt to individual developmental changes over the life course, and, as such, there is continuity in parent–child solidarity and religion. We see this also in the Evangelical Christian Wilson family.

The Mormon Young family demonstrates the deleterious effect of G3 Chuck's authoritarian parenting style on his son Brandon's unsuccessful religious mission. However, we also see how Brandon's close relationship with his mother softened this negative effect and may yet contribute to the possibility of religious continuity. Brandon's mother still holds out hope that her son will return to the Latter-Day Saints Church. But with his marriage to a non-Mormon woman who is not inclined to convert, this seems unlikely.

In the Jackson family we find little in the way of religious transmission but many indications of conflict in parent–child relationships. In one generation after another, we see relationships fraught with criticism, anger, dysfunction, and distance. A close look at the Jacksons' stories suggests that negative ways of relating and parenting are transmitted across generations.

In the Catholic Garcia family we see how close mother–child relationships can promote religious transmission despite distant or authoritarian father–child relationships. This pattern is particularly evident across the patriarchal older generations in this family. What we notice is how the women in the Garcia family intervene in the father–child relationship, serving as moderators of their husbands' strict parenting styles to facilitate the transmission of their Catholic faith. G3 Luis said that he would routinely refer to his mother as the arbiter of his relationship with his "stern" father. Similarly, he said that his wife is the "go-between" whenever he and his children have conflicts.

In the Sanchez family, also Catholic, we see a persistent pattern of strained marital relations and distracted parenting that had consequences for socializing children into their Catholic religion. Within the context of a machismo culture and high rates of infidelity and divorce, along with the limited support they felt from the church during their marital difficulties, the G3 Sanchez women left the Catholic Church. These women, who believed the church was unable to help them solve their problems, turned to Evangelical Protestantism instead.

The quality of the relationship between parent and child is a crucial component of the degree to which transmission of religion occurs. When children perceive their relationship with parents as close, affirming, and accepting, they are more likely to identify with their parents' religious practices and beliefs, while relationships marked by coldness, ambivalence, or preoccupation are likely to result in religious differences. Furthermore, the linkage between warmth and religious transmission is not only a feature of parent–child relationships: we see it across three and even four generations as well, as we discuss in the next chapter on the unexpected importance of grandparents and great-grandparents in religious socialization.

CHAPTER 5 | The Unexpected Importance
of Grandparents (and
Great-Grandparents)[1]

Generation (G) 3 Beverly Johnson, now sixty, says she was raised
by her grandparents. She still attends the "family church" that her
grandfather helped to found. She notes that he is the one who had the
greatest influence on her life. Her daughter Erika, thirty-two, says,
"My mother still maintains [a strong religious] attachment because my
great-grandfather was involved with founding the church." Beverly is
highly religious. She says that she tried to raise her children as she was
raised by her grandparents, with the Ten Commandments at the center
of their instruction. She appears to have succeeded; Erika and her three
siblings are of the same faith, and in this family we see four generations
of religious continuity.

When asked who in his family has had the greatest influence on his
values and beliefs, thirty-one-year-old G4 Lucas Sabelli replied, "My
great-grandfather. Just his presence and everything about him was
so positive. And sharing some of the stories from my mother about
his character makes me want to be more like him, more caring, and
strong, and fun, and dependable, and just rad." Lucas's mother and
aunt also described their grandfather Leo as the greatest spiritual and
moral influence in their lives.

Increasingly Relevant Grandparent

Gen Xers and Millennials will have greater involvement with their grand-parents—and, for some, their great-grandparents—than any previous gen-eration of grandchildren in American history.[2] There are several reasons for this. The first involves demographic developments. Because of the increase in life expectancy over the twentieth century, grandparents have longer lives than ever before, and grandchildren can enjoy many years with living grandparents. This has increased the chances for grandparents to play a significant role in the lives of grandchildren.[3] Thus it is not sur-prising that a majority of grandchildren report being emotionally close to their grandparents, as well as sharing similar views and values with grand-parents.[4] Moreover, grandparents and grandchildren today have more time to interact, share, and lend support. They have more time to learn from each other and more opportunities for mutual socialization. Though there is sometimes greater geographic distance between generations now than in the past, grandparents and grandchildren have more ways to communicate as well, with the pervasive use of technologies such as cell phones, Skype, and Facebook—often with grandchildren teaching their grandparents how to use them—an instance of "reverse socialization" between generations.

Characterizations of grandparents as distant, detached, or irrelevant run counter to what recent research shows.[5] Most grandparents have a continu-ing presence in the lives of their grandchildren, providing emotional sup-port, assistance, advice, and a first-hand witness to family and historical events.[6] This enhances grandchildren's learning about themselves, their kin, and their cultural context.[7] Furthermore, their interactions with grand-parents are likely to influence how they themselves enact relationships with their own grandchildren.[8]

In addition, more grandparents are in better health longer than their predecessors, so more are directly involved in the lives of their grand-children for longer periods of time. With the majority of mothers work-ing and a growing number of single-parent households, as documented in chapter 1, a larger number of grandparents have been providing direct care for grandchildren than ever before.[9] More grandparents have been assist-ing grandchildren financially, not only through gifts during childhood and adolescence but also with college tuition, wedding expenses, and purchas-ing a home. More than just altruism, this reflects the "generational stake" discussed in chapter 4 in which the older generation continues to invest resources of time and treasure in younger generations throughout the life course. It is also perhaps an example of the norm of generativity associated with aging that is part of Erik Erikson's theory of stages in the life cycle.[10]

There are also increasing numbers of grandparents who are raising grandchildren full-time because their own adult children are unable to parent. This can occur for various reasons, including imprisonment, illness, drug or alcohol addiction, or court-defined abusive parenting. The percentage of grandparents raising grandchildren has increased substantially in recent decades; in 2008, 2.5 million grandparents were primarily responsible for the care of one or more grandchildren, and 49 million Americans (16% of the total population) were living in a family household that contained at least two adult generations or a grandparent and at least one other generation.[11]

This evidence concerning the growing importance of grandparents suggests that there should be more research examining these relationships, looking at the religious influence of grandparents on grandchildren. Yet research on grandparenting in America began only recently, in the 1980s,[12] and we lack any long-term information about grandparental influences on the religious outcomes of young adult grandchildren.

In addition, the influence of grandparents is often considered inconsequential because it appears to be indirect, operating through the much stronger religious influence of parents. This ignores the fact that some grandparents—perhaps an increasing number—may be more directly involved in religious socialization than are parents. Grandparents can provide a stabilizing influence in their grandchildren's lives in situations of parental divorce, incapacity, addiction, or emotional distancing. In these contexts grandparents' influence may be highly salient for the development of children's religious values and beliefs. In other situations, grandparents may play a larger role in influencing children's religious orientation simply because they have more time to do so, or religious instruction is not a priority for parents, or parents are religiously indifferent. Regardless, the result is what we describe later in this chapter as the "skipped generation" effect of grandparental religious influence.

Continuity Between Grandparents and Grandchildren, 1970 and 2005

What is the extent of continuity across three generations in the dimensions of religiosity explored in this study? How has this changed over the

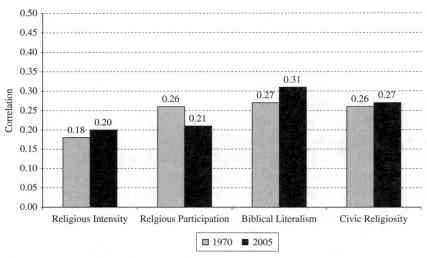

FIGURE 5.1 Similarity Between Grandparents and Grandparents on Four Dimensions of Religiosity, 1970 (G1–G3) and 2005 (G2–G4)

past thirty-five years, given the many recent changes in culture, families, and religion in American society as reviewed in chapter 1? In Figure 5.1 we illustrate findings from our longitudinal survey data concerning these questions. (See the Notes and the Appendix for more information on the statistical procedures used in these analyses.)

First, we look at the evidence for intergenerational transmission as seen in the degree of religious similarity between grandparents and grandchildren. As shown in Figure 5.1, grandparents and grandchildren are similar to each other on all four dimensions of religiosity.[13] The second issue is whether there has been a decline in grandparent–grandchild similarity over 35 years. For each of the four dimensions—religious intensity, participation, Biblical literalism, and civic religiosity—we compared 1970 and 2005 grandparent–grandchild correlations to see if there was a significant difference in similarity between the two time periods. Clearly, there was not. Transmission rates have remained remarkably stable between these two generations over the past thirty-five years.

We turn next to religious affiliation. In 2005, the proportion of grandparents whose grandchildren shared the same religious tradition was 43%, a degree of continuity across the three generations that was higher than we had expected. In 1970 the figure was somewhat higher at 53%. In Figure 5.2 we present grandparent–grandchild resemblance rates separately for five

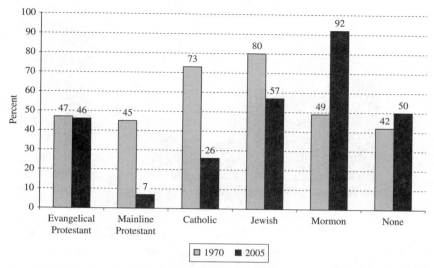

FIGURE 5.2 Percentage of Grandparents Whose Young Adult Grandchildren Have the Same Religious Tradition, 1970 (G1–G3) and 2005 (G2–G4)

religious traditions and the nonreligious "nones." The extent to which grandparents and their grandchildren have the same religious affiliation, and how this has changed over the past thirty-five years, varies by religious tradition. We see here a pattern similar to the parent–child results described in chapter 3—but even more so. Among Evangelicals there was no change. For Mainline Protestants, percentages of grandparents whose grandchildren shared their religious tradition decreased considerably between 1970 and 2005, and for Catholics the decline was even sharper. While we can't rely on the percentages shown for Jews and Mormons in Figure 5.2 because of the small sample size of grandparent–grandchild dyads from these groups, they do have the highest rates of religious continuity across generations in our study, and in chapter 9 we suggest a number of reasons for this.

In the "none" or nonaffiliated category, half the grandparents in 2005 had grandchildren who also were nonaffiliated. This is an increase over 1970. The parent–child similarity rates for "nones," by contrast, increased considerably, from 40% in 1970 to 63% in 2005 (see chapter 3). These figures provide one explanation for the rise of the religiously uncommitted in America since the 1970s: intergenerational transmission (see chapter 8).

We wondered about the extent to which there are gender effects in these comparisons—that is, whether there were stronger similarities between grandmothers and grandchildren than between grandfathers and grandchildren.

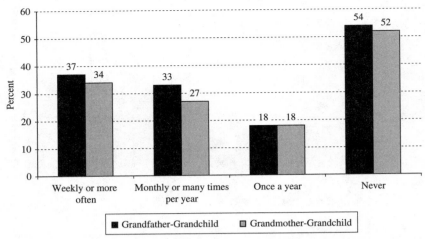

FIGURE 5.3 Percentage of Grandparents and Grandmothers Whose Grandchildren Attend Religious Services with the Same Frequency, 2005

We found that it varies by religious dimension. For religious participation, (Figure 5.3) the differences were slight: Resemblances between grandfathers and grandchildren were about the same as between grandmothers and grandchildren.

For religious intensity, however, we found some interesting gender differences (see Figure 5.4). Here we illustrate the responses to the question "Taking everything into consideration, how religious would you say you were?" Possible responses ranged from "very religious" to "not at all religious."

While the degree of similarity varies across the response categories, for youth who say they are "very religious" there is higher similarity with grandfathers than grandmothers. For those "not at all religious," there is greater similarity with grandmothers. Thus very religious grandfathers may be a particularly important influence on grandchildren's religious values.

Types of Grandparental Religious Influence

To summarize, when we look at these data on the religious orientations of grandparents and their young adult grandchildren, we see strong evidence of transmission from grandparents to grandchildren, and we see no diminishment in the degree of that transmission over the thirty-five years of this study. How do they do this? What are some ways in which grandparents influence grandchildren in religion? In examining processes of religious

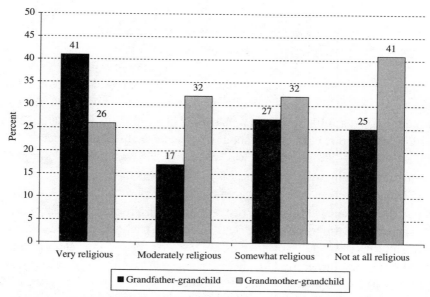

FIGURE 5.4 Percentage of Grandparents and Grandmothers Whose Young Grandchildren Have the Same Levels of Religious Intensity, 2005

influence across generations in the twenty-five families of our interview study, we came to appreciate four themes, or types, of religious socialization that occur between grandparents and grandchildren.

The "Skipped Generation" Influence: Grandparents Substituting for Parents

In some cases, grandparents' influence on their grandchildren's religious lives is so extensive that they serve as replacement figures for the children's parents. G3 Shari Sabelli, fifty-four, said she felt "extremely close" to her Catholic grandfather, G1 Leo, though she did not feel close with her own parents. Shari's warm relationship with her grandfather developed in the context of a difficult childhood. The proximity of her grandfather, who lived in the same neighborhood, allowed for regular interaction, which was a source of stability during her parents' divorce and her mother's frequent hospitalizations. Shari took comfort in the predictable routine of attending Catholic mass with her grandfather:

It meant we were all going to be in the same place together. I mean, you go to mass. And, you know, my grandfather had a carnation in his lapel. We sat in the same seats. It was really predictable. And most of what was going on in my family life just wasn't really that predictable, except when I was with the whole family. It was predictable. And we liked that.

The positive involvement of her grandfather during her childhood enhanced the closeness of their relationship and contributed to her grandfather's influence on her religious beliefs. Shari saw him living his faith daily. "He didn't just go to church or talk about it; he actually lived the tenets of the faith," she says. "I thought—he was wonderful. He was like a rock for me. You know, when everything was going bad, he was the rock."

Shari's fond memories of her grandfather took place within the Catholic Church, which may explain the reason for her return to that faith years later. "Even when I wasn't a practicing Catholic, I was a Catholic in my heart," she explains. "Every significant event of my life took place on the steps of that church. In fact, I took my kids there for my grandfather's funeral and had to take a picture of them on those steps because it all happened right there."

Her comments in the longitudinal surveys over time indicate the loss she felt years after her grandfather's death. In 1997 she told us that "talking again about family influences reminds me how much I miss him. In past surveys, I looked forward to answering this section—NOT being able to answer it [because of Leo's recent death] reminds me of the loss. I still really miss him, and think of him every day. I loved him very much."

Shari's cousin G3 Nina, age fifty-four, reports the same kind of close relationship with their grandfather as Shari did. She says Leo influenced the importance she gives to religion in her life today. In contrast to the close relationship she had with her grandfather, Nina's recollections of her childhood tell of the emotional distance she felt between herself and her father, who "worked constantly. He was probably a very typical husband of the fifties and the sixties. I was kind of neglected—not neglected, that's not the right word—kind of shunned upon by my dad, I think. My father was so withholding."

The lack of closeness in the father–child relationship and the absence of parental religious influence as a consequence made Nina's religious experiences with her grandfather that much more salient. Asked about the role of religion in her home when growing up, Nina said there was "none... nothing. It wasn't a Godless home, per se, but we never had any conversations with my father or my mother. My mother never went to church with us and my father didn't. It was my brother and I. We would go to [our grandparents'] house, we always went to church." Her grandfather Leo encouraged her religious beliefs during her childhood, sending her inspirational things "to uphold me and keep me spiritually fed." Her grandfather's religious influence continued into Nina's adulthood:

> When I was an adult, my children were young, and I had lost my job and I was really anxious. . . . My grandfather took me to church. I remember that that was the most comforting thing, was to be there with him in church, knowing that God was in control. It was shortly after that that I was okay and got another job and moved on from there.

A warm and affirming grandfather, Leo was highly involved in the lives of his grandchildren and as such developed close relationships with them and played an important role in their religious development. The close bonds he developed with his grandchildren provided intergenerational solidarity that was missing in the emotionally distant relationships each young woman had with her own parents—a "skipped generation" effect in religious socialization. These two lines in the Sabelli family illustrate the different ways in which skipped generation effects can influence a family's religious transmission trajectory.

Grandparents Reinforcing or Enhancing Parents' Religious Influence

In other families we found grandparents whose adult children and grandchildren shared their religious tradition and beliefs. In some families, there was clearly a grandparent–parent mutual reinforcement, each generation enhancing the religious teachings and practices being passed on to younger generations. Also, as we see in the following section, there are grandparents whose adult children and grandchildren shared their nonreligious tradition and beliefs.

The Wilsons, the Evangelical Protestant family we met in the last chapter, exemplify the grandparents-as-reinforcement theme. They have been conservative Protestants for more than five generations. When G2 Carolyn, seventy-six, was asked who was most influential in her religious development, she credited her grandparents and her parents. "Both my parents and my husband's parents believed the same way. We just grew up with that belief . . . So it has just been our way of life."

From grandparents, to parents, to Carolyn—and from Carolyn to her children and grandchildren—this is a story of significant continuity in religion. Carolyn succeeded in passing on the same evangelical tradition she inherited to the next generations. The similarity among the Wilson generations is significant. We saw examples of this in chapter 4 and discuss it further in chapter 9. In each generation, the Wilsons say that their faith is based on a "personal relationship with Christ." As Carolyn's son G3 Ken, fifty-five, says, "He's a personal God....You can relate to him, you can talk to him...[T]he Holy Spirit is the personal side that comes and dwells in us." We asked Ken where he thought his family's significantly similar religious beliefs and practices came from. He talked about his grandparents' example and what they taught: "It just all boils down to that relationship with Jesus Christ. That's the main thing they passed down [to us] and everything springs from there." The Wilsons are very warm and supportive of each other, and their belief in a personal relationship with God is the core issue in this family. It has been reinforced from generation to generation, and the youngest Wilsons are highly committed to transmitting their evangelical Christian faith to the next generation.

But we have found that nonreligious orientations—spirituality, values, and ethics that are not encapsulated in institutional or traditional practices and beliefs—can also be transmitted successfully just like participation in established religious traditions. Here grandparents are often important links in that chain. The Smith family provides an example of such nonreligious intergenerational continuity. Beginning with the grandmother several decades ago, the Smiths have made intentional efforts to pass on an ethic of "none," the socialization of nonreligion. G2 Doris Smith was raised a Lutheran but, in her 1985 survey, shortly before she died, said she was a "none." Her daughter Cheryl, fifty-one, says she is "agnostic at best." Granddaughter G4 Crystal, twenty-nine, told us, "I generally say I'm spiritual. If I had to connect to a particular religion, oh my gosh...probably something Middle Easterny. At times in my life I've said I was atheist, but not so much anymore." She says she was not raised in any particular religion and that her mother "didn't really want us going" to religious activities or services.

Crystal also talks a good deal about her grandmother Doris, who was a significant presence in her life. She was "a very strong woman" who relocated to be closer to them in her later years. As recounted by Crystal, her grandmother played an important role in influencing her daughter's and her three grandchildren's nonreligiousness:

My grandma Doris was very much against religion. So we [never] mentioned Jesus or the Bible. She didn't believe. She thought the Bible was full of sh—, as she put it. She would explain how the Bible was written by man and that it was transferred from person to person. She was her dissertation away from having her PhD in the social sciences. I think it was her that started us in this nonreligious "spiritual" outlook. She was definitely very much against religion.

In these two examples from our sample we see that a grandparent with strong religious views, or strong nonreligious views, can create a highly influential moral socialization environment that continues across two or more generations.

Grandparents Challenging or Subverting Parental Religious Socialization

In the third pattern of grandparental influence in our sample, we find that sometimes devout grandparents participate in religious instruction or sacraments for grandchildren (or great-grandchildren) in ways that go against the implicit or explicit wishes of the children's parents. G1 Gladys Sanchez, age ninety, is a devout Catholic who would very much like her grandchildren and great-grandchildren to follow in her Catholic faith. However, some of her great-grandchildren have not been baptized, a situation she finds quite distressing. Only half-jokingly, she told us she might have to take things into her own hands in baptizing her great-grandchildren, even at her advanced years, since she fears her granddaughter Naomi, whose religious faith is described by Gladys as "nothing," will not baptize them, denying Gladys's great-grandchildren a sacrament:

> They don't baptize their kids.... I told them, it's not right. Naomi's mother [Gladys's daughter] should tell them, why they don't baptize? My other granddaughter, she did the same thing. [Her] kids are not baptized [either].... I wish I could get one of the [boys], and take them to be baptized. Maybe I'll do it.

In another family G2 Harriett Holmes, seventy-eight, actually did take things into her own hands. A devoted Lutheran, she was dismayed when her son married a woman who belonged to a nontraditional church. When her granddaughter was born, Harriett was determined that the infant would receive the sacrament of baptism one way or another:

> They didn't believe in baptism. I did, and I was visiting them when the first child was born in their home. And when they handed her to me I went in a corner of the room and I performed the baptism, which is not recognized by the church as a whole, but it can be done if there is a home delivery, as in this case.

Sometimes such grandparental intervention doesn't work. G4 Adam Goldman, twenty-six, is an evangelical Christian whose mother Elizabeth is a fervent Evangelical and whose father Lawrence describes himself as "the most Jewish Methodist guy I know." They divorced when Adam was a young child. On his father's side, Adam comes from a family of Jewish immigrants. While his great-grandparents were secular Jews, their son, G2 Len, became more religious.

Len and his wife, Hazel, attempted to pass on their Jewish religious beliefs and traditions to their children. "We celebrated all the holidays and were involved in the Temple," Len recalls, and they provided their children with a Jewish religious education. But their efforts to transmit their Jewish heritage to their son Lawrence did not succeed. He began to rebel against his parents. His rebellion included marrying Elizabeth, a born-again Fundamentalist Christian convert.

G3s Lawrence and Elizabeth had three children together, but their marriage did not last. After they divorced, Elizabeth continued her active involvement in her Evangelical Christian faith; she succeeded in transmitting her religious tradition to all three of her sons.

G4 Adam talks about why he and his siblings followed their mother's Christian faith and not their father's Jewish traditions. When he and his siblings were growing up, they would attend family gatherings at their Jewish grandparents' house, participating in Jewish holiday rituals. Len and Hazel attempted to teach their grandchildren the traditions and stories of their Jewish heritage and even some Hebrew. But this created conflicts. Adam's mother Elizabeth did not want her children to embrace the Jewish faith. "When we did go over there my grandmother was always trying to teach me Hebrew, trying to teach me things about the Torah, to try and bring me toward the Jewish religion," Adam recalls. "Then my mom would always get mad and try to correct everything that she said [was] wrong. You could totally tell they didn't like each other."

When Adam and his siblings returned home following these gatherings, their mother would talk to them about what they had experienced at their grandparents' house and then tell them about her own quite different religious views. This created an effective barrier, blocking the transmission of his paternal grandparents' and great-grandparents' Jewish religious heritage. In this case, the grandparents' attempt to substitute their religious socialization for that of the children's mother was not successful.

Grandparents Ignoring Grandchildren's Religious Socialization

A fourth pattern is reflected by grandparents who play no role in their grandchildren's religious socialization. Some are indifferent to religion and have no interest in whether or not their grandchildren are involved. Others have made the determination not to interfere or participate in their grandchildren's religious choices. Still others are ambivalent, not sure what to do but not having strong feelings one way or the other. Note that this category does not include nonaffiliated grandparents such as atheists, agnostics, and nondeists who, like Doris Smith mentioned above, are explicit in efforts to socialize children and grandchildren in their own nonreligious perspectives.

The Jacksons are a family in which grandparents have little to do with their grandchildren's religious training or beliefs. When asked what she learned from her grandparents, G1 Myrna replied, "Not a great deal. We just grew by ourselves." Likewise, Myrna seems to have little impact on her own grandchildren's religiosity. In part this was due to the geographic distance separating her from her grandchildren; her children are dispersed across the country. But conflict in the Jackson family also prevented effective transmission. Regarding religion, G3 Karen said "that was just one subject that wasn't brought up, wasn't talked about, because there were too many different beliefs, I guess." According to Karen, G1 Myrna was the source of discord at family gatherings:

Well, Grandma [Jackson] would just—like nothing was right or good enough for her. So if you went and you showed up to the family reunion or not, you might be the topic of—I'm not even going to say conversation—it was more like ridicule. Well, those weren't very happy times. And as we got older, we just all tend to not show up at those events.

Arguments with Myrna about religion were especially common. Karen explains, "If I did believe something, it was best to just keep it quiet, keep it to yourself to avoid coming under attack for believing or not."

Rediscovering Religious Grandparents

Most research on religion in industrialized societies has ignored the role of grandparents in religious transmission. This is an unfortunate oversight because, as we've seen, grandparents are playing an increasingly significant role in their grandchildren's lives. About four in ten of the grandparents and grandchildren in our sample share the same religious tradition. This was a higher level of transmission than we expected. Our data show little change in the past thirty-five years in the degree of grandparents–grandchild similarity and we were surprised by the relatively strong evidence of cross-generational influence in religiosity. Such religious influence can be a great stabilizing factor in grandchildren's lives when their home life is precarious, as we saw in the case of the Sabelli family and encounter again in the next chapter, when we explore the debilitating impact of divorce on the transmission of religion from one generation to the next.

CHAPTER 6 | How Interfaith Marriage and
Divorce Affect Continuity[1]

Generation (G) 3 Ken Wilson, fifty-five, talked about the hazards of
marrying outside his Evangelical faith: "What you're taught is, don't
be unequally yoked, meaning you're really fighting at odds if one of
you is a believer and a Christian and the other one isn't. If you do,
now you have the issues of children, how to raise them and all that."
He is thankful that he married within his faith, and today, all three of
his adult children are Evangelicals.

G3 Nancy Young is a devout Mormons who in 1970 reported
that she had just been married in a Mormon Temple ceremony. In
her survey she said she hoped "[f]or each child to marry within our
[Latter-Day Saints (LDS)] church." Through the years, her surveys
and those of her husband's indicated a similar dedication to the
Church and similar efforts in raising their children in the faith. In her
2008 interview, we learned that her five children had married Mormon
spouses and that all nine of her grandchildren were also LDS.

Nominally a Catholic but raised in a nonreligious household, G4 Daniel
West married a Catholic, Sue. When their marriage experienced problems,
they both started going to an Evangelical church and found what he calls
a "solid and stable foundation to build a marriage on." Together they are
transmitting their new faith to their children, now teenagers.

WHOM ONE MARRIES, AND whether marital partners have similar religious traditions, is significant for religious socialization and the transmission of religion across generations. Interfaith marriage is a concern of parents, priests, ministers, and rabbis. Divorce and remarriage are likely to diminish prospects for passing on family religious traditions to a younger generation. Thus it is not surprising that religious institutions discourage marrying outside the faith and have prohibited divorce.

In looking at stories of family members in our study, we were struck by how often marriage, divorce, or remarriage led to a change in religious affiliation. What do such changes in marital status imply for religious continuity over time? In this chapter we explore how marriage serves as a key mechanism for the successful transmission of religion across generations by focusing on several configurations of religion and marriage. A *same-faith marriage* is one in which both spouses have an affiliation within a similar religious tradition (Protestant, Catholic, Jewish). Interfaith marriages may be of two kinds. An *interfaith marriage with conversion* is where one partner converts to the religion of the other or where both partners convert to the same faith after marriage. *Interfaith marriage without conversion* occurs when each partner goes his or her own way. An interfaith marriage in this context also can be seen when one of the partners has no religious affiliation while the other is religious.

Interfaith Marriages and Religious Transmission

First, we look at evidence about marriage and religious affiliation nationally and in our study sample. Interfaith marriages are very common in the United States today. More than a quarter of all adults who are married or living with a partner are in relationships of mixed religious traditions.[2] If we include marriages in which spouses are from different Protestant denominations, such as a marriage between a Presbyterian and a Methodist, then the proportion of couples in religiously mixed marriages today is 37%. The unaffiliated or "nones" are the most likely (65%) to have a spouse or partner from a different religious background, while those least likely to marry or live with a partner outside their religious tradition include Mormons (17%), Catholics (22%), Jews (31%), and Evangelical Protestants (32%).

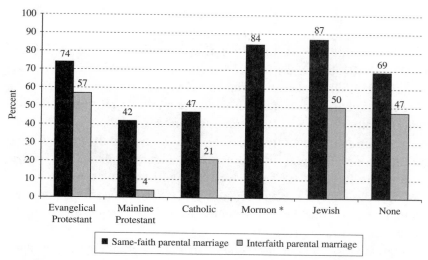

FIGURE 6.1 Percentage of G3 Parents in Same-Faith and Interfaith Marriages Whose G4 Children Share Their Religious Tradition, 2005 (G3–G4)

* There were no interfaith marriages among the G3 Mormons in our sample.

Same-faith and interfaith marriages show significant differences in the extent to which parents and children share religious traditions. Figure 6.1 presents parent–child similarity by religious tradition for same-faith and interfaith parental marriages. For same-faith marriages, 68% of G3 parents[3] have G4 adult children who share their religious tradition. For interfaith parental marriages, by contrast, only 38% of parents have adult children who share either the father's (40%) or the mother's (36%) religious tradition.

For parents in same-faith marriages, we see higher parent–child similarity for three religious traditions: Evangelicals, Mormons, and Jews. This is not surprising, because these are tightknit religious traditions that strongly encourage same-faith marriage (see chapter 9), which in turn promotes socialization of children into the same religious faith. We also found that for parents where both are nonaffiliated—one might regard these as "same-faith" marriages of sorts—69% have adult children who are also "none." The unexpected degree of parent–child similarity among the nonreligious is discussed in chapter 8. Same-faith parents who are Mainline Protestants or Catholics are less likely to have children who share their religious tradition and much less likely if in a mixed-faith relationship.

When parents have different religious traditions, are their children more likely to share their father's tradition or their mother's? As seen in Figure 6.2, when parents in our sample have an interfaith marriage, their children are more likely to have the mother's religious tradition than the father's. At the same time, fathers and mothers with no religious tradition are equally likely to have young adult children who are also none. The proportion of Jewish fathers and mothers whose children are Jewish is the same. However, with so few cases, we do not want to overestimate the significance of these findings; there were not enough cases of interfaith Mormon marriages in our sample to make comparisons meaningful.

In our survey, the G3 fathers and mothers in interfaith marriages come from different religious traditions. Among fathers, 9% are Evangelicals, 7% are Mainline Protestant, 14% are Catholic, and 3% are Jewish. For mothers, 25% are Evangelicals, 33% are Mainline Protestant, 16% are Catholic, and 3% are Jewish. What is remarkable is the high proportion of fathers in interfaith marriages that are nonreligious: more than 65%. This

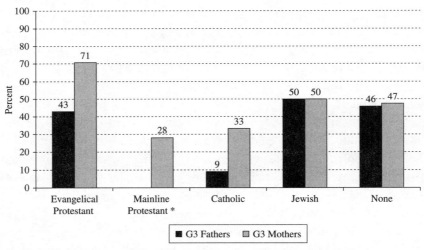

FIGURE 6.2 Percentage of Fathers and Mothers in Interfaith Marriages Whose Adult Children Share Their Religious Tradition, 2005 (G3–G4)

* There were no Mainline Protestant G3 fathers in interfaith marriages in our sample.

is much higher than for mothers (22%). In the absence of a religious identity, there is probably little pressure for marital religious homogamy—to marry within one's religious faith.

Divorce and Religious Transmission

Parental divorce can also affect the likelihood of parents and their children having the same religious tradition (see Figure 6.3). In the 2005 Longitudinal Study of Generations (LSOG) sample, 55% of G3 parents had not divorced; of these, 63% had the same religious tradition as their G4 children. But among the 45% of G3 parents who had divorced, 53% had the same religious tradition as their G4 children, a 10-point difference. Whether or not parents divorced seems to matter most for parent–child resemblance among Evangelical Protestants (a 19 percentage point difference), Mainline Protestants (an 18 percentage point difference), and Catholics (a 20 percentage point difference). There is very little difference between divorced and nondivorced parents for Jewish parent–child resemblance and for nonaffiliated parent–child resemblance. Of the Mormons who responded to our survey, there were too few to make comparisons that would be statistically reliable.

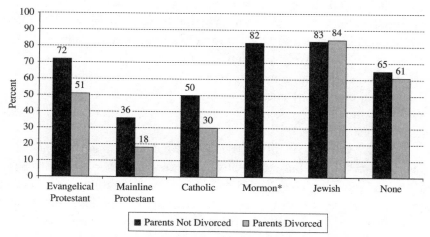

FIGURE 6.3 Percentage of Parents Whose Young Children Share Their Religious Tradition by Whether or Not Parents Divorced, 2005 (G3–G4)

* There were too few parental divorce cases among the G3 Mormons in our sample to measure make a meaningful comparison.

During our interviews we discovered many family stories that illustrate the ways that divorce and remarriage can disrupt religious transmission. In older generations of the Sanchez family, for example, there was a long tradition of same-faith marriages with the Catholic Church, and there was no record of divorce. But starting with the G3 Baby Boomers, there began to be marriages to non-Catholics as well as an increase in divorce and remarriage. Some remained Catholic, others switched to Evangelical Protestantism, and some drifted away from religion. For these G3 family members who switched their religious allegiance, divorce and remarriage interrupted the passing on of their family's Catholic tradition to their G4 children.

We see this clearly in the case of the Sanchez great-granddaughter G4 Natasha. Her parents divorced during her childhood, and her father, a non-practicing Catholic, remarried a newly converted, zealous Evangelical Protestant. Natasha spent weekends alternating between her nonpracticing Catholic birthmother and her father and Evangelical stepmother; on the weekends when she was with them she attended an Evangelical church with her stepmother. In her mid-teens, Natasha stopped attending her stepmother's church. She seemed not to have developed a commitment to either the Catholicism of her mother and father or the Evangelical Protestantism of her stepmother.

Yet Natasha's childhood experience in her stepmother's religion left a residue of influence. Thinking back, Natasha reflects, "We are still the people we are because of all those days. Because of what we were taught, and because we still have it in us, we haven't completely lost God in our life." Now divorced herself, Natasha has decided that her young G5 children should be exposed to religion and is introducing them to the Evangelical church she knew as a child. It is too soon to know whether Natasha's stepmother's religious orientation will be transmitted to her step-grandchildren.

Natasha's story and many other accounts of divorce in our sample demonstrate that divorce has a disruptive effect on parents' attempts to pass down a religious heritage. In our findings on divorce's effects on religious transmission, we also discovered an interesting exception to this trend. This occurs when both partners convert to a new common faith in an effort to grow closer together and stave off divorce.

In the Brigham family, G3s Marjorie and Karl married in their early twenties while Karl was in the service. Growing up in different religious traditions (Marjorie was Methodist; Karl was Catholic), they initially represented an interfaith marriage. However, a few years after starting their family they both converted to Mormonism. Each indicated that the decision to convert was fueled by their persistent marital problems and their hope that the Mormon faith with its strong support of marriage and families would help their relationship. This conversion defined the religious trajectory of their G4 children into adulthood and that of the next generation, the G5s. However, after thirty years of marriage Marjorie and Karl finally divorced.

While Marjorie and Karl's conversion to the Mormon faith ultimately did not save their marriage, their story offers an interesting twist on how religion can be passed on when a decision to divorce is prolonged. All their children were socialized into the Mormon tradition, some more successfully than others. Marjorie and Karl's divorce affected the religious paths of their children in different ways, in part because of their respective ages when their parents divorced and the stresses they experienced. The older G4 children were strongly socialized into the LDS Church and in adulthood remained very committed to their religious faith, passing it on to their own children. However, the younger G4s all left the LDS Church in their late teens for periods of time—though all eventually returned. Marjorie, now age sixty, recalls that "all of the youngest decided for a while not to go to our church... [and one] had a couple of boyfriends who were not members of our church." Ten years after her divorce, Marjorie reported that every one of her children had married in the LDS Church: "All my children, even if they had strayed away... have come back to deciding that this [a Temple marriage] was very important in their lives. To me it's a miracle."

Same-Faith Marriages and Religious Transmission

It is not surprising that same-faith or religiously homogenous marriages provide the most favorable context for consistent religious socialization of children leading to transmission of their faith, or that divorce can undermine that socialization. However, the likelihood of there being a same-faith marriage in the first place varies by religious tradition. Same-faith marriages were most evident in the Mormon, Jewish, and Evangelical families in our sample. In these families children were taught to value marrying someone of the same faith and discouraged from marrying outside it. The children learned these lessons well, as reflected by Marjorie Brigham, who put it this way: "You have a better chance of living your religion if your spouse or your important person in your life believes the way you do and has the same values."

In these families we observed that grandparents and often great-grandparents had admonished their grandchildren to marry within their faith—a fact that reinforces some of what we saw in the last chapter, about how unexpectedly strong grandparents' religious influence can be. In the Lieberman family, fifty-three-year-old Vicki reflected that being Jewish "was very important to my grandparents." Her mother, Ruth, seventy-six, recalled how her parents were very strict about marrying within the Jewish faith and staying within the Jewish community: "I wasn't allowed to bring somebody who wasn't of my own religion home, or even date them."

In the Wilson family, marrying within their Evangelical faith has been embedded in the family's religious training for generations. Seventy-six-year-old Carolyn Wilson described how she and her husband met at church. She said, "I would not have considered marrying anyone that wasn't a Christian."

For the Mormons in our sample such as the Young family, marrying a Mormon in a Temple ceremony is central to religious continuity over the generations. Whereas earthly marriages are "till death do us part," Mormons believe they will be married to their spouse eternally if they are married in a Mormon temple and live worthily. Great-grandparents Henry and Ruby Young married in the Mormon temple and were successful in transmitting this religious tradition to four generations of their offspring. Their daughter, G2 Nancy Young, remembers being raised with the expectation that she and all her siblings would marry in the faith, an expectation she imparted to her own children. In Nancy's first LSOG survey in 1970, when asked what good things she would want in her life, she replied, "for each child to marry within our church." When asked what bad things could happen to her, she responded, "for one of my children to marry outside of the church." Her wishes were granted: All five of her children have been "sealed" to their spouses in the temple and are raising their children in the Mormon faith. Her granddaughter, G4 Nicole, twenty, looks forward to marrying in the temple: "It is in the Mormon religion that families are forever so when you get married it's such a huge deal because you're going to be with this person forever, you with your entire family."

Jews also place a high value on marrying within their religion. For generations, members of the Rosenberg family have married within their Jewish faith. G3 Howard, fifty-five, talked about the importance of a Jewish marriage in his family:

> [T]hat's the way you ensure Jewish continuity....You look at who people select as marriage partners. So how many generations do we have? One, two, three, three generations. The family life for each of those generations, I guess, has had as a priority the continuation of traditional Judaism, practiced in one form or another, but a fairly consistent strain of that religion, in three generations. You could probably take it back to my grandparents on my father's side and make it four, four generations....It didn't matter much what your parents believed, but you knew what you were doing on certain Jewish holidays.

Howard's wife, Kathy, says that her parents always expected she would marry a Jew. They assumed "that we would stay within the religion, that we would adopt some forms of traditions that were similar. We never even talked about it...[I]t was expected." She understands how important same-faith marriage is for maintaining a Jewish identity; you have to "stay within and adopt traditions in some form." Her parents' lessons and expectations clearly took hold: All of Kathy's siblings "are married to Jewish people, and they all live Jewish lives."

These cases illustrate that marrying someone from the same faith significantly increases the likelihood of religious transmission across generations. This is particularly true in the context of a religious tradition in which homogamy is buttressed by high cultural or institutional boundaries, such as in Judaism, Mormonism, or conservative Protestantism (as discussed in chapter 9). In these traditions, religious homogamy is also cultural homogamy, and religious socialization by parents is reinforced by experiences children receive at church or synagogue, with friends, at school, and in the community.

Same-Faith Marriage Does Not Guarantee Religious Transmission

However, there is another, less expected aspect concerning the linkage between religion and marriage: Devout belief can cause individuals to stay in an unhappy marriage, which might negatively affect religious socialization of their children and thus religious transmission. Although G3 Charlotte Jensen and her husband, Alan, are in a same-faith marriage, the long-term strains in their marriage have hindered efforts to pass on their Mormon religious tradition to their children and grandchildren. Growing up in a home where her parents' Mainline Protestant faith was weak at best, Charlotte embraced the LDS Church while in her teens because it "had everything in it that I was looking for as far as family values and it just had everything in it that I personally believe." A new Mormon convert, Charlotte married a nonpracticing Mormon and worked to bring him back into the Mormon fold, and he became as faithful as she was. They began raising their G4 children in the Mormon faith. Over time, their marriage became increasingly strained, yet their Mormon teachings kept them together in marriage. Today, however, their young adult children question the wisdom of their parents' decision not to divorce. According to their son, Dustin, who says he is non-religious, their Mormon faith is the dubious reason his mother stayed married to his father:

> [One] reason why we're so rough on my mom about her religion is that a big thing in the Mormon religion is divorce.... There's no such thing as divorce. Once you're married, you stay married for life. You stay with your life partner no matter [what], you know, through thick and thin, and we all believed that she should have left him a long time ago and she just stuck with him side by side and she rode through it all

While Charlotte and Alan's marriage survived, we'll see in the next chapter that their efforts to transmit their Mormon religion to their children were not successful. By the time they were teens, all of their children had stopped practicing the Mormon faith. One son married a Catholic, and another married a nondenominational Christian. The other two remain unmarried in their late twenties, another departure from Mormon tradition, as Mormons tend to marry at younger ages[4] and have the lowest rates of "never married" of any religious group in the United States.[5]

Interfaith Marriages and Religious Continuity

Interfaith marriages—marrying someone from a different religious background—fall into two categories: conversion of one partner to the religion of the other or no conversion, with each partner continuing to go his or her own religious way. It would seem likely that religious transmission would be higher in marriages with religious homogamy—that is, where one partner converts to the other's religion.

Interfaith marriages with conversion can proceed along different pathways, though each can lead to religious congruence and religious transmission. One consideration is timing: whether the conversion occurs before the wedding or after. A second is whether the conversion involves a family religious tradition. In some cases the religion of one spouse may represent a continuation of traditions in his or her family of origin. In others, both spouses may move in an entirely new religious direction, independent of the tradition of their respective families. A third consideration is the meaning behind religious conversion: One or both spouses may be seeking spiritual development, they may be seeking to save their marriage through mutual religious involvement, or religious conversion may occur simply for convenience with no real commitment to religion by either spouse.

Converting to a Common Faith Before Marriage

In the West family, the previously nonreligious G4 Cindy converted to her husband's Evangelical faith just before they were married. Referring to the absence of religion in her family of origin, Cindy talked about how she felt something was missing in her childhood. Her parents came from different religious traditions. (Her father was Catholic, her mother Presbyterian.) Because her father in particular was dismissive of his own family's religion, and because her parents were unable to reconcile their different religious views, they stopped practicing any religious faith; religion was of little importance in the West household during Cindy's growing-up years. She describes how the Evangelical religion of her future husband and his family became very appealing to her and how they and their pastor led her to religious faith. She says it was a "really big, life-altering experience" to go through this with her new husband at the beginning of their marriage and was a "turning point" in their being guided together. Meeting and marrying her husband helped to shape her religious beliefs and involvement, Cindy says, and she admired the religion of his family of origin. "His family had a different way about their family dynamic, because all of them are churchgoers. And so we started attending church." She pauses, then adds, "So the Lord definitely brought him into my life, to bring me closer to Him."

Since their marriage twelve years ago, Cindy and her husband have been active in their nondenominational Christian church. Their family bonds are enhanced by church involvement. They attend services with his parents and family members, and then after church they all have lunch together. "And even the family members that go to different churches still meet with us Sunday afternoons for lunch," notes Cindy. She and her husband are raising their two young children in their Evangelical faith.

The young couple's decision to be active churchgoers pleased his family and surprised hers. "I think they kind of are impressed," she says of her own parents. "I really do think that they admire the fact that we've taken it upon ourselves to become more involved with the Lord, and to teach our kids."

Converting to a Common Faith After Marriage

Marriage can be strengthened and transmission made more likely if parents who come from different religious traditions jointly find and adopt a new faith as they develop their marriage. We see an example of this in the Holmes family. For G2s Raymond and Harriet, as well as their G3 son Cliff and his wife Stephanie, we see a pattern of a marriage that starts out as mixed-faith and then, several years later, while their children are still young, involves conversion by one or both spouses to a common religious affiliation. Based on their interviews and survey responses over the years, both of these marriages appear to be strong and loving.

When they married, Harriet was a strong Baptist and Raymond's background was Church of the Brethren. Although Harriet's Baptist parents were disappointed that she didn't marry in her own faith (her father was a Baptist pastor), they accepted their daughter's interfaith marriage. Harriet recalls:

> I met Raymond and I don't know, just something about him said, "this is it!" I think that when we talked seriously about who we were and what we wanted in our lives...that we were pretty much on the same page. He wanted a home and family and so did I and he was *[pause]* I won't say he

was very religious, because Ray wasn't, but he did go to church and he did believe in the same way that I did. So it was not a stretch at all and I was just comfortable with him.

For Harriet, having a spouse who shared the same religious affiliation was less important than having a spouse who shared similar religious beliefs. Harriet said she was not fazed by her husband's religion because he attended church regularly and was religious. Several years later when Raymond and Harriet and their children moved to a new town, their experience of being welcomed into an Episcopal Church after feeling rebuffed by the local Baptist congregation caused both Raymond and Harriet to convert to the Episcopal faith. The Holmeses' adult children and grandchildren attend the Episcopal church with their now-widowed mother whenever they visit her.

G3 son Cliff Holmes continues to be actively involved in the Episcopal church of his youth to which his parents converted. He married Stephanie, who at the time of their marriage was not affiliated with any church but interested in a nontraditional spirituality. Eventually, Stephanie did convert to her husband's Episcopal faith but not until their children were nearly school age. Stephanie talked about her initial resistance to converting:

> But I didn't want to do it, and I just, I mean I really, really, really bucked doing it, because I really don't like institutional religions. And when I finally did, that was kind of the moment of epiphany. The answer really kind of came very cleanly, clearly, and very simply to me that it's just, you know, like it's not going to change our conversation. And it was like, oh, thank God, okay.

Stephanie's conversion delighted her husband and her mother and led to a thoroughgoing church involvement by every member of the family. "We made sure that the kids were both baptized, because God forbid if [we] didn't have them baptized," she says. "So we did all the obligatory right things, you know . . . and from my perspective, mostly we did that for family needs. And then, as we've been kind of reconnected to our church, which has been really lovely for my husband, it's been a good thing for me, because it's kind of allowed me to really finally understand my relationship to God, without it having to be about the church."

While Cliff and Stephanie have raised their G4 children in the Episcopal Church, as adolescents these G4s are beginning to question their religious faith, as their mother did when she was their age. As yet it is not clear whether Cliff and Stephanie's children will become participants in their parents' and grandparents' Episcopal faith. The religious orientations of the G4 Holmeses' future marital partners may be what most determine their religious commitments going forward.

Interfaith Marriage Without Conversion Weakens Religious Transmission

Interfaith marriages that did not involve religious conversion occurred in one-third of our interview families. In most of these marriages, the spouses belong to different Protestant denominations or one spouse professes a religious tradition while the other has none; in both types there is little evidence of religious transmission to the next generation. Many of the parents of these marital partners, themselves religiously committed, had hoped their adult children would marry someone who shared their religious faith, even as they acknowledged this was beyond their control. At the very least they wanted their children to marry someone who believes in God.

G3 Tom Holmes (the brother of Cliff mentioned above) reflects this pattern of interfaith marriage without conversion. Raised an Episcopalian, he married someone from a different Protestant background. Tom noted that religion was not important in his interfaith marriage. He said that he had discussed religion with his wife and "told her it was not necessary" for her to be religiously involved. "[I]f it was something she wanted to do, fine. But it was entirely her decision," he said. They later divorced.

Tom's parents tolerated the fact that he and his siblings married people of different religious Christian denominations, but they drew the line at marrying a non-Christian or an atheist. He noted that his parents were not accepting of his sister dating a Jew. Now in his fifties, G3 Tom attends church infrequently and does not regard himself as religious. Tom did not pass his Episcopalian religious heritage down to his son, Jon. Asked if he and his son share the same perspective concerning religion, Tom replied, "I wouldn't necessarily say it's the same because I don't really know why he might feel the way he does. But I never made him go to church, so I really, honestly don't know how he feels about that. I don't think he goes to church now." However, Tom does not believe his son is an atheist or agnostic: "No, no, no, no. No, he's definitely not an atheist. I know he believes in God." It appears that Tom seems to share his parents' attitude toward atheism, who "drew the line" at nonreligion.

For the Liebermans, as we noted earlier, marrying within the Jewish faith is of paramount importance. When twenty-seven-year-old G4 Lindsay was asked about a pivotal moment in her life relating to her religious beliefs and values, she replied that it was her traditional Jewish wedding, a celebration she wanted "just because it's beautiful and it's tradition... you know, we wanted to keep with tradition." But there have been exceptions in the Lieberman family. Lindsay recalls how her cousin, Marcia, took a different religious path and married outside of her Jewish faith: "[She] married a Catholic, and that's important." Lindsay explains:

> Their children are just probably going to be very confused, because both sides of their family are important. Like they're going to temple, and they're going to Bible lessons, so it's like, whatever.... I just think they're going to be so confused.

Whether Judaism will be passed down to the children in this line of the family is questionable. Lindsay acknowledges that her cousin's interfaith marriage and the religious upbringing of her children have caused her G1 great-grandmother, Imogene, great distress.

The Importance of Same-Faith Marriage

Whom one marries and whether there is religious similarity between spouses is important for effective religious socialization of children and the transmission of religion from one generation to the next. In our sample, more than two-thirds of the same-faith marriages produced children who followed their parents' religious tradition, whereas less than one in four mixed marriages resulted in a child who followed either the mother or the father's religious tradition. Thus, we find that parents in a same-faith marriage are most likely to perpetuate religious continuity across generations. This is especially likely if there is high religious commitment, the partners regularly attend religious services together, and religion is highly salient in the lives of both partners.

Another important result from our data is that religion can strengthen marriages—same-faith marriages—leading in turn to stronger religious socialization and a greater degree of religious transmission. But same-faith marriage is not a guarantee of religious transmission, particularly when the marriage is strained—even when there is a high degree of church involvement in the religious socialization of children.

Because of the multigenerational nature of our sample, we were also able to see change in the value placed on religious homogamy over time within the same families. The importance of marital partners sharing a similar religious faith has declined over generations, except for the Evangelical, Mormon, and Jewish families. In our survey data, for parents who said their efforts to teach their children about important values included allowing their children religious "choice," it appeared that "believing in God" is a more desirable religious outcome than "going to the same church as one's parents."

Divorce and remarriage complicate parents' religious socialization efforts. In our study divorce frequently disrupted religious transmission to the next generation, even if the parents were similar in their religious identity. Yet divorce did not always fracture children's continuity with their parents' religious tradition. In several families, the divorced parent with high religious commitment was successful in transmitting his or her religious faith. This often occurred when the decision to divorce had been delayed until after the children's primary religious socialization had been accomplished.

However, many young adults who break away from their parents' religious traditions do so for reasons that have nothing to do with family structure or their parents' marital situation. We next describe young adults who are taking a path that is different from their parents: the Religious Rebels, the Zealots, and the Prodigals.

PART THREE | Will They Leave, or Will They Stay?

CHAPTER 7 | Interruptions in Religious Continuity

Rebels, Zealots, and Prodigals[1]

Generation (G) 3 Charlotte Jensen, age fifty-three and a devout Mormon, is what we term a "Zealot." That is, she is much more religious than her nonreligious parents and the only one in her family to embrace a religion of any kind. She is a fervent convert to the Church of Jesus Christ of Latter-Day Saints (LDS). She has four children. She has resolutely raised them in the Mormon faith, but not one has followed her in that path. They are what we term "Religious Rebels."

Twenty-six-year-old G4 Sarah Turner was raised in a tightknit Evangelical family and as a child was highly involved with her parents in their church. But in high school and college she became increasingly uncomfortable with what remembers as church members' tendency to be judgmental and their intolerance toward others who did not believe exactly as they did. She also was disturbed by their hypocrisy, preaching one thing and then doing another. She left the church, a low-key religious rebel. But her parents hope and pray that she will come back to the church again and turn out to be a "religious prodigal," returning home.

WHY DO SOME CHILDREN break away from their parents' religious tradition and take a very different direction in spiritual expression? How do others become more intensely religious than their unchurched parents or siblings, and what causes still other young adults to leave their family's religious tradition, drifting away or converting to another religion, only to return later to the faith of their parents?

Failures in Religious Transmission

The data we presented in chapter 3 show that almost 6 out of 10 young adults in our sample were similar to their parents in religious affiliation, a rate higher than we expected in light of the many changes that have occurred in American society over the past few decades. That religious transmission is this high might be comforting news to religious families and religious leaders, especially among conservative religious groups, for whom youths' leaving the faith of their parents is a source of much concern (see chapter 10).

The other side of the coin is this: More than 4 out of 10 youth are different from their parents in faith; the rate of religious nontransmission in our sample is also high. In these families, some quite religious, parents and children differ in religious affiliation, participation, and belief. Why does this occur? In this chapter we discuss several types of nontransmission, focusing on the families in which religion is salient and a youth's falling away from the family faith is a disappointment to parents. From our interviews, we have identified three outcomes reflecting nontransmission—that is, categories of young adults who have taken a very different spiritual path than a highly religious parent:

1. *Religious Rebels* are young adults who actively reject the beliefs and practices of religious parents. Some convert to a quite different faith or practice; others reject religion altogether; still others drift off into religious indifference. Mormons use the term "apostasy" to describe this; "backsliding" is used by Southern Baptists and other conservative Protestant circles; "disaffiliation," a much less colorful term, is found in the writings of sociologists.
2. *Religious Zealots* are young adults who are considerably more fervent in their religious commitment than their parents. "Zealotry" is a term used to refer to individuals who are passionately committed to a cause or idea, usually political; however, we use it here in a comparative sense to indicate that a family member's religious intensity is much greater than his or her parents.' Religious Zealots are usually converts to a religion different than their parents. A majority of the Zealots in our sample were also Rebels, having rejected their parents' religious

tradition in converting to another. But some were from religiously indifferent families, the first to embrace a religion of any kind.

3. *Religious Prodigals* (or "boomerangs") are those who started out as Religious Rebels but whose departure from the faith turned out to be temporary. They rejected the religious beliefs and practices of their parents but, after a period of time, came back to them—as in Jesus' parable of the Prodigal son, who returned home to his father after wasting his inheritance on riotous living in another land.[2]

There have been few studies about youth who might be Religious Rebels, Zealots, or Prodigals. Of those that have examined "disaffiliation," or apostasy, only a few have looked at family factors. One study found that the chances of young adults' dropping out decreased with the events of marriage and becoming a parent.[3] Another showed that if religious faith had been important to parents, there was less chance of children leaving the religious tradition of their childhood.[4] Both studies showed significant contrasts between religious traditions in disaffiliation, with what they called "low tension" or less exclusive religious identities (such as Mainline Protestant traditions) showing more dropouts and "high tension" or tightknit communities (such as Evangelicals and Mormons) showing more retention. This was because, according to the researchers, "more liberal religious groups offer ample room for youth to claim their own religious faith."[5]

In this chapter we focus on families of young adults who have rejected familial religious traditions or have become much more religiously involved than their parents, as well as those who have left their family's faith only to return to the fold later in life: Religious Rebels, the Zealots, and the Prodigals.

Charlotte Jensen: Zealot with Four Religious Rebel Children

G3 Charlotte Jensen, whom we met in the last chapter, is, at fifty-three, highly religious, a zealous convert to the Mormon faith. She strongly rejected the religious indifference of her parents and grandparents. Her grandfather, Melvin, was in the military so the family moved around a lot; her father, G2 Charles, says, "Not having a specific church, we just got away from [religion]." He adds that he and his wife Clara believed their children should make their own choices regarding religion: "It's always been where they have a choice. They could pick and have what they wanted. Maybe that is because I wasn't so definite in [religion]."

Charlotte recounts that "we went to the community church as kids and my parents encouraged us to go there, but they never went with us." When she was a teenager she started becoming involved in the nearby Mormon Church: "I grew up with a lot of kids that were in the Mormon Church and they were—I can't really say looked down upon, but made fun of." Paradoxically, this led Charlotte to identify with her Mormon friends' sense of being different; she says she wanted to learn more about them and their ways. She also had a Mormon teacher in high school that influenced her.

Charlotte converted to the LDS Church in her late teens and then married Alan, a man from a devout Mormon family who had drifted away from the faith. Alan, now age fifty-seven, said that when he was growing up, "Just about everything I did was based around the Church." He was baptized and confirmed in the Church, and he attended seminary early every morning before high school started. But Alan strayed from the faith as a youth, and it was Charlotte's influence that brought him back. This makes Alan's religious biography quite interesting—a case in which we see each of the concepts introduced in this chapter. He was a religious rebel who became a prodigal, returning to his family's faith through the influence of a Zealot spouse. Today Alan's faith is firm: "I believe in the Gospel and I believe in Jesus Christ. I wouldn't be where I am without Him."

Charlotte is active in the LDS Church and very sure in her beliefs. She talks about how different she is from her parents and siblings, personifying what we call a Zealot: "Out of my whole family, I've gone a different direction. I'm the only one that has a church. We have different beliefs, different morality." She wishes that they had the same confident faith that she enjoys.

Charlotte and Alan have four children, three of whom have been active participants in the Longitudinal Study of Generations surveys throughout the years. Despite their parents' fervent faith, none of the four children is a Mormon today. Their oldest child is G4 Dustin, age thirty, who says, "I have no religion at all." He told us he changed his religion because of the pressure toward conformity felt in the LDS Church and toward his highly religious parents for forcing him to participate:

I was eighteen when I moved out. I decided I was my own person and I didn't have to follow everything my parents [believed]—you know, the typical. I was definitely against going to church. [They] were so into conformity. I was forced to go most of my childhood. I didn't really go of my own accord and so [later] I stopped going.

Dustin says his three siblings feel the same way about their mother's intense devotion to her faith: "They kind of resent the Mormon religion the way I did when I was younger, so they kind of look the other way and kind of brush [our mother] off when it comes to her religious beliefs."

Dustin's younger brother, G4 David, echoes these sentiments. He says, "I have not participated in any religion whatsoever since I was eighteen. I have not gone to church." His parents were "too strict" in their religiosity and "wanted us to conform too much." He said that religion was the source of most conflicts in the family:

> Not necessarily religion, but just the strict fact of going to church. Church was always forced upon us when we were younger. I'm a strong believer that you should take your children to church when they're super-young and aren't really knowing any better, but once they begin to understand and know what's going on with church and with religion, then they should be able to make their own choice.

Like his siblings, twenty-eight-year-old David says he is not religious and has not been in a Mormon church since he moved out of his parents' house.

What we see in the Jensens is a mother from a religiously indifferent family who converts to a new religion, influenced by Mormon high school church friends and the LDS parents of the man she married. She becomes highly involved in the LDS Church and as a parent is highly committed to her children's religious welfare. She raises her children in the Church and follows all the Church's precepts for religious education. But what she hoped for—to see her faith transmitted in the lives of her young adult children—does not occur. Her children say that she overdid it; none of the four is following in her religious tradition. For them, their mother's religious zeal was "too much of a good thing."

Sarah Turner: Religious Rebel Whose Parents Hope She's Just a Prodigal

G4 Sarah Turner, age twenty-six, told us she was the "black sheep" of the family, but she added that she does not want to make any waves or cause trouble. Recall from the opening vignette in chapter 1 that Sarah comes from a devout Evangelical family and was active in the church when she was growing up. Today as a young adult, however, she feels uncomfortable with her family's fundamentalist church, and this isolates her from the rest of her family. Her parents, G3s Irene and Eddie, describe themselves as born-again Christians and are highly involved in their church. The same is true of her grandparents, G2s Rob and Eleanor, as well as her great-grandmother, G1 Grace. Her parents and grandparents nurtured Sarah in their Evangelical faith and involved her in the many activities her church had to offer children and youth.

But Sarah says that when she went to college she started having doubts and questioning her religious beliefs. She also came to feel the burden of an oppressive atmosphere of judgment in her church tradition. Although her outward behavior in college did nothing to merit such judgments, she began feeling guilty about her increasing doubts about the literal truth of the Bible and the teachings of her church. She has struggled to free herself from the shame this aroused. "I pretty much stopped going to church after high school," she says. "I didn't want to have to answer to anybody. I didn't want to have to feel guilty about what I was doing. I felt like I would constantly be in conflict with—'Is God judging me?' I just felt like I wanted to be free from all that."

The nondenominational Evangelical church in which Sarah grew up maintains very strong convictions about what is right and wrong, good and evil. But Sarah came to feel that what they defined as "sin" was arbitrary and based on an inconsistent use of the Bible (e.g., prohibiting women from teaching while ignoring prohibitions against eating shellfish). Such inconsistency made Sarah want to withdraw even further in self-protection. "I didn't want to have to worry about sinning, going to hell, and all this guilt that's put on you when you're really religious," she explains. "I didn't want to deal with that, so I just stopped [going to church]." She also became convinced of what she felt was hypocrisy in her church—contradictions between what people were preaching and what they were doing. This was particularly true about their lack of Christian love and acceptance of those who believed differently than they did.

When we interviewed Sarah, she was working as a nurse in the pediatric ward of a cancer hospital. She says she was raised with Christian values of helping others and that her parents influenced her "through their actions [showing] the importance of service and doing what you could to help other people." In many ways Sarah is following the ethical values of her Evangelical parents and grandparents—but not their religious practices and beliefs. When asked about her religious affiliation, Sarah said she didn't have one.

Sarah's relationship with her parents and grandparents appears to be guarded and ambivalent. On the one hand she talks about them with considerable warmth and affection. On the other hand, she says,

> I feel like I hide a lot or I don't say a lot or I hold back a lot when I'm around my family. To avoid conflict, to avoid being judged by them, and to avoid them trying to convert me, just that hassle. I have to stand back a bit, protect myself.

Sarah's mother, fifty-six-year-old G3 Irene, is keenly aware that Sarah has taken a different path and that she is no longer religiously active. But she attributes Sarah's reasons for leaving their church to social rather than religious concerns: "[She was] not getting along with some of the people that were in her youth group at our church. I don't think it's so much the religious belief."

Moreover, Irene feels that her daughter has incorporated much of her familial and religious heritage into her adult life, surmising that "she has not fallen far from the tree." Irene is obviously proud of Sarah's achievements and the importance her daughter places on service to others. Irene feels that in the not-too-distant future, perhaps in the course of marriage and having children, Sarah will come back to the church and back to the faith of her family:

> I see her in her career, in her life, and I see her acting on those [Christian] beliefs we taught her. The things that she does come from a Christian perspective on the way you treat people and what you do for people.

Sarah's father Eddie, who is fifty-eight, is even more explicit in believing that his daughter will return to the church: "It's a phase she's going through." He says he has attempted to discuss Sarah's religious beliefs with her but "she gets defensive...and [says] 'I don't want to talk about it.'" Eddie does not know what to do about his daughter's crisis of faith, which stands in contrast to the strong and enduring conviction of other Turner family members.

Within the context of her born-again Christian family we can see Sarah as a religious rebel but a very low-key rebel who wants to avoid conflict with her family. Sarah discontinued her involvement in her family's church because she felt oppressed by its judgment, intolerance, and hypocrisy.

Her mother and father hope and pray that, given time, Sarah will come back to the fold as a prodigal returning home. They take heart in the fact that her values of service and helping others are similar to those taught by their church. While saying she resents her family's "hassling" about religion, Sarah does acknowledge the appeal of her religious heritage: "Some part of me goes back to that childhood [experience], just everything you learned, your whole life. So I'm kind of torn right now." Because of Sarah's wish to avoid conflict in their close-knit family, and because of her current ambivalence about religion, her mother's prayers might be answered.

Lawrence and Elizabeth Goldman: A Rebel and a Zealot with an Interfaith (Ex-)Marriage

We mentioned earlier that fifty-two-year old G3 Lawrence Goldman had described himself as "the most Jewish Methodist guy I know." He has had a varied religious career. While his parents were conservative Jews, Lawrence chose as a teenager to be different:

> I wanted to be something else, whatever that would be[a] Buddhist, or maybe [a] Hindu, or anything else, anything else. I grew up in a very conservative Jewish household where everything was centered around the Temple, and part of the rejection of all that says I get to be something different. Where I'm at now is I go to a Methodist church and my kid goes to a born-again Christian school and I'm married to something else.

Lawrence comes from a family of Jewish immigrants. His grandparents, G1s Dinah and Boris, were secular Jews who were highly active in the socialist movement during the 1920s. Their son, G2 Len, now eighty, followed secular Judaism until he married a woman from an Orthodox Jewish background and, because of her, became more religious. We met Len and Hazel and their grandsons in chapter 5. Len said he and his wife Hazel worked hard to pass on their religious beliefs and their Jewish culture to their children: "Because of my wife's influence, we celebrated all the holidays and were involved in the Temple." Len and Hazel also provided their children a Jewish religious education. But this did not prevent their son G3 Lawrence from turning away from his Jewish heritage.

Lawrence says that it was when he was a teenager that he began to rebel against his parents, getting into trouble in multiple ways. His rebellion included marrying women from other faiths. His father Len lamented that none of his son's three wives have been Jewish. The first marriage lasted only three months; the second, with G3 Elizabeth, lasted ten years and produced three children. Lawrence says that Elizabeth was a "born-again fundamentalist Christian, all the way, along lines of anointing with oil, having people come into the house to exorcise demons. All that."

They are now divorced, and Elizabeth is still a fervent born-again Evangelical Christian. When we interviewed her, years after she had divorced Lawrence and remarried, she said, "The only reason that I exist [today] is to serve God and to be a good wife and good mother and grand-mother." She talks about what triggered her conversion from a Catholic upbringing to become a born-again Evangelical Christian: "I had a drinking problem, and the Lord just sent some people into my life, and it changed me from night to day."

Elizabeth has harbored a deep hope that, despite their pluralistic religious background, the G4 sons she had from her marriage to Lawrence would choose to follow her in matters of faith. "If I could only give them one thing that would be it: a belief in God and Jesus Christ," she says. "If they have that, and walk with Him, they're good." To that end, she brought her children to church twice on Sunday and during the week.

Elizabeth's influence on their children's religious orientation was successful; today each of the three follows her Evangelical Christian faith. While Lawrence perceives his ex-wife as excessively religious and believes she forced her beliefs onto their children, the children do not feel this way. Their oldest son, twenty-six-year-old G4 Adam, a devout Evangelical, says he has a close relationship with his mother and that she guided him and supported his religious development when he was a teenager:

> She was always making sure that I understood that Jesus died on the cross for me, that I knew I was forgiven for my sins....If I was doing something that was a sin, she'd always try to correct me on it. We always had Bible studies at the house. We'd sit down and read the Bible for like an hour.

Adam has reflected on why he and his siblings followed their mother's Christian faith and not their father's Jewish traditions. He recalls that when they were growing up they would attend family gatherings at their Jewish grandparents' house, participating in Jewish holidays and rituals. But, as was mentioned in chapter 5, when Adam and his siblings returned home following these gatherings, Elizabeth would speak to them about what they had experienced there and then share her own quite different religious views. There was another reason Adam and his siblings followed their mother's conservative Christianity: Their father, Lawrence, was inconsistent in his own religious beliefs and practices. "He says he'll be Christian, and then he switches. I think he went to Science of Mind for a little bit, and then Buddhism." Lawrence has had a difficult adult life, with periods of unemployment, marital instability, and depression. Today, however, he is married for the third time, this time happily; while he has not returned to the conservative Judaism of his parents, he and his father Len have reconciled.

Overall, in the Goldman family we see that a break occurred in a long Jewish intergenerational heritage, where the Jewish religious tradition of the immigrant G1 great-grandparents appears to have been broken in the rebellion of G3 Lawrence, not to be transmitted to the G4 children.

Marjorie Brigham: A Zealot Mother Whose Prodigal Children Returned

G3 Marjorie, age sixty, is a convert to the Mormon faith. She married Karl, also a Mormon. She is highly religious, much more than her own parents, G2s Edith (a Methodist who did not attend church much while Marjorie was growing up) and Kenneth (a Methodist who is more religious than his wife). Marjorie's grandparents, G1s George and Elaine, were Christian Scientists who did not believe in medicine. In her first survey in 1970 Marjorie said she had just converted to the LDS faith and that "becoming a Mormon was the good thing that made me happy." But her conversion created conflicts between Marjorie and her parents. Kenneth said, "I feel that in today's world families should be of a reasonable size, one to three children. [My daughter] Marjorie has seven. This would be a cause of tension we have had." Edith said, "Our daughter Marjorie and her husband are converted Mormons, and my husband and I do not agree with aspects of that religion. They do not exercise birth control, but [their] child rearing and guidance are excellent."

Marjorie describes her religion as the main source of guidance in her parenting practices:

We went to church on Sundays and we had Family Home Evening, which is once a week to get together. So maybe we would have a lesson and use the scriptures about being Godlike and kind to each other. Maybe have a story in there or from our own personal experience of how that makes people feel bad. Ask the children questions so they would be involved...Raising our children to be good people and to want that religion as part of their lives is very, very important. I just think my children would see emptiness without it, and just wandering around, and with it [religion] they could feel strength.

However, Marjorie's children did not stay in the church. Marjorie and her husband were having difficulties; he was not participating in church activities, and his non-Mormon parents moved closer to them. The influence of their father Karl's not going to church anymore, coupled with the influence of non-Mormon grandparents, caused Marjorie's children to become "I could say confused, but maybe not. They just made a choice...and all four of the youngest decided not to go to our church." The oldest was away from the Church for seven years, dating young men who were not Mormon. Another child, G4 James, stayed away for three years, and his younger sister G4 Jill struggled for a time with drugs and alcohol before she "decided to become strong in the Church again" after more than a decade out of the fold. G4 Holly, the youngest, simply decided for a time that religion didn't matter to her.

This was not the end of the story for Marjorie's children, however; they all fulfilled their mother's hopes and moved from being Rebels to Prodigals. "Holly will be married in the Temple this summer; it's really quite a miraculous thing," Marjorie exalts. "All my children, even if they had strayed away from it, have come back to deciding that this was very important in their lives. To me it's a miracle!"

What brought Marjorie's children back to the fold? Why, after leaving their faith, did these Prodigals from the Brigham family return?

Marjorie's older son G4 Nathan, age forty, talked about this. A committed Mormon, he noted that his brothers and sisters now shared his religious commitments: "They're all active and have strong conviction in the Church." When asked whether his parents had an expectation that he carry on in their faith, he said,

Yes...but they never pressured. Never pressured us. And they still don't. Especially now that we have our own kids—when it comes to our religious conviction in the church, we're very consistent [with them].

I know in a lot of churches you get a family where they put too much pressure on their kids, to where they don't want even to look at the religion anymore. My parents were great. They allowed us to have our own agency to choose what we wanted to believe.

Three Outcomes

In this chapter we explored the stories of offspring who differ substantially from the religious practices and beliefs of their parents. The Rebels, the Zealots, and the Prodigals represent three types of outcomes reflecting the *non*transmission of religion across generations. Rebels are those who reject their parents' religion. They might convert to a different faith, reject religion altogether, or drift into religious indifference. Zealots are those who are much more religious than their parents. Most are converts to another religion, deeply committed to their new faith. Prodigals represent a temporary type of nontransmission. These are children who grow up in a church family and then depart from that family's faith, converting to another religion or dropping out of religion altogether. But later they come back to the parents' faith or something closely resembling it. These categories are not mutually exclusive. Those Rebels who convert to another religion could be considered Zealots in their new faith, at least for a time; many Prodigals who come back to the family faith were rebels for a time.

The family histories of Rebels, Zealots, and Prodigals constructed from LSOG data contribute to and extend recent research on the "religious transformations among youth."[6] By situating these individuals' shifts in religion within a family context, we learn more about the potential contributors to religious development and have a deeper understanding of adult religious outcomes.

The examples of nontransmission we found in the twenty-five families that comprise our sample suggest four conclusions. First, the Rebels came from strongly religious families where there was "too much of a good thing," as parents' religious socialization efforts were experienced as excessive or intrusive. When highly religious parents pushed their resistant children to participate in religious activities (such as church, Sunday school, Bible study, youth activities, etc.) or to conform to church doctrine or moral dictates, this was experienced by some children as having religion "shoved down my throat." The result was religious rebellion. We saw this in Charlotte Jensen's children's rejection of their mother's Mormon faith and in Sarah Turner's perceptions of the judgment and hypocrisy of her family's Evangelical church. There are, of course, exceptions; we see many examples of intergenerational transmission for highly religious parents in our sample, particularly those in tightknit religious groups— what have been called "quasi-ethnic denominations."[7] (See chapter 9 on Mormons, Jews, and Evangelicals.) Nevertheless, we were struck by how often we found parental religious fervor associated with the child's religious rebellion.

Second, the Zealots in our sample—adult children who are highly religious compared to their parents and often converts to a different faith— often produced Rebels—children who find a different faith from their fervently religious parents or who drop out of religion altogether. We have seen this in the case of Charlotte Jensen and her four children. There are exceptions to this as well as in the case of Elizabeth Goldman—a Zealot whose children remain committed to her faith. Yet in our sample, zealots often tend to produce rebels, and occasionally the Rebels become zealots—a sort of intergenerational dialectic of intense religious expression and reaction.

In our sample of families there were some Prodigals who rebelled from their parents' faith but then came back. In chapter 10 we comment on some of the reasons for this and describe suggestions from religious leaders on how to encourage Prodigals to return. But in the case of Marjorie Brigham's four Prodigals, all of whom left their Mormon faith for several years and then returned, it appears that three things were operating. First, she was a warm, affirming mother who had a close relationship with her children.[8] Second, she allowed them considerable religious latitude: her son Nathan notes that she didn't pressure them but "allowed us to have our own agency to choose what we wanted to believe in." Third, they had a strong religious foundation to build on, one created by their mother, whose religious role modeling was consistent, with regular Family Home Evenings focused on church teachings. Her warmth, openness, and example left them with the freedom to leave, and then return to, her faith.

Another issue is reflected in these cases, and that is how important transmission is to religious parents and how disconcerting evidence of nontransmission can be. Charlotte Jensen hopes her nonreligious children will return to the fold. Irene and Eddie Turner believe that Sarah's devotion to service for others reflects the Christian beliefs to which she will soon return. Marjorie Brigham feels that "to want religion as part of their lives is very, very important." Such passion about the religious outcome of children is probably mystifying to people who are religiously indifferent or nonreligious, but it is one of the driving forces in these parents' lives.

However, the priority some parents place on a child's following them in religion can also have a negative effect on the parent–child relationship. When an adult child's religious orientation runs counter to the parents', this may prompt the child to withdraw or to be less open and more guarded about revealing inner thoughts and values. Sarah Turner, the quiet religious rebel, "hides a lot" to avoid conflict and judgment by her parents. This sense of alienation may also prompt children to disengage from family activities to avoid confrontation. Not wanting to hurt one's parents can in fact lead to withdrawing from interaction with them.

We have seen that nontransmission of religiosity to children can be very painful for highly religious parents and grandparents. They have invested much of their time and energy in the religious education of their children and often express the hope that they will meet their children in heaven. These religious parents pray that their rebel children will eventually become Prodigals and return to the family faith, where they will be welcomed back with prayer and rejoicing. Occasionally that does happen but not—at least among the families in this study—as often as the parents would like.

Often the Religious Rebels in our study were religious "nones"—young adults who would have responded "none" when asked their religious affiliations. It is to them and their family backgrounds that we turn in the next chapter.

CHAPTER 8 | The "Nones"

Families of Nonreligious Youth

Generation (G) 4 Gina Adams, who is thirty-six, describes herself
as an atheist who values a humanistic point of view. But she is not
rebelling against a religious upbringing: "I think that all comes from
my family." Her mother G3 Dawn says, "I don't go to church... [But]
I feel like I'm religious. I just feel I can have a religious connection
without that."

    G4 Laura Baker, thirty-one, says she has no religious affiliation but
is "spiritual... I think I [got] my values from my grandparents when
I was young."

    G4 Brianna Shepherd, thirty-one, is not involved in any church.
She says she is "more of an agnostic than anything." She contrasts
herself to her mother, a "really, really religious" woman who
"shov[ed] religion down my throat."

THE COMMENTS ABOVE ARE from people who do not fit into traditional religious categories, those who answered "none" in response to our question
"What is your current religious affiliation?" As the quotes above indicate,
these nonaffiliated individuals are not of one type. There are varieties of
religious "nones" as well as differences in family backgrounds. The first
young woman is spiritual but not religious; she has a sense of spiritual
connection to something beyond her, which she attributes to the influence

of her grandparents, who were also uncommitted to any church. The second is an atheist with secular humanist values whose mother is not affiliated with a church but says she is religious. The third young woman is an agnostic; she rebelled against a highly religious parent.

In this chapter we examine the family backgrounds of those who are nonreligious or nonaffiliated in our sample and ask: Where do those who say they have no religion come from, and how does this occur? What are the family dynamics that can lead to, or reinforce, a lack of religious involvement in one of the world's most religious nations? We look at how parents (and grandparents) can influence their children's nonreligious orientation, either by actively transmitting their own skepticism of organized religion or by unintentionally fostering their children's rejection of the family's religious tradition. We expand the scope of existing research that focuses on adult children leaving or staying with the religion of their parents[1] by applying a multigenerational family lens to the transmission of nonreligion or nonaffiliation.

The Diversity of Nonreligion

It is standard practice in survey research[1] to identify respondents' religion by their response to the question "What is your religion?" Those who are not affiliated with a church, synagogue, or temple or who do not identify with a religion are usually assigned the code "none"[2,3] Recent national data indicate that about one-quarter of the nones are atheist or agnostic and the rest are "nothing in particular."[4] But as William Bainbridge notes, the reasoning underlying these responses can be difficult to discern:

> Some of these nones may actually be atheists who conceal their beliefs in fear of reprisal from the religious people in their environment. Others may be agnostics who are ignorant of the term or of the philosophical arguments associated with it. Others may simply be uninterested in religion, having no opinions about it.[5]

Furthermore, while some nones may simply be passively indifferent to religion, others are actively engaged against it, perhaps intensely so. Paul Pruyser suggests that "irreligion is not merely the absence of something. . . . It can be zealous, militant, declarative, and dogmatic. Like religion it can be the product of training, existential decision-making, or drifting. And often it is the product of religious instruction itself."[6]

This broad and often vaguely defined category—variously termed the "nonreligious," the "unaffiliated," the "unchurched," or the "nones"—represents a wide variety of orientations toward organized religion and individual spiritual experiences, or their absence.

Within the families in our study, we identify four types of unaffiliated individuals or nones:[7]

1. *Atheists:* Individuals who explicitly deny the existence of God (nontheistic).
2. *Agnostics:* Those who say they do not know whether God exists, perhaps adding that there is no way to know whether God exists.
3. *Religious but unaffiliated:* Those who say they are believers, or religious, but are not affiliated with a church or temple; this includes (a) those who are "seekers" but haven't found a church they want to affiliate with, (b) those who believe but who do not like organized religion with its churches and priests, and (c) the growing number of persons who say they are "spiritual but not religious."
4. *Religiously indifferent:* Individuals who do not think about religion, who feel religion is not important for them, or who have been "turned off" by religion.

It should be noted that these categories can be fluid and not mutually exclusive; individuals can and do shift back and forth between them. Moreover, as Nicholas Vargas has shown, there is a substantial difference between those who seriously consider leaving religion and those who actually do disaffiliate. In his national sample, 13% of religious Americans said they were contemplating leaving religion, while three years later only half of these had actually left.[8]

The Changing Demography of Nonbelief

In American society today more than 93% of adults say they believe in God or a higher power,[9] and about 38% say they attend religious services weekly.[10] Among the world's advanced industrialized countries, the United States is the most religious in terms of belief in God and in organized religious participation.[11] Compared to the 7% in the United States who are nonbelievers, 22% of Canadians do not believe in God, 39% of those in Great Britain, 56% of the French, and 56% of Swedes.[12] At the same time, public opinion polls show that religious involvement such as church membership has declined considerably since the 1970s and is significantly lower than its zenith in the post–World War II period.[13] The number of adults who never attend religious services or attend less than once a year increased from 18% in 1972 to 28% in 2008.[14]

More noteworthy, the proportion of the adult population that reports no affiliation with a particular religion has increased dramatically in the past two decades, nearly tripling from 6% nationwide in 1990 to 20% in 2012.[15] These changes are much greater in younger age groups. Millennials today are significantly less attached to organized religion than their elders were in their youth. In 2012 almost one-third of young adults ages eighteen to twenty-nine were unaffiliated with a religious institution, while in the 1970s only 13% of young adult Baby Boomers were unaffiliated. Young men are much more likely to be unaffiliated than young women.[16]

These trends are occurring in a society in which there has been, and still is, a stigma attached to being nonreligious. It turns out that atheists are one of the most disliked groups in America. In a poll asking which of the following groups "shares my vision of American society," out of a list that included Muslims, homosexuals, Jews, Hispanics, and immigrants, atheists were in last place. Asked if they would disapprove of their child's marrying someone from a list of minority groups, atheists again were last.[17]

Why have the nonaffiliated in younger age groups increased so substantially? One factor has to do with demographic changes: Today's young adults marry and have children later than their predecessors and also enter the workforce later, extending the life cycle phase (the college years) when religious attachment tends to wane. Increased rates of higher education may be another factor. A Harris Poll reported that 86% of Americans without a college education believe in the resurrection of Jesus Christ, while only 64% of those with a postgraduate degree believe so.

A third explanation for the rise of Americans claiming no religion is the increasing politicization of religion. Michael Hout and Claude Fischer argue that the political right has become so identified with a conservative religious agenda that it has alienated moderates who consider organized "religion" a synonym for an antigay, antiabortion, procivic religion agenda. At the same time, while they may feel disenfranchised from organized religion, many of them remain privately religious or "spiritual."[18] This reaction against the politicization of religion is seen particularly among young adults.

A fourth important factor, one that has not before been pursued in detail, involves intergenerational transmission: the increase in the number of religiously nonaffiliated parents who raised their children without a religious tradition. National data show that the number of adults raised without a religion increased from 2.5% in the early 1970s to over 6% in the 1990s.[19] However, these and similar results are based on cross-sectional survey data and respondents' retrospective reports and are open to the risk of recall bias. The most convincing test of non-religious transmission would be based on data from parents and data from children.

In the Longitudinal Study of Generations (LSOG) surveys, the changing distribution of the nonaffiliated from 1970 to 2005 follows the pattern of that observed in the nationally representative public opinion poll data described above.[20] However, because the LSOG is a southern California sample, the proportion of nones is higher than in a national sample including Southern and Midwestern states, where there are fewer unaffiliated persons. Figure 8.1 shows the LSOG sample distribution of unaffiliated and nonreligious individuals in each generation in our study, comparing the 1970 and 2005 surveys.

In 1970, the total proportion of LSOG participants who said they had no religious affiliation was 11%; by 2005, this had increased to 36%. This represents a more than 300% increase in just thirty-five years. As we can see in Figure 8.1, there are striking generational differences in these distributions. In 1970, 5% of the G1 parents (born before and during World War I) reported they were unaffiliated, compared to 6% of their G2 children (born in the 1920s and 1930s) and 18% of the G3 grandchildren (Baby Boomers, then in their late teens and early twenties). In 2005, of the surviving G1s, the percentage of unaffiliated had grown to 17%; the percentage of G2s had increased almost fourfold, to 32%. The percentage of G3 unaffiliated doubled, to 38%, a proportion equal to the youngest generation (G4s). Thus, over the thirty-five years

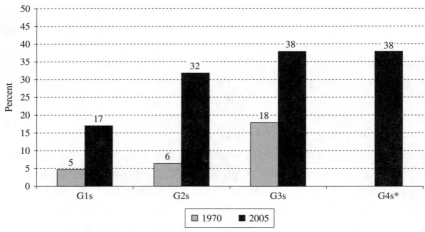

*The G4 youth were added to the LSOG panel beginning with the 1991 survey wave as they turned 16.

FIGURE 8.1 Distribution of Unaffiliated Individuals in the LSOG by Generation, 1970 and 2005

* The G4 youth were added to the LSOG panel beginning with the 1991 survey wave as they turned sixteen.

of this study there has been a remarkable increase in the unaffiliated category for each generation.

Intergenerational Transmission and Nonbelief

We have relatively little previous research to draw upon concerning the family backgrounds of nonreligious, unaffiliated, atheist, and agnostic individuals. There have been only a few social science studies carried out on these groups. One is Phillip Zuckerman's groundbreaking study *Why People Reject Religion.* Zuckerman suggests that "most of the nonreligious people in America today were actually raised with some religion, and then at a certain point they opted out. They rejected their religion. They became apostates."[21] Another example is Frank Pasquale's[22] research exploring the social characteristics and origins of secular humanists and atheists. His data suggest that the nonreligious humanists are "overwhelmingly the product of religious upbringings." About 8 out of 10 of the 951 respondents in his study said both of their parents were religious, and 7 of 10 reported conflicts with their parents over religion.

Chrystal Manning's study of the impact of atheism and secularity on families and children is a third example. She concludes that "most contemporary secularists are individuals who were themselves raised with religion."[23]

Earlier studies came to similar conclusions. Caplovitz and Sherrow[24] conclude that "apostasy [defection and disaffiliation from a religious group] is to be viewed as a form of rebellion against parents." Leavy[25] suggests that "atheism may be an expression of liberation from the domination of one's parents." Hunsberger[26] finds that individuals from religious backgrounds who turned against religion had more distant relations with parents than those who remained religious.

Our data suggest a different picture of the religious backgrounds of the nonaffiliated, one in which family continuity and transmission is more likely to be involved than discontinuity and rebellion. Referring back to Figure 3.2 in chapter 3, where we illustrate the percentage of parents and young adults who have the same religious tradition or are nones, we see that in 1970 it was 40%, but by 2005, the proportion of unaffiliated parents with unaffiliated young adult children had increased to 63%—a remarkable increase in just over three decades.

From where did this new generation of nones come from, religiously, and how has that changed over time? We can begin to understand this if we shift our perspective to that of the unaffiliated young adult children and then identify the religious tradition of their parents in 1970 compared to 2005. We show this in Figure 8.2.

In Figure 8.2, two things stand out. First, we can see a significant change over the time period among unaffiliated young adults in terms of the religious tradition of their parents. Second, in 1970 unaffiliated young adult children were most likely to have abandoned the religious tradition of parents who were Mainline Protestants. In the tumultuous decades of the 1960s and 1970s, the Mainline Protestant churches appear to have been the big losers to the growing secularism of American culture. But this pattern of shifting was of limited duration. By 2005, unaffiliated young adults were much more likely to have inherited their parents' unaffiliated religious orientation.

In 1970, only 14% of unaffiliated young adults (the G3s in our sample) had parents who were nones, indicating that most had switched from their parents' religious tradition to none. Almost half of the unaffiliated

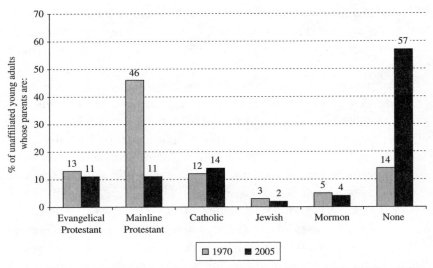

FIGURE 8.2 Parents' Religious Tradition and Unaffiliated Young Adult Children, 1970 and 2005

young adults had G2 parents who were Mainline Protestants; about one in eight unaffiliated young adults had parents who were Evangelical Protestant (13%) or Catholic (12%); and very few had parents who were Jewish (3%) or Mormon (5%). By contrast, in 2005 almost 60% of young adults with no religious affiliation had parents who were also nones, indicating they *inherited* their parents' nonaffiliation; 11% had parents who were Mainline Protestant, while the proportions of unaffiliated young adults whose parents were from the other religious traditions were essentially unchanged from what they were in 1970.

Thus we now find nearly 6 out of 10 unaffiliated young adults come from families where their parents were also unaffiliated, indicating that nonreligion is indeed transmitted from one generation to the next. We also find some indications of parent gender differences in young adults' religious origins: In 2005, 62% of the unaffiliated adult children had fathers who said they were not involved in a religious organization, while 52% had mothers who were nones (data not shown here). As we see in the next chapter, these data also indicate that Jewish and Mormon parents have been more successful than other groups in transmitting their religious tradition to their children, or at least in preventing their children from leaving their religious tradition to become unaffiliated or nonreligious.

The Nonreligious: Generational Continuity and Discontinuity

What we see in our data is that the intergenerational transmission of nonaffiliation with a religious institution, and perhaps non- or antireligiousness in general, is significantly greater today than in the past. How and why does this nonreligious transmission occur? Looking at some of the stories of people in our study can give us some clues.

The Adamses: "A Humanistic Point of View that Comes from My Family"

In some cases we found that a non-religious identity had been imparted intentionally and specifically from one generation to the next. Gina Adams, thirty-six, is an atheist, but she is not a religious rebel who turned against the religious beliefs and practices of her family. Instead, she perceives that she is part of a family tradition, a generational heritage of secular humanism and nonreligious values. "I put a lot of value on a liberal, humanistic point of view—not dogmatic—and I think that comes from my family," she explains.

The Adams family exemplifies the varieties of nonreligion in our society. Some members are atheists, some are agnostic, some are "spiritual but not religious," and some are "religiously unaffiliated" Christian believers who do not go to church. We also noticed considerable fluidity among these categories of nonreligion by some family members as their religious self-identities shifted to accommodate new experiences or relationships. Many drifted in and out of organized religious involvement as they moved from one church to another or away from religion all together. Yet at the time of their interviews, all the family members were quite articulate about what they believed. They talked about values being passed down from generation to generation, and we detected continuity in spiritual values and behaviors despite their apparent disparity in religious beliefs and practices.

We begin with the story of the G1 great-grandfather, Ted, a labor union leader who moved his family to California during the Depression.

Describing his father as a nominal Catholic in his youth, Ted's G2 son Victor, now age seventy-eight, said he was a Social Democrat. "We would call him a socialist today. But they believed in a great measure of private freedom—you know, like freedom of the press and so on. As a result of that heritage, he really denied the existence of the need for a church." Victor did attend church regularly with his mother, and his father did not stand in the way of that.

Victor sees his mother as having been the most influential in terms of his religious views. But when asked whether his father's values of helping others had anything to do with his own social activism, he responded,

> Oh, absolutely. But it wasn't so much that as it was my [religious] training. But my father was a great humanitarian. Forget the religion. But anybody around who needed—and this is during the Depression, when nobody had anything....He would find a family. We'd bring them some groceries—as little as we had. So, I learned a lot from that. I'll never forget that day we brought some groceries to this lady's house with a little kid. And they just cried....And so, in addition to the church going, I grew up with the kind of idea that [if] you've got it made, you need to give back.

This tradition of helping is woven throughout the stories of each generation of G1 Ted's descendants. Today, Victor is not a church member, so he would be defined as a none although he is not antireligious. During his interview, he mentioned several religious books that he is currently reading and talked enthusiastically about what they had to say.

Like her father, Victor, G3 Dawn also has taken an eclectic and unconventional religious pathway throughout the ups and downs of life. She had some exposure to religion in her family while growing up, through her mother and grandmother. As an adult, she married an abusive man, which led to the end of organized religion for her. "I stopped going to church and I was really mad at God," she says. "I just couldn't do it....And all the stuff that, in church, didn't offer me any comfort. It didn't make any sense." Because she knew some alcoholics who were "driving [her] crazy," she started attending Al-Anon. "And that is kind of where I get my religion these days, from AA." Now fifty-six, Dawn says that she believes in God but that she just does not go to church.

"I just feel like I can have a spiritual connection without that. But it's important to me. I mean, in my personal life, it's something that I think about quite often."

Dawn's daughter, thirty-six-year-old G4 Gina, defined herself as an atheist. In her interview she told us how highly she values the liberal, humanistic point of view she received from her family. She describes how she and Gabriel, her husband, who is also an atheist, view religion:

> Religion is not important to us. In fact, I would say that we are antireligious....You can teach morality without having to involve God. The Golden Rule is pretty simple and you don't need God to come down and tell you that. Religion is so dogmatic, so it contributes a lot to people hurting each other and not understanding each other.

When asked what religious values and beliefs she would like to pass on to her young children, Gina replied, "I value reason and science and treating people the way you would want to be treated, and I think that's a good basis for teaching my children the right values." Gina commented further that she would want her children to be atheists like herself and her husband:

> Honestly, yes, I do. I'm not going to try to force them into anything, because I think that's wrong, but I will definitely be disappointed if they end up with some beliefs that I think are not very enlightened. So yeah, I'm going to raise them that way....I think there are kinder religions out there than Christianity. I think I would be most disappointed if they came and wanted to be like Baptists, Evangelicals, or something.

Gina affirmed she does not think her sisters are still going to church or are religious: "I don't think they are....My family is very centered around humanistic values, like enlightenment values, like being open to ideas and being aware of history and science."

In the Adams family we see a tradition of nonreligious, secular humanist values over several generations. G4 Gina defines herself as an atheist who married an atheist. She has not rejected the values of the older generation; rather, it appears that she has made them even more explicit. The Adamses, within and across generations, display a range of religious beliefs (or lack of religious beliefs) and practices, and they seem to celebrate their diversity. Consciously, but more often implicitly through example, they have transmitted—over several generations—the values of being open and tolerant in religion, as well as a pattern of religious seeking. These values have helped them through many crises. Although this is a family whose members have faced a wide range of challenges including divorce, financial reversals, disabilities, and long-term illnesses, they show affection for each other and have a high degree of contact and interaction, despite geographic distance.

The Bakers: "Drenched in Atheism and Socialistic Values"

G4 Eric Baker, age thirty-one, has a negative view of religion. As we saw in chapter 2, he is an atheist who thinks religion is only interesting from a sociological point of view. "It's amazing the stuff we've created out of our heads, as a human race," he says. But unlike the findings of earlier studies that would suggest that atheism like Eric's arises as a backlash against an intensely religious upbringing, he sees his atheism as part of his family's secular humanist tradition. "My grandfather was [a] liberal academic and my great uncle was [a Communist]," he says. "So we're pretty much drenched in atheism and socialistic values."

The Bakers are a Jewish family with strong intergenerational traditions of social and political activism as well as Jewish cultural identity. But with the exception of G1 Donald Baker's mother, G0 Golda, none are religiously observant Jews and none follow the practices and beliefs of any branch of Judaism. Donald's daughter, G2 Robyn, told us that her grandmother was "the only one that I felt carried on the Jewish traditions in her life. Nobody else did." This is a very close family made up of strong personalities who are intensely committed to humanistic values and liberal ideals that are rooted in the history and experiences of previous generations of the family. As Donald's son-in-law, Frank, put it, "They're lefties from way back."

They are decidedly nonreligious. Donald and his wife, Lydia, the latter of whom was ninety-seven when we interviewed her, were political activists who met at an antiwar organization meeting during World War II. They were "socialists and not religious"; they never went to synagogue or practiced Jewish religious traditions, even though they routinely joined Donald's parents, who lived close by, for Hanukkah and Passover. But Lydia emphasizes that she is not *anti*religious:

No, I'm not an atheist. I believe in a spiritual something that has been a miraculously fantastic idea. But I never believed in a God. I would love to. But I think if there had been a God, I cannot imagine that He would allow this kind of brutal killing of each other.

Lydia and Donald's seventy-two-year-old daughter, Robyn, who said she was "none" in each of her LSOG surveys throughout the thirty-five years of our study, talks about her religious identification in ambiguous terms. "I don't know if I am a spiritual person. I still kind of leave myself open. I think if something came along, maybe like Unitarianism or something, I would still be open if I felt the need for something additional in my life. [I'm afraid] not to believe.... God knows, when my daughter was sick, and my husband was sick, I was afraid not to."

Robyn's G3 daughter, Laura, age fifty-two, has no religious affiliation and does not believe in God or a higher power but says she is a spiritual person. Laura attributes her morality to what she learned from her grandparents:

I think [my values came] from my grandparents when I was young— certain values of equality and justness, what's right and what's wrong.... Those values were definitely put on us or passed on to us through their efforts, their political efforts ... to make social change for the benefit of all. That definitely was part of their lives, and I think that was passed on to us.

When we put the Baker family stories together, we find this is a liberal family across five generations with a very strong legacy of political activism and critical thinking about what it means to be religious, nonreligious, and antireligious. Their Jewish background is part of the family narrative, but the importance of this identity is cultural, not religious, and this is consistent across generations. High intergenerational solidarity is evident in their longitudinal surveys. For several years Robyn and her children lived with Robyn's parents. The political discussions around the kitchen table laid the foundations for the younger generations' ethical and secular humanist values that were subsequently passed on to their own children and grandchildren—down the generational lineage. On the other hand, there are reports of periodic disagreements and feelings of distance between the generations—for example, the tension mentioned by several family members between Robyn's mother, Lydia, and her daughter prompted by her marriage to a non-Jew.

The Wagners: "I Have My Own Religion"

G3 Daphne Wagner was a teenager in 1970 when the LSOG surveys began. When she was asked, "What is your religious preference?" she responded, "I don't subscribe to a particular religion. I have my own religion." When we interviewed Daphne thirty-six years later, she had this to say:

> I'm not at all religious. But I am spiritual . . . [which] involves taking control of my life and my beliefs versus waiting for someone else to. . . . Spirituality is something that comes from within, and you decide yourself how you're going to believe.

For Daphne, now age fifty-two, religion is something entirely different from spirituality. "Religion to me is organized, and in a building, and being dictated to by another person telling you how to believe, and if you don't do this, that's wrong," she says. "I don't need someone in the church interpreting a book to tell me how to live or be."

She sees moral values and ethical behavior as unrelated to religion. "I think honesty is the most important, and being open, and helping people, and being of service to those in need. . . . You don't need a church to tell you that."

Over the almost four decades that Daphne has participated in our study, her views on religion and spirituality have remained very consistent, despite disappointments with marriage and children, ups and downs of employment, and problems with health and finances. She has never had any involvement with a church or religious group. Another feature that has remained constant is Daphne's close relationship with her parents and grandparents, the legacy of a family lineage that is very affectionate, very supportive—and very nonreligious. The portrait of the Wagners emerging from the interviews is a family that is "spiritual but not religious." There is remarkable similarity across the generations in their nonreligious identification and in the way they express their beliefs and values. They are quite clear about the differences between spirituality and religion. Each describes the values they hold as being important with an almost "religious" intensity—values of freedom, individual choice, and living an ethical life.

Daphne's grandfather, G1 Irving, also reported his religious affiliation as "none" in each of his LSOG surveys before his death in the early 2000s.

His wife, Fanny, was ninety-two when we interviewed her in 2008. When asked how she would describe her religion, she briskly replied, "Don't have any—only my own." She then added, "Believing that you have to go attend church to believe in God, that's not important....I've seen a lot of religious persons that thought they were religious, and I thought they were hypocrites."

Fanny participated in various religious education activities when she was growing up, but none appeared to have had any lasting effect. In high school she went to the Latter-Day Saints (LDS) Church "because all the kids I ran around with were Mormon, and they liked to dance, and I liked to dance." She recalled being interviewed by the LDS bishop for membership, but when a church member came to her door to ask for her monetary donation, "I got turned off....I decided if I want to pray I'll do it at home." In early adulthood she attended a nondenominational Evangelical church, but not for long. All this resulted in a distaste for organized religion: "I never could tolerate self-righteous people."

Fanny and Irving's daughter, seventy-three-year-old G2 Bernadine, told us that she was Mormon as a child. However, Bernadine reported "none" as her religious affiliation in most of the LSOG surveys she completed over the years. In her recent surveys, she wrote "spirituality" when asked her about her religious affiliation. She believes in a higher power but defines it as being outside any church or organized religion. Using words almost identical to those of her mother, Bernadine explains:

> I don't subscribe to a particular religion. I have my own....I feel I have a connection, a force within me that connects to the higher self. It's just my string that goes from me to my God...to power. I don't see why people would go to a building and have men telling you what to believe.

Bernadine's value orientations have been very consistent over the eight waves of data collection. In each survey she selected "an ethical life (responsible living toward all)" from a list of personal values as being most important in her life. She also ranked highly "service to mankind" and "equality" and "a world at peace"; she ranked "religious participation" as the least important value in her life. Other important values for Bernadine are "freedom" and "individual choice," which she mentions in talking about what she wanted to pass on to her daughter, Daphne. Children should be able "to choose and decide what's right and wrong, what to do and not do. My parents never tried to push their values on me and I didn't want to [push mine] on [Daphne]." Despite this emphasis on independence from parental values and freedom of choice—or perhaps because of it—Bernadine's values are remarkably similar to those of her parents, as are her daughter Daphne's.

In the Wagner family we find a tradition of no religious involvement across four generations. Instead, the members of each generation emphasize spirituality, "something that comes from within," in contrast to religion, or "another person telling you how to live." There is also a tradition of placing a high value on ethics and morality. Being honest, staying open-minded, encouraging children to choose for themselves—these are mentioned as important values that have influenced the Wagner children. These values, in deed and word, appear to have produced similar views of spirituality across several generations.

Where does the Wagners' generational continuity in nonreligious spirituality come from? One likely explanation is the high degree of family solidarity evident across generations and the successful modeling of spirituality these close emotional bonds may have engendered. These close bonds and mutual high regard are evident in all the survey data provided by members of the Wagner family. Since 1970, in every survey Bernadine reported that she feels "extremely close" to her mother, Fanny, and to her daughter, Daphne. Similarly, in each of her surveys Daphne says she feels "extremely close" to her mother, Bernadine, and "very close" to her grandmother, Fanny, a sentiment Fanny holds toward her daughter and granddaughter as well.

The Shepherds: "Stop Shoving Religion Down My Throat!"

Previous studies have suggested that one of the most common pathways to atheism is family religious conflict; in this scenario, atheists actively reject the religious constraints and rigidities of their zealously religious parents. Thirty-one-year-old Brianna Shepherd is a none, as is her brother Ivan, age thirty-six. They say they do not believe in God or a higher power. But their mother, Nora, is a very religious woman who says her life is centered on being a Christian. When we asked Ivan "Is there any role that religion plays in your life?" he replied, "Yeah, it irritates me." His childhood allowed for no individual choice in matters of faith. "I was forced to go to church for, like, the first twelve years of my life by my mother and grandparents. That was a negative as far as religion is concerned because [of] no religious choice," he says. "The more I wanted to ask questions the less I got answers. I kind of got bitter towards the whole thing. Now I'm an atheist."

Ivan and Brianna's parents divorced when they were very young, and they were raised by their mother. Ivan describes his mother as "very religious" today, as she was during the years he grew up. He adds that her intense religiosity has caused conflict in their relationship in the past and would do so now if he allowed himself to get into a discussion of religion with her. As a child he attended a religious school associated with his mother's church. He said he fully believed in the religious messages he was taught until as a teenager, when he started questioning religion along with parental authority. In each of the LSOG surveys he participated in since joining the study eighteen years ago, he mentions religion as a key area of disagreement with his mother and lists his religious preference as "none" or "atheist."

Ivan's sister Brianna is also nonreligious. She too sees this as a reaction to her family and her mother's heavy religiosity, but she calls herself more of an agnostic than her brother: "I mean there could be something, but I don't know, I really don't know, and so I don't really choose to put all my energy into something that I don't know." Like Ivan, Brianna rebelled when she was a teenager. "I didn't want to go to church three times a week, and she was really strict," Brianna explains. "She wouldn't let me hang out with my friends. . . . I couldn't go out on dates and stuff." Brianna ran away from home but came back after her mother agreed to "stop shoving religion down my throat."

Their mother, G3 Nora, fifty-four, is a devout nondenominational Christian. She attends church several times a week and says she is "very religious." Her own parents were highly religious, although their fundamentalist religion is different than her faith today. She says it is painful that both of her children have rebelled. She doesn't understand how this could have occurred since she always followed her faith and tried to be the best parent she could:

> I've raised my daughter with a strong Christian value which at this point in her life she is adamantly rejecting. It has been extremely disappointing as a parent not to successfully impart to your children what you hold to be most precious and important in life. . . . Our lifestyles and reasons for living

are diametrically opposed. My life is very much centered on my beliefs as a Christian.... Her belief system brings me a lot of sorrow.

In the Shepherd family story we see two members of the younger generation who broke with their mother's intense fundamentalist Christianity. Both Ivan and Brianna reflect what has in previous eras been regarded as the most common pathway to religious nonbelief in America. Raised in a highly religious family context, they are Religious Rebels who have rejected the rigidity and constraints of their background (see chapter 7). Such an explanation would be plausible if we limited our comparison to just two generations. In our interview study, however, we have data from three and four generations, so we can trace religious influences farther back than the two-generation parent–child relationship. When we do so, we see a three-generation tradition on their father's side of nonsectarian moral and perhaps spiritual values but without religious content. Ivan and Brianna are aware of these influences, primarily from their paternal grandmother, and believe that they have had a positive impact on their lives. Ivan explains:

> [My grandma] studied cultures...And her values—she really enjoyed studying different religions and stuff mainly for the stories...She was more accepting of a lot of stuff than my other grandparents and my mom. And I'm sure that had a lot of influence on me.

Thus, while Ivan and Brianna might be Religious Rebels in reaction to their mother's fervent Christian piety, their father is nonreligious while their paternal grandparents seem to have served as role models for religious openness and an evolving antireligious perspective.

Family Contexts of the Nonreligious

Where are the increasing numbers of nones coming from? What are the family backgrounds and dynamics, across generations, which augur a switch from the religion of one's youth to nonreligion or nonbelief? As we saw earlier in the chapter, the limited research available stresses that many who have taken the path of nonbelief have rejected their parents' religious faith, often because it was too demanding or their parents were overly zealous in their religious socialization.[27] Scholars have observed that atheism in particular can be the result of religious rebellion. Atheists are often considered the "black sheep'" of the family. However, another possibility is that atheism is not a break from a family's religious tradition but actually represents continuity with the family's moral and ethical value orientations. We've seen that there is a high degree of intergenerational similarity—continuity—in nonreligion today, and the transmission of nonreligion from parents to their children can be seen to a far greater degree than in the recent past.

The big question for sociologists and psychologists studying origins of adult nonbelief in a culture that strongly emphasizes belief is this: How do nonreligious traditions evolve in the absence of social institutions—something similar to churches, synagogues, temples, parochial schools, or summer Bible camps—that would promote or reinforce unconventional views? A large number of our nonreligious respondents said that their parents (or grandparents) taught them or exemplified the values they chose to emulate. As we reviewed the interview data, it was clear that most of the nonreligious parents in our sample were quite articulate about their nontheistic ethical standards and moral value systems. In fact, many nonreligious parents were more coherent and passionate about their ethical principles than some of the "religious" parents in our study. The vast majority appeared to live goal-filled lives characterized by moral direction and a sense of life having purpose. The values expressed by these nones were aligned with many of the basic values espoused in the Bible, the Torah, and the Qur'an: We heard "do unto others as you would have them do unto you"; "give generously to those in need"; "help those who need help"; "love your neighbor as yourself"; and "heal the sick, give to the poor, do justice to all." Or, as Phillip Zuckerman puts it, among the nonreligious he interviewed, "There is less concern with the specific do's and don'ts [of organized religion], what *is* important is *how they treat other people*."[28]

But secular and atheist parents describe a challenge that is very different from what worries most of the religious parents in our sample: How to impart their values and beliefs without "brainwashing" their children. Zuckerman notes that

[Many] apostate parents realize that they initially became religious [as children] only because their parents raised them to be religious. While they certainly want to pass on their own secular values, secular opinions, and secular beliefs to their children, they don't want to "commit the same crime" of indoctrinating their kids to think just like them. They'd like their children to come to their own decisions, about religion, life, death, and morality—something they themselves weren't allowed to do.

For religious parents—especially the strongly devout and heavily involved—it is a joy and a duty to bring up their children in the fold, to teach them the tenets of their religion with earnest devotion, and to do all they can to ensure that their children become enmeshed in their religious tradition. It is just what a good parent ought to do. But for parents who are apostates, there is much more self-doubt when it comes to raising children to be secular or not.[29]

One last point: The high levels of family solidarity and emotional closeness with parents evidenced by most of the nonreligious youth in our study were a surprise to us. They shouldn't have been. We may have been influenced more than we realized by popular stereotypes of atheists (for example) as "others," very different from most people in our society, including the family. As Penny Edgell notes, atheists are frequently defined as "others" in American society, placed outside conventional moral boundaries and thus denied cultural membership.[30] Indeed, many Americans who believe in God might regard irreligious families with the same suspicion as the Psalmist: "The fool has said in his heart, there is no God" (Psalm 14:1).

In these data, however, again and again we see that warm and supportive intergenerational relationships enhance the role modeling of parents, creating the sharing of beliefs and values as described in chapter 4. Although similarities between parents and children are obviously related to other characteristics (such as similarity in social class, education, or temperament, each of which is often related to religion), a close parent–child relationship may be the single best explanation for high intergenerational continuity of nonreligious beliefs. Such is the case in each of the four families discussed in this chapter; consistent with the findings presented in chapter 4, the presence or absence of a warm, supportive relationship between parents and their children is the most plausible explanation for intergenerational similarity or difference in nonreligiosity.

CHAPTER 9 | # The Power of Community
Families of Mormons, Jews,
and Evangelicals[1]

The Wilsons are a close-knit Evangelical family. They talk about each
other with affection, are in frequent contact with one another, belong
to the same kind of church, and are in agreement in their political
views. Generation (G) 2 Carolyn, seventy-three, says, "Both my
parents and my husband's parents believe the same way. We just grew
up with that belief. So it has just been our way of life." When twenty-
five-year-old G4 Kristin was asked who in her family has had the
most influence on the development of her religious views, she replied,
"My mom and dad. They're a team."

"My Jewishness is very important to me, and as far as my family
is concerned and who my children would marry, Judaism would rank
number one," says G3 Miriam Bernstein, age fifty-nine. "Because
I want to continue the tradition of being Jewish and I feel like our
family and our history has gone through a lot in order to survive and
be Jewish, [and] I don't want to give it up, I don't want to lose it. And
so I would want my children to be married to someone who's Jewish
and raise children who are Jewish.... Being Jewish is not simply a
religion, being Jewish is a way of life."

IN OUR SAMPLE, THREE religious traditions showed the highest degree of family continuity in religion across generations: Mormons, Jews, and born-again Evangelical Christians. Though these groups differ in beliefs and practices, they share several sociological characteristics relevant to faith transmission across generations. First, they and their families are members of a distinct religious community. Practicing Mormons, religious Jews, and faithful Evangelicals often stand out because of what they believe and what they do. Frequent attendance at religious services, prayers and religious rituals in daily life, volunteer activities in religious organizations, and significant financial support for their churches or synagogues—each of these features distinguish them from many other religious groups in the United States.

Second, they reflect some of the characteristics of minority groups within a broader society. Their groups often have been singled out for ridicule or oppression. Mormons and Jews today are inheritors of a history rife with prejudice and persecution; Conservative Protestants are the spiritual descendants of nonconformists who were often discriminated against in predominantly Catholic or Anglican Europe. The possibility of being singled out like this again lingers; the group bands together for mutual encouragement or protection. Further, such groups often form cohesive communities with a high degree of internal interaction and a sense of distinctiveness that create boundaries between them and others, who in some cases are called "gentiles" or "worldly."

Third, and most relevant to our study, in each of these groups religious practices are highly interconnected with family activities, and there is a high value placed on families and family continuity. Their religious practices and traditions emphasize family membership. Their churches or synagogues have well-established institutional mechanisms (such as Sunday school, youth groups, summer camps, coming-of-age celebrations, and marriage rites) that are celebrated as a means of socializing younger generations into the beliefs and practices of their faith. For Mormons, Family Home Evening each Monday is an intergenerational gathering to share scriptural stories and pray together; the weekly event assumes almost sacramental meaning. For born-again Evangelicals, daily family prayer and Bible reading are hallmarks of a devout family.

For the reasons listed above, it would seem plausible to find considerable religious continuity in the Mormon, Jewish, and Evangelical families in our study. At the same time, in light of the remarkable secular changes we discussed earlier—the recent erosion of institutionalized religion, the hypothesis that individualism has weakened the family as a social institution—then it may be that even in high-boundary religious communities there is less intergenerational continuity than there was several decades ago. How successful are tight-knit religious groups in passing on their religious tradition to younger generations? What do they do to promote religious continuity in children and grandchildren, and—of perhaps utmost urgency, for devout members of these faith communities—why does religious transmission fail, and what can be done about it?

Mormons: Families of the Saints

The Latter-Day Saints (LDS) faith is reported to be the fastest-growing religious community in the United States. In 2011 the Church[2] reported 6.2 million members in this country, up from 3.4 million in 1977.[3] Mormons have missionaries in most countries in the world, typically college-age men and women who volunteer between eighteen months and two years of their lives in missionary assignments. Family Home Evening, described above, is a sacred ritual. So is family attendance at Sunday services. Teenagers and college students rise early each weekday to attend "seminary," or religious school, before the regular school day begins. Eternal marriage is celebrated by temple weddings that are open only to members in good standing with the Church. Temple work assures the eternal bonding of the family unit, including performing baptisms by proxy and "sealings" for family members who have passed away, even centuries ago, so they too can partake in eternal family life. Members have a command from Church tradition to raise their children in the faith.

Young Mormons have many opportunities daily to demonstrate their faithfulness in living according to Church teaching. Put differently, pressures to conform are high. For young men, going on a mission is essential, and failure to complete it is an embarrassment not only to the individual but to his family—as we saw in Brandon Young's example when he was sent home early for health reasons (chapter 4). For couples, failure to have a Temple marriage would be a source of family sorrow. For a rebellious young person the consequences can be dire, since apostasy (leaving the faith) can lead not only to excommunication from the Church but even, in some cases, to shunning by the family, a termination of all contact with one's community.

For Mormons the transmission of religion across generations is extremely important, and there are many ways in which the Church and family work together to encourage religious continuity across generations. How do they succeed in this goal, and what happens when transmission fails?

The Shepherds: Mormon Continuity and Discontinuity Within the Same Family

The Shepherds are the largest family in our interview sample, and we have Longitudinal Study of Generations (LSOG) survey data from twenty-five family members spanning four generations. What makes the family particularly interesting for our purposes here is that there are two lineages or "lines" that have followed very different religious profiles starting with the G2 generation. In the one line, family members are deeply religious and show high intergenerational continuity within the Mormon faith. In the other line, most are highly nonreligious or indifferent to religion, but this too seems to reflect intergenerational continuity.

The story of this family starts with G1 Ira, now deceased, who was born shortly after the turn of the twentieth century. Ira had been a highly regarded leader in the Mormon community and at the time of his interview was obviously proud of the religious continuity in his family. He said that "my religion" was the most important thing his parents had passed on to him. In several previous generations, the men in his family had been Mormon leaders. When asked what he would like to pass on to his children and grandchildren he replied, "My testimony. That God lives and that Jesus is the Christ." When asked about raising his children Ira said,

> Religion pretty much established the principles of living for us, our purpose of being here on earth and what our goals should be throughout life, and we believe in the life hereafter, so that the principles of the Gospel were essential and had a far-reaching effect on the lives of all of us.

Of course Ira and his wife, Dorothy, raised their children to be active Mormons; for one of their daughters, the transmission of their faith succeeded very well: Lucille had five children, all of whom are Mormons. But Lucille's sister, Sharon, took a different religious pathway, and this has been reflected in the religious biographies of her children and grandchildren. Sharon married a Mormon but he left the Church, and she soon followed him. Their three children are nonreligious, and of Sharon's six grandchildren, three are agnostic, one is Jewish, one is Catholic, and one seems to be vaguely "Christian."

What led to the "great divide" in the intergenerational transmission of religion in this family that started out devoutly Mormon? What accounts for the strong religious conformity or continuity across generations in one line of the family and the intentional and perpetual rejection of that faith across generations in the other lines?

G2 Lucille and Her Mormon Lineage

Lucille's children and grandchildren talk about many activities in the Mormon community that have kept them together as a family and faithful to Church teaching. Along with the high emphasis placed on family cohesion, these activities integrate church and family and represent very effective socialization contexts for the intergenerational continuity of religion. Lucille's son, G3 William, fifty-five, describes his growing up experience this way:

> I was very active in my Church. We went to Church on Sundays. We had activities throughout the week. We held family nights together as a family [Family Home Evening]....We went to a children's activity all through my growing up—we call it Primary for Children. And then, as you become a youth, age twelve to eighteen, it's called Mutual.[4] It was just a constant amount of activity we had....Oh, and every single morning...at 6:00 in the morning, we have about an hour of a religious class...where we discussed topics of our gospel, and I was active in that all through my growing up years.

Throughout their lives, Lucille and her husband, Ernest, tried to set an example for their children in the Mormon way of life. Ernest served as a bishop, the equivalent of the minister or pastor of a congregation, a role that is very time-consuming—and unpaid. They encouraged and supported their sons in serving missions for the Church. They served together on Mormon missions after they retired, hoping to set an example for their grandchildren and great-grandchildren to do the same. They emphasized the importance of their children marrying within the Church, and each has had a Temple wedding. All of Lucille and Ernest's thirteen grandchildren are reported to be practicing Mormons, and the three married grandchildren who are in our study are raising their children in the Mormon tradition as well.

G2 Sharon and Her Non-Mormon Lineage

Meanwhile, on the other side of the Shepherd family, there is Sharon and her line. Like her sister Lucille, Sharon was raised as a Mormon, always participated in Church activities, married a Mormon man, and had a Temple wedding. But there the similarity ended. Sharon's husband Aiden stopped practicing Mormonism and became what his grandson described as "a closet atheist." He became a successful corporate lawyer. Sharon went to college and obtained an advanced degree in a field related to religion. When her children were small she took them to Mormon church activities, but she did not encourage them to continue after childhood, and none did.

Sharon's son, sixty-two-year-old G3 Elliott, might be called a life-long "seeker." He says he is "an atheist who has been a Mormon, a Jew, a Christian, and an agnostic." He goes on to say that he was "born an atheist" like his dad, Aiden, but briefly converted to Mormonism, the faith of his grandparents, while a teenager. His conversion occurred while he was staying with his Mormon aunt, Lucille, and her family for a time, and so he was "very active" in the LDS Church during adolescence. However, Elliott gradually stopped being a practicing Mormon through college and graduate school. He married Sara, a Conservative Jew, and converted to Judaism. They had two children, G4s Luke and Noah, whom they began raising as Jews. But the marriage was filled with conflict and led to divorce. Elliott then married a conservative Christian.

Looking back, Elliott says his becoming a religious seeker was in part due to the religious freedom his parents, G2s Sharon and Aiden, provided him—a conscious departure from the suffocating religious conformity Sharon felt her own parents, G1s Ira and Dorothy, had imposed. "They wanted us to think for ourselves," he says. "And we did." Similarly, Sharon's younger son, Mitch, claimed no religious affiliation yet married a highly religious woman, whose conflicts over religion with their children, Ivan and Brianna, are described in chapter 8.

In summary, the Shepherds are a family from a long Mormon tradition that exemplifies both high continuity and low continuity in religion across generations. While descended from a respected line of Mormon leaders, the two branches of the family have diverged significantly in recent years, starting with the G2s in our study. In one family line, G2 Lucille's, the Mormon faith has prevailed in all of the adult members in our study, a striking example of the intergenerational transmission of religion. There are clear reasons for this high continuity: the strong mutual reinforcement of family and Church activities, very high Church involvement, conformity within the family in beliefs and practices, and complete homogony in marriages within the Church. Most continue to live within the same highly Mormon community they grew up in. There is also strong solidarity within the family, with family members living near each other and reporting close relationships.

In the other line, adherence to the Mormon faith died out after Sharon and Aiden left the Church—a decision prompted in part by Sharon's undergraduate and graduate studies, which caused her to question and look critically at religion. She and her husband also moved away from the primarily Mormon community of her parents and her sister Lucille. Sharon's children and grandchildren have made their own ways in religion, taking varied pathways through atheism, agnosticism, Mormonism, and Judaism. The reasons they give for this line's religious individualism are clear: rejection of what was experienced as Mormon rigidity, parental emphasis on freedom of choice rather than conformity, higher education, exposure to role models of different faiths, and parental ambivalence toward religion.

In Lucille's line of the Shepherd family we have a prime example of intergenerational continuity in religion. In Sharon's line we see discontinuity in the beginning, as she drifted away from the strong Mormonism of her parents and grandparents. However, there is a pattern of continuity here as well, which is evident in the prevalence of agnosticism, atheism, and "nones" that have persisted over three generations now.

The break with Mormon tradition by Sharon and her family resulted in a family rift that changed relationships as well as religion and has already persisted through three generations. Despite the strong Mormon emphasis on family relationships, both nuclear and extended, none of Sharon's grandchildren today appear to be acquainted with Lucille's grandchildren. Our interviews with family members in both lines offered no indication of any efforts to reconcile this division.

Jews: Families of a Chosen People

Judaism began to take shape almost 4,000 years ago when, according to the Jewish, Christian, and Muslim scriptures, God told Abraham that his descendants would be His own "chosen people." Unfortunately, over the centuries to be a "chosen people" has often meant to be chosen for persecution or extermination. This has resulted in two characteristic responses: on the one hand, a movement toward assimilation and even intermarriage with the majority culture or religion, and on the other a movement toward affirming Jewish identity and culture as distinctly different from the majority society.

American Judaism has three major branches, each reflecting to one degree or another these strategies. The Orthodox branch follows biblical dietary laws (keeping kosher), maintains strict observance of the Torah, and emphasizes traditional Jewish life. The Conservative branch was established "for the preservation in America of historical Judaism,"[5] so Conservative Jews generally keep kosher, wear prayer shawls, and use Hebrew in temple services. The Reform branch views such practices as strict dietary laws and the wearing of distinctive clothing such as prayer shawls as anachronisms that isolate Jews from the rest of humankind. Reform Judaism's conviction is that Judaism should "alter its externals to strengthen its eternals."[6]

In 2008 there were 5.76 million Jews in the United States.[7] Precise numbers of members in the three major branches of Judaism are difficult to determine, since American Jews sometimes move from one branch of Judaism to another during their lifetime. One estimate is that 6% of American Jews identify with Orthodox, 40% with Conservative, 39% with Reform, and the remaining 15% with "no denomination."[8] The latter are most likely to identify with Judaism as a culture, a historical and social entity with distinctive traditions, rather than a religious system of beliefs and practices about relating to God. As we see later, Jews who are nonreligious still answer "Jewish" when asked the question "What is your religion?"—which makes matters complicated for the researcher seeking precise religious categorization. Should they be classified as "nones" or as Jews?

Finally, how do American Jews, living in an increasingly modern and secular culture, attempt to pass on their religious traditions to a younger generation, and how well are they succeeding?

The Liebermans: Jewish—But Not Religious

The Liebermans reflect a pattern similar to many Jewish families in the United States since 1900[9]: while the first generation to immigrate to the States was highly religious, subsequent generations have become less so, with the major shift occurring in the second generation.

In the 1970 LSOG survey G1s Benjamin and Imogene Lieberman identified themselves as Orthodox Jews, and both said they were "very religious." They practiced Jewish rituals such as weekly synagogue attendance, keeping a kosher home, and observing Jewish holidays in a religious manner. They earnestly hoped to see their beliefs and practices passed on to subsequent generations of their family. However, their G2 daughter, Ruth, felt that her parents were too forceful in their attempts to impose their religious perspectives as well as their negative views regarding non-Jews.

Ruth says that she is "not very religious." One reason for the shift is because her parents "were very strict" about being Jewish; another is that they did not teach her the meaning behind their religious practices. "Instead of explaining things to me, they just told me what to do and what not to do, and not why," she says. "I was a very good little kid, and I obeyed, but I didn't know what it was all about. If I asked a question, they told me that they really didn't know what the prayers were. They read it in Hebrew, they didn't understand what they were saying, and they didn't bother to learn."

Still another reason Ruth says she distanced herself from her parents was their cultural insularity. "They were bigoted. I was never allowed to date anybody that wasn't Jewish.... [They] refused to talk to someone who had married a non-Jew." Ruth says she could understand why her parents were intolerant toward non-Jews: "They were persecuted in Russia, so they felt that way.... [But] I vowed not to be like that and to bring my children up differently." Her values differ from those of her parents. She calls herself "very liberal-minded" and not very religious. Culturally, she is Jewish, but she's uncertain whether she believes in God.

Despite her unrewarding experiences with Judaism while she was growing up, Ruth says she has tried to influence her children and her grandchildren to maintain a Jewish historical and cultural identity, though not a religious one. She seems to have been successful. Her fifty-three-year-old daughter, G3 Vicki, says, "I'm definitely Jewish. But, I'm not a religious Jew." When asked about believing in God she replies shortly, "No." Similarly, Vicki's daughter G4 Lindsay, twenty-seven, identifies as Jewish and says, "I don't necessarily believe in a god who created the world. I don't subscribe to that."

Regardless of the lapse in Jewish religious observance over four generations of the Lieberman family, all have continued to follow Jewish cultural traditions, celebrating Jewish holidays by gathering as a family for Passover, Rosh Hashanah, and Yom Kippur in order to "keep the traditions alive." Moreover, religion still surfaces. Vicki explains that "when the holidays came around, that's *[pause]* sort of, you know, when you realized you were Jewish.... Being Jewish was about celebrating the holidays as a family, eating certain foods and knowing Yiddish words."

One factor reinforcing Jewish identity was the Jewish neighborhood community where the Lieberman children socialized with other Jewish children. Vicki says that being Jewish played an important role in her life and that of her family because she grew up "in a pretty Jewish neighborhood, and so most of my friends were Jewish." Her daughter Lindsay says,

> Having a group of friends who were raised the same....That was the most important part of belonging to a temple. It wasn't really a religious thing, it was a social thing. It was nice to know other people in your community who had been through the same things [and who] understand the same things, and were brought up the same.

A Jewish identity was also passed on through religious education. That is where the Lieberman children learned about their Jewish heritage. G2 Ruth sent her children to a religious school to learn Hebrew so they could complete their bar and bat mitzvahs. G3 Vicki did the same for her children, and G4 Lindsay anticipates doing so for her future children as well. Vicki adds, however, that religious school was more about their learning the "Jewish way of life" than it was about being religious.

Instances of anti-Semitism and discrimination also influenced the Liebermans, reminding them that they were different, that they should stick together as a family and support their community. Ruth remembers: "[It was during] World War II and I had kids chasing me home saying, you're a

Jew, you killed Christ and you made this war happen and that's why they're killing the Jews." Her husband also experienced persecution growing up. He remembers "a neighbor who wasn't Jewish and I remember her saying to me, 'You killed Jesus Christ.'"

For the eldest Liebermans, marriage to a non-Jew was prohibited. In her 1970 survey, G1 Imogene wrote that Jews should marry in their faith "so the Jewish way of life will not be forgotten." But the next generation took a different stance when G2 Ralph, Ruth's brother, married a non-Jew. The consequences were dire: G1 Benjamin, his father, disowned him. According to Ruth, he did not talk to his son until a few years before his death. In later generations the proscription against marrying outside the Jewish faith had weakened considerably. Ruth's G3 daughter, Vicki, says, "I would prefer that both my kids married somebody Jewish, but if they don't, then that's okay too."

By the third and fourth generations of the Lieberman family, being Jewish had become a cultural but not a religious identity. Vicki, as noted above, says she is Jewish but not a religious Jew. Her G4 son, Erick, says that more important than his Jewish religious tradition is the continuity in culture he feels: "I see that I am Jewish, and I see my parents are Jewish, my grandparents are Jewish, and I see that this is the way they did it—this is the way I'm supposed to do it."

The Rosenbergs: Increasing Religiousness Across Generations

Other Jewish families in our sample showed a generational progression of Jewish observance but in the opposite direction: first-generation immigrant Jews who were not very religious with increasing religiousness for the generations thereafter. The Rosenbergs provide an example. While the great-grandparents were Conservative Jews, all four great-grandchildren are religiously Orthodox, some fervently so, and they have influenced their parents to become more religious as well.

G1s Milton and Hattie Rosenberg were Conservative Jews but not very religious. They emigrated from Romania and after living briefly in New York moved to Los Angeles where Milton got a job in the film industry. Their daughter, G2 Rosemary, identified herself as a Conservative Jew in our 1970 LSOG survey but said she was "not very religious" though somewhat active in the Jewish community. Rosemary's fifty-five-year-old son, G3 Howard, recalls that his grandfather was not strict in his religious practices. "We drove to synagogue and he didn't study Torah a lot.... That just wasn't what he was about."

Howard and his wife, Kathy, identified as Conservative Jews in their 1970 survey but did not identify with a synagogue until later when they had children and joined an Orthodox temple. As their children were growing up, Howard and Kathy were drawn more and more into their children's Orthodox synagogue activities. When their children became teenagers they decided to move to a neighborhood with an Orthodox synagogue so they could walk to services on Friday night and Saturday morning in accordance with Jewish laws for Shabbat. When asked his religious affiliation in 2007, Howard replied, "Conservadox... somewhere between Conservative and Orthodox."

Their son, G4 Ethan, is stricter in his Orthodoxy. "When I'm at my parents' house [on Shabbat] they will turn on and off lights, but I will not. That's certainly fine; no one gets bothered by that." The G4 Rosenbergs have influenced their parents to follow in their own lives what the children had been taught in the religious schools to which Howard and Kathy sent them—that is, as Ethan put it, "consistently living a Jewish way of life... it is the way you live that makes you a Jewish person."

These two families, the Liebermans and the Rosenbergs, provide examples of a strong Jewish identity passed down through the generations, but they differ in the importance they place on *religious* as distinct from *cultural* Judaism. This is, of course, the same distinction that is reflected in the major branches of American Judaism today, from Orthodox to Reform, as described earlier in this chapter. Tracing the transmission of religion down through Jewish generations in America poses a particular challenge to researchers because "Jewish" can refer to religion, culture, or both.

In the Lieberman family, religiosity shifted from Conservative, Orthodox practices that valued centuries-old Jewish rituals and prayer toward a cultural and nonreligious (and, in some cases, antireligious) Jewish identity. This identity was reinforced by family rituals that were rooted in ancient religious rites—bar mitzvahs, weddings, holy days— but now lack deeply religious meaning. In the Rosenberg family also, the Jewish cultural identity has persisted strongly following immigration, but the religious dimensions of Judaism have grown stronger across generations. What accounts for the two different paths that religiosity has taken in these two families over successive generations? We return to this question at the end of the chapter.

Evangelical Christians: Families with a Personal Relationship with Christ

While the term "Evangelical" goes back to the Greek used for the preaching of John the Baptist and to Luther and the sixteenth-century Reformation, in America today it has its antecedents in the religious revivals of the late nineteenth century that urged sinners to be "born again."[10] American Evangelicals since the mid-twentieth century have emphasized three doctrines: (a) the Bible as the literal and divinely inspired Word of God; (b) humankind as sinful but for whom eternal salvation is possible through belief in Christ and spiritual regeneration (i.e., being "born again"); and (c) personal devotion such as Bible reading and prayer and a zeal for Evangelicalism and missions.[11] Some Evangelicals today believe it is their moral duty to defend "Biblical" teachings and practices in the face of worldly secularism, leading them to activate politically for teaching creationism in schools, criminalizing abortion, mandating prayer in schools and Christian symbols in civic buildings, and limiting civil rights such as marriage to homosexuals. Their political power is viewed as a major factor in American politics today.

The perception exists that Evangelicals are growing rapidly in America today. This is not quite the case; their numbers grew in the 1970s, remained relatively stable until and then slightly declines. This was followed by an increase in 2004, then another slight decline.[12] Nevertheless, Evangelical Protestants represent the largest religious tradition in the United States today, at about 27% of the adult population, larger than Catholics (24%) or Mainline Protestants (18%).[13] Evangelicals constitute a powerful force in contemporary American society religiously, culturally, and especially politically.

For Evangelicals "family values" are important, and the transmission of their faith to younger generations is considered an aspect of Christian stewardship. Evangelical churches devote much time and energy teaching their children and youth to "grow in the Lord." Sunday schools are large and carefully organized. Many churches have organized preschools, and some of the larger ones sponsor K–12 academies. All invest considerable resources in youth groups and prayer meetings. Dating within the faith is expected and reinforced by parents and youth counselors. In high school, organizations such as Young Life and Youth for Christ provide opportunities for dating, religious affirmation by peers, and witnessing; this is continued in college by Campus Crusade for Christ, InterVarsity Christian Fellowship, The Living Word, and the Vine. These groups are prolific: At the University of Southern California, for example, a campus of 17,000 undergraduates, in 2012 there were 106 religious organizations registered on campus, involving over 8,000 students; 78 of them were Evangelical Christian.

Despite this apparent strength in numbers, many Evangelicals feel themselves to be a beleaguered minority in American society, denigrated by and discriminated against by a secularist majority. In fact, research by David Kinnaman[14] reveals widespread antipathy toward Evangelical Christians, particularly by unaffiliated youth, who view Evangelicals as "judgmental," "hypocritical," "insensitive," and "out of touch with reality." Kinnaman concludes that Christians are best known for what they are against—such as limits on the ability of gays and lesbians to marry—and that this perception must be changed by Christians acting in ways that are consistent with Christ's message of grace, love, and compassion.

The Wilsons: An Evangelical Family "Connected...Through Our Love of God"

The Wilsons have been Evangelicals for over five generations, as we saw in our profile of them in chapter 4. It is interesting how thoroughly the younger Wilsons have internalized the religious faith of their parents, grandparents, and great-grandparents. They use almost identical words and phrases to describe their "relationship with Christ" (the phrase they prefer, rather than the word "religious") and the meaning of their faith. Note the similarity over generations in response to the question "How would you describe God?"

> He's who we worship and Jesus is the Holy Spirit who guides us and directs us...in a personal way. (G2 Carolyn)
>
> He's a personal God....You can relate to him, you can talk to him. [T]he Holy Spirit is the personal side that comes and dwells in us. (G3 Ken)

It's a personal relationship with Jesus, who knows the details of my life, who knows my struggles, who has plans for me. (G4 Kristin)

Spiritual is the personal relationship with God and…you have a relationship with him. (G4 Susan)

In no other family in our study did we find such literal congruence as members described their views about God or the ways they put their faith into practice.

Where did this remarkable similarity in religious views and actions come from? When asked what values his grandparents tried to instill in their children and grandchildren, G3 Ken responds, "It just all boils down to that relationship with Jesus Christ. That's the main thing they passed down, and everything springs from there."

Each family member participates in church every Sunday. Church has meant not only worship and faith development but also fellowship and being part of a community of like-minded people. G3 Elaine says,

[Going to church is] to continually grow. If you're not continually growing as a Christian, you're stagnating and you're not feeding your soul. So we go there as a time to worship, as a time to spend time with God. And also for fellowship. It's a time to see other Christians, to be surrounded by other Christians, to boost us up for the week.

Marrying within the faith is strongly promoted, and interfaith dating is strongly discouraged. Each of the youngest generation has married an Evangelical. But religious homogamy does not ensure marital harmony. After G4 Kristin married an Evangelical Christian, he was unfaithful, and they are now divorced. This was a shock to the Wilson family, but they all rallied to support her and her G5 children. Kristin interprets the breakup as God's will and says that He is teaching her to put more trust in Him. "God is testing me, I know that," she explains. "I couldn't get through this without my relationship with Him. When I'm down, His Spirit fills me and I can bounce back up again."

The Wilsons are a very close family, both emotionally and geographically. Each of the youngest generation lives within a few miles of their parents, and they see or talk to each other daily. They and their families attend the same Evangelical church. G4 Susan says, "We're connected—through our love for God and to each other."

The Wilsons' religious upbringing has been reinforced by many activities bridging church and family. Across the generations, they attended Sunday school as children and then taught Sunday school as parents. They have family prayers before each meal and before going to sleep. G2 Carolyn says that she watches religious programs on television. G3 Elaine describes how her parents taught Sunday school as a couple when she was growing up and how her father, Thomas, had a leadership position in their church, which impressed her greatly.

But not all has been peaceful in the Evangelical Wilson family. Despite their deeply held faith—or perhaps because of it—there have been conflicts among members of the family who do not see things the same way. G3 Ken recalls this about his father:

> I used to have these questions [about religion] and we'd talk about them and he'd start raising his voice and getting a little excited....If I had questions about this interpretation, this part of the Bible, something Dad didn't quite agree with, he couldn't discuss it, he would just get mad that you're trying to entertain some different way than what he would do.

Furthermore, there is a bit of a mystery about Ken's brother, G3 Peter, who declined to be interviewed. We learned about him from G4 Kristin, who mentioned that one of her uncles was no longer a church member, adding that she had not seen him since she was in the third grade. Then there is Ken's sister (we don't know her name), whom G4 Kristen says she has seen twice in the past ten years. About her Ken says, "My sister's a strong believer, but we just don't relate. We just don't communicate that much. And then my brother, he's just so different than I am that we just don't have a lot in common." Evangelicals have been accused of exclusiveness and intolerance in their tightknit religious community, and this might be the case here. The examples cited above are in sharp contrast to the glowing description given by those Wilsons that we interviewed: "We are a very close and loving family," as G4 Kristin put it.

In fact there is a somewhat insular quality to the Wilson family that seems to flow from their Evangelical Christian lifestyle and their intense involvement with like-minded members of their church and community—and is possibly related to an exclusion of family members who are not similarly devout. The Wilsons we interviewed are very intimate, rallying for family members who need support. Their belief in a personal relationship with God is the core issue in this family, around which all activities and relationships are built, and they are highly committed to transmitting their faith to the next generation.

Tightknit Faiths and Tightknit Families

Mormons, Jews, and Evangelicals are in many respects religious minority groups within American society—whatever their size in the population. They each constitute a group that is identifiable to outsiders in terms of religious practices and beliefs. They form cohesive communities with well-defined borders separating themselves from outsiders. They place a high value on the family and incorporate rituals and traditions that help to maintain the continuity of their faith across generations. In the families reviewed in this chapter, we see examples of both success and failure in the goal of religious continuity across generations.

In the Evangelical Wilson family and in Lucille's line of the Mormon Shepherd family, there is a high—unusually high—degree of religious continuity extending over four or more generations. For the Wilsons, at least for those whom we interviewed, each family member regardless of generation uses remarkably similar words to describe having a "personal relationship" with God. For the Shepherds, each family member in Lucille's line mentions the importance of living worthy of the faith and of having a temple wedding. There are several things that these families have in common that seem to have led to high intergenerational continuity of their religious tradition.

First is the strong reinforcement between family and church, with religious activities built around family activities and high family involvement in religious education. Second is the strong role modeling by the previous generations' involvement in religious organizations and in the articulation of beliefs. A third factor is a high degree of family closeness, both emotionally and geographically, characterized by frequent family interaction, help, and assistance. In addition, we see reliance on the strong social bonds within the religious community, exemplified by a prohibition on marriage or even dating outside of the faith. All of these factors suggest strong in-group solidarity and a degree of insularity from the outside society.

For the Jewish Lieberman family, the intergenerational continuity is cultural, not religious. "I'm definitely Jewish. But I'm not a religious Jew," as G3 Vicki puts it. While the Jewish religious identification in this family decreased over the four generations, their Jewish ethnic identity did not. The intergenerational continuity of cultural Judaism can be attributed to several factors that have already been mentioned in connection with the Wilsons' and Shepherds' religious continuity: (a) defining religion as "spending time together as a family"; (b) an emphasis on passing on the cultural traditions and heritage through the observance of holidays, ceremonial family dinners, and coming-of-age rituals; (c) growing up in a Jewish community with Jewish neighbors and playmates; (d) an emphasis on the importance of family and family interactions; and (e) a ban on marrying outside the faith. For the Liebermans and other Jews, another factor strongly influences intergenerational continuity: a Jewish history involving ethnic identification and persecution that binds the family together in a common cultural identity.

The patriarch and matriarch of the Shepherd family were surely disappointed that Sharon, their second daughter, did not follow her parents' and grandparents' Mormon faith. Likewise, the G1 Liebermans were undoubtedly upset that their son did not follow their Orthodox faith. What happened to disrupt the intergenerational continuity in these cases? The picture is less clear here, because we have less complete data; religious parents understandably talk less about their failures than their successes. However, several factors seem to undermine religious continuity across generations:

1. Marriage outside the faith or to someone who leaves the faith, as discussed in chapter 6.
2. Parental religiosity—too much or too little socialization of religion by the parents, particularly the perception by children that parents attempt to force religion on them—an issue we address in chapter 8.
3. Perceptions of hypocrisy when parents do not act in congruence with their religious teachings, or when parents follow the letter but not the meaning of the law, such as parents insisting on praying in Hebrew but being unable to explain what the prayers mean.
4. Other role models—aunts, uncles, grandparents—who discourage religious transmission.

Looking at families within high-boundary religious communities such as Mormons, Jews, and Evangelicals can provide many insights about the intergenerational transmission of religion. Particularly useful are the lessons about how and when the transmission of faith does *not* work. We turn to this in the next chapter, where we review what we have learned in this study and look at some practical applications for families and religious organizations interested in supporting religious transmission.

CHAPTER 10 | Conclusion

What We Have Learned and
How It Might Be Useful

WE HAVE LOOKED AT families and faith using data collected across thirty-five years to explore questions such as these: How effective are parents in passing on their faith? How influential are parents today, as compared with several decades ago, in transmitting religion to their children? What things differentiate parents who are successful in transmission, and parents who are not? In this closing chapter, we review what we have found and summarize it in a theory of intergenerational religious momentum describing how parents' behaviors can encourage or impede continuity of faith across generations. Then we discuss implications from this study, practical applications of the results for parents, parents, pastors, priests, and religious educators interested in fostering religious transmission across generations.

Research Results: Momentum and Transmission Across Generations

Religious families are surprisingly successful at transmission

There is concern within some religious communities today that families are not very strong, nor very effective, in shaping their children's moral and religious values. At least this is the message of many outspoken religious leaders (as well as some politicians), in ways that are reviewed in chapter 1. These decry what they see as a decline in parental moral influence and call for a return to "traditional family values." Religious educators too voice concern about the loss in participation by youth, warning about the need for churches to build better ways to keep young people within the faith.[1]

Yet the results of this study show a different picture. In our data on religion and families the message is more about family continuity than differences, about stability over time rather than decline. A majority of the parents and young adults in our sample share similar religious identities, practices, and beliefs. For example, six out of ten parents have young adult children who report they have the same religious tradition as their parents—or share their parents' preference for no affiliation at all.

Parental influence has not declined since the 1970s

Significant changes occurred in American civic and religious life in the decades between 1970 and 2005, as noted in chapter 1. Many appeared related to the ability of parents to influence their children's religiosity. There were far-reaching changes in American culture, legacies of the 1960s "Decade of Protest" that led to the "generation gap" becoming a byword of the era, a symbol of increasing distrust for social institutions such as organized religion.[2] There were alterations in family structures, rising rates of divorce and an increase in single-parent households. There were changes in America's religious practices. Starting in the 1960s, there was a decline in church membership, lower rates of church attendance, growing numbers of the religiously unaffiliated, and an increasing diversity of faith in our society—an expansion of religious pluralism especially prevalent among youth.

One result of such cultural, familial, and religious trends has been, according to many religious and social commentators, an erosion of the moral and religious influence of families. With our longitudinal data on religion from both parents and young adult children, we could examine if this was true. To our surprise, it was not. The degree of intergenerational similarity in four dimensions of religious practice and beliefs had not changed between 1970 and 2005. The extent to which religious families are successful in passing on their faith to younger generations appears to have remained stable over time.

In short, our results indicate that the decline in parental influence assumed by many has not occurred in religious beliefs and practices.

Rather than rebelling against or abandoning their parents' values and beliefs, a majority of younger-generation members today appear to have retained those values and beliefs—while also adapting them into a new historical context (as described in chapter 2).

Parental warmth is the key to successful transmission

As seen in chapter 4, certain patterns or themes in parent–child relationships seem to be particularly relevant to religious transmission. We found four types of parenting that were related to intergenerational continuity or discontinuity of faith: (a) warm, affirming parenting that the child sees as a consistently close relationship with one or usually both parents; (b) cold, distant, or authoritarian parenting; (c) ambivalent or mixed-message parenting, when a parent is perceived as sometimes warm, sometimes cold, or where one parent is seen as warm and the other as cold or distant; (d) strained or preoccupied parenting, as when parents are distracted by marital, financial, health, or substance abuse problems.

The warm, affirming relationship pattern was most likely to result in the successful transmission of religion. Children responded best to parents who were unconditionally supportive, who provided consistent role modeling of religious practices, and who did not force their beliefs or practices on their children. For example, in the Wilson family (chapter 4) we saw that a consistently close relationship with parents created continuity in their Evangelical faith—across four generations. In addition, we found that the most successful parents in religious transmission showed love, respect, and patience for those children who took a different path in religion; these often turned out to be "Prodigals" and returned (chapter 8). By contrast, the other three parenting styles (such as the cold or distant, ambivalent or mixed-message) appeared to decrease the likelihood of religious transmission and increase the likelihood of rebellion. The stern judgmentalism of Brandon Young's father, for instance, was a decided turnoff for Brandon and a key factor in his decision to leave the Mormon faith. Parental piety does not, it seems, make up for a distant though devout dad.

Grandparents are more important than we recognize

Grandparents have seldom been considered in research on religious influences of children. But they should be, because the role grandparents play in the lives of grandchildren will be much more influential in the twenty-first century. About four in ten grandparents and grandchildren in our sample share the same religious tradition, while slightly less than this report the same frequency of religious service attendance and agreement on religious beliefs. This is considerably higher generational continuity than we had expected. Moreover, comparing 2005 to 1970, there has been no significant decline in the degree to which grandparents and grandchildren are similar on the aspects of religiosity measured in our surveys.

Clearly, cross-generational influences are important in religious socialization. From our interviews and family case studies we identified four types of grandparental religious influence patterns in our sample: (a) grandparents replacing or substituting for parents' religious socialization—the "skipped generation" effect; (b) grandparents reinforcing or accentuating parents' religious socialization; (c) grandparents challenging or subverting parents' socialization; (d) grandparents avoiding or ignoring the religious socialization of grandchildren.

With the first two of these patterns we saw successful transmission results. Beverly Johnson, who was raised by her grandparents, cleaves to their Protestant traditions, while Shari Sabelli's close relationship with her devotedly Catholic grandfather Leo was a major force in her decision to return to the church as an adult. Chrystal Smith, who is strongly nonreligious, talks about the influence of her atheist grandmother, Doris, who was very much against religion. However, the third pattern—grandparents attempting to replace or subvert parents' efforts—was not as effective and in fact was counterproductive. In the Goldman family, devout Jewish grandparents could not undo the maternal influence of their fundamentalist Christian daughter-in-law, and the grandparents' attempts to do so caused tension within the family.

Interfaith marriage and divorce deter religious transmission

Our results show that parents in a same-faith marriage help perpetuate religious continuity across generations. This is most likely if there is a strong religious commitment, the partners regularly attend religious services together, and religion is highly salient in the lives of both partners. Moreover, religion can strengthen same-faith marriages, leading in turn to more effective religious socialization of children in the family.

Interfaith marriages are increasingly common in the United States, and couples handle religion in such cases in different ways. In our study, marriages where there is conversion by one partner to a common religious faith increased the likelihood of transmitting a religious tradition to the next generation. In other interfaith marriages, where each spouse continues to go his or her own way, we found that the stronger the faith of one partner, the more likely the transmission of that faith.

Divorce is often a disruptive factor in the transmission of religious tradition to children, as we saw in the gradual loosening of the Sanchez family's bonds with Catholicism as divorce occurred more frequently through the generations. Yet divorce did not always fracture that continuity: In some families the divorced parent with high religious commitment was successful in transmitting his or her faith.

Religious Rebels, Zealots, and Prodigals are outcomes of nontransmission

Religious Rebels, Zealots, and Prodigals refer to young adults who are significantly different from their parents in religious practices and beliefs. Religious Rebels are those who reject their parents' religion by converting to a different faith, settling into religious indifference, or renouncing religion altogether. This is often called apostasy, particularly in the Mormon tradition. Religious Zealots are those whose intensity in belief and practice is greater than that of their parents, most being new converts to another religion and deeply committed to their new faith. Prodigals represent a special kind of Religious Rebels, children who grow up in a church family and depart from their family's faith in young adulthood but eventually return, sort of like a religious boomerang.

The Generation (G) 4 Religious Rebels in our study came from strongly religious families in which parental piety had been "too much of a good thing," where the parents' efforts at religious socialization were experienced as excessive or intrusive. Think of Brianna Shepherd, an agnostic who reacted strongly against her mother's determination to "shove religion down [her] throat." When highly religious parents pushed children against their will to participate in religious activities (church, Hebrew school, Bible study, youth groups, etc.) or to conform to church doctrine or morality, some perceived the parents' piety as oppressive and rebelled.

We found it interesting that, when the Zealots in our sample themselves became parents, they often produced Rebel children who sought a different faith from their fervently religious parents or who simply dropped out of religion. That is, many of the Zealot converts were unable to transfer their strong faith and devotion to their children (often due to a lack of support by their spouse, who had not followed them in conversion). The Prodigals in our sample were Rebels who later came back to their family religion; in almost every case we found that their parents had been patient and supportive—and perhaps more tolerant and open than they had been before the Prodigal's departure.

The cases of nontransmission in our study provide examples of how important religious transmission is to many parents, and how difficult it can be when their children choose a different path. Seeing their children leave their religious tradition can be painful and sometimes a source of shame for highly religious parents. They have invested much time and energy in the religious education of their children. Many have the hope that they will reunite with their children in heaven after they die. These parents pray that their children are only temporary Rebels who will eventually return to the family faith.

Religious "nones" are also products of intergenerational transmission

Over the past two decades, there has been an unprecedented increase in the number of Americans who are "nones," atheists, agnostics, or those unaffiliated with any church, synagogue, or temple. Previous research has suggested that a majority of atheists or those who have taken the path of nonbelief have rejected their parents' religious faith.[3] Many atheists describe themselves—or their family members describe them—as the black sheep of the family.[4] However, among the nonreligious in our study it was more common to see intergenerational similarity, children following in the same path as their parents as nonreligious nones. The degree of such parent–child similarity has increased over time. In the 1970 Longitudinal Study of Generations (LSOG) survey one in seven unaffiliated young adult children had parents who also professed no religious affiliation; thirty-five years later, in 2005, this had increased to six in ten.

High-boundary religious groups have high rates of transmission

Mormons, Evangelicals, and Jews share characteristics that distinguish them from other religious groups within American society. They have well-defined beliefs and practices that make them distinctive. In our study families from these groups showed the highest rates of religious transmission. We found three factors that seemed to explain their success in passing on the tradition. First are strong and intentional bonds between family and church or synagogue, in which religious activities are built around family activities with high family involvement in religious education. Second is an emphasis on parents' role modeling, evidenced in their investment in the tradition and their articulation of its beliefs, Third is the value given to family solidarity, characterized by warm emotional relationships, frequent family interaction, help, and assistance. There is also a reliance on strong and exclusive bonds within the religious community, exemplified by a prohibition on marriage or perhaps dating outside of the faith. All these factors suggest strong in-group solidarity and a degree of insularity from the outside society that, in turn, contributes to intergenerational continuity.

These communal forces also involve risks. We also saw failures in transmission within the Mormon, Evangelical, and Jewish families in our study. In these cases, several factors seemed to lead to generational discontinuity. One was parental religious intolerance, too much or too rigid socialization of religion. We saw this in the Lieberman family, when G2 Ruth abandoned the strict Orthodox Judaism of her parents in part because of their "narrow-minded rejection" of non-Jews. A second factor was the child's perception of hypocrisy when parents did not act in congruence with their religious teachings, or when parents followed the letter but not the meaning of the law. There were also accounts of cold or authoritarian parenting, a particular problem in conservative patriarchal religious communities, such as in the case of Brandon Young and his father. Each of these resulted in a failure to pass on the religious tradition, creating exceptions to the rule of strong continuity in high-boundary religious groups.

Generations differ in their perceptions of God and spirituality

The progression of generations—that is, youth coming of age in a succession of historical periods with different events and challenges can be a useful way to understand the origins of the religious trends we have discussed throughout this book.[5] In our study we identified seven generations, from those born in the 1890s to those born in the 1980s, focusing on the years in which individuals entered adolescence and came into adulthood. We looked at the expressions of religion and spirituality by members of these generations, and identified significant cross-generational trends that emerged in one age group and then continued to develop through successive groups.

One theme that developed over time concerns the increasing separation of religious practice from religious institutions. In the oldest age group, the World War I (WWI) Generation respondents associated religious practice primarily with a house of worship; they appeared apologetic if illness or lack of mobility had forced them to give up religious attendance. Depression Era respondents appeared to begin a trend that distinguished between going to a church or other place of worship and leading a religious life where churchgoing was unnecessary. For many within the silent generation, God and religion were described as residing within the human spirit. With each successive age group, from those born earlier to later, we see a trend reflecting a slightly changing image of God, from the transcendental to the internal.

A second cross-generational trend concerns the growing differentiation between "religion," specifically organized religion, and "spirituality," meaning an internal, personal relationship with God. Emerging first in interviews with Older Boomers, the emphasis on spirituality served to further separate religious practices from religious institutions. The emphasis on spirituality helps in understanding the personal and highly individualized "relationships" with God developed by Generation Xers and Millennials.

A third generational trend involved the increasing complexity of religious and spiritual experience over time and the departure from the more clearly defined institutional boundaries of religion of the past by successive age groups. As the accounts of the Millennials most notably suggest, older terms for religion may no longer work for younger individuals, who with others in their age group develop new concepts and contexts for religious and spiritual practice.

Yet the differences between age groups noted above may not be the result of generational (age cohort) effects but instead be linked to aging (life cycle) effects. There are factors related to growing up and growing old that might well explain a shift from tending to view God as individualized and personal in youth, to transcendent and eternal in old age; or a progression from dismissing religious tradition as a source of meaning in life, to embracing it as comfort and guidance. It will be interesting to see how the current young adult generation will modify their religious and spiritual expression as they grow older— and whether they will continue to modify religion in the United States. Time will tell whether the "Whatever God" of today's Millennials will gradually develop into the "Transcendent God" that characterized our WWI generation respondents. Perhaps when the Millennials themselves are celebrating their ninetieth and ninety-fifth birthdays, their spirituality will resemble what we have seen in our WWI generation sample today.

Intergenerational Religious Momentum

We now tie together the findings from this research about families and religious transmission and examine their implications. In reviewing the thirty-five years of data we had collected from over 3,500 family members, we were struck by how often we saw persistent patterns of religion (and sometimes nonreligion) across generations. Something about religion seems to "stick around" families over generations, more so than other characteristics we had compared across generations in an earlier study—characteristics such as political and social attitudes, values reflecting humanism and materialism, and psychological attributes such as self-esteem and depression.[6] We propose a concept that summarizes and ties together our findings: *intergenerational religious momentum.*

Intergenerational religious momentum is valued highly in many families. Parents invest a great amount of time and effort encouraging their children to stay in the faith. When interruptions in religious momentum occur, as in the case of Religious Rebels, it can be painful. Religious organizations and their ministers also have an investment in maintaining intergenerational religious momentum, though as we discuss below programs in most churches touch only tangentially on helping families do this.

A theory, or model, of the factors we have found to encourage or impede intergenerational religious momentum is presented in Figure 10.1. It is a

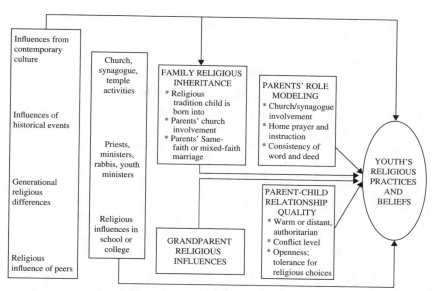

FIGURE 10.1 A Theory of Intergenerational Religious Momentum: Influences on Youth's Religious Practices and Beliefs

theory, in social science terms, because it is an attempt to explain what we have found about family influences on youths' religiosity. The outcome, depicted on the right-hand side of the page, is the young adult's religious practices and beliefs. On the far left are contextual factors surrounding the young adult and his or her family: influences from contemporary culture, historical events, generational differences in religious expression that can reinforce or detract from the intergenerational religious momentum, the probability of the child following in the parents' religious footsteps. These are societal and cultural factors discussed in chapters 1 and 2. The next column shows influences from religious organizations: programs and worship activities of churches, synagogues, and temples and inputs from religious leaders such as pastors, priests, rabbis, campus ministers, and religious educators. Religious influences encountered in education, and the influence of friends on religious beliefs and practices, can also reinforce or detract from intergenerational religious momentum.

At the center of this theory are family influences, starting with the religious inheritance of children, what they are born into—the religious tradition of their parents, their parents' religious involvement, and whether the parents were of the same religious faith at marriage. Being born into a household that is Pentecostal, Methodist, Mormon, or Jewish will become relevant to many religious choices of children as they become young adults, as will their parents' involvement in these religious traditions. At the bottom of this column are grandparents' religious influences. In some families, it is grandparents who maintain and sustain intergenerational religious momentum.

Most important in the theory are parental behaviors that influence religious development. The first category we call "role modeling"—what parents do in setting examples for religious practice and belief, such as attending church regularly, participating in church activities, and encouraging faith development at home through prayers, scripture reading, and religious stories. This is what churches and religious leaders teach that parents should do. Moreover, it is important, as seen from our interviews, that parents show consistency between belief and practice: "walking the walk and not just talking the talk," as expressed by G4 Lauren Walker.

The second category concerns the quality of the parent–child relationship, what we have called "intergenerational solidarity." Our data show the affective (emotional) dimension of parental behavior is very important in influencing religious transmission. Parents who are warm and affirming are more likely to have children who follow them; parents who are cold or authoritarian, ambivalent or distracted, are less likely to do so. Also affecting transmission is the level of conflict between parents and children. Moreover, we have seen that parents who are perceived as open and accepting of their child's religious choices are more likely to achieve transmission. Particularly important, according to our data, is the role of fathers' warmth. Parental piety—religious role modeling, setting a good example—will not compensate for a distant dad.

The theory of intergenerational religious momentum depicted here summarizes our research results, showing how various influences throughout childhood and into young adulthood affect development of a religious orientation. For example, the data show that positive inputs on the part of a parents (such as warmth and affirmation or positive role modeling) lead to more likely transmission of faith, while negative inputs (an authoritarian style of parenting or inconsistency in role modeling) lead to a lower probability of transmission. The theory can also depict change, for example, if a father alters his authoritarian religious style, becomes a more consistent role model, or allows his child more freedom of religious choice, then the outcomes could be an increased probability of transmission. How might such change come about? What are some practical implications from these findings, for families and religious leaders who wish to encourage religious momentum across generations?

Applications: What Can Families Do?

This project started out as a traditional academic study, with hypotheses and data analyses that could be published in scholarly journals. However, what we discovered has practical implications as well—applications that can be relevant to a variety of groups.

First are families—parents and grandparents interested in the religious future of their children and grandchildren. Second are pastors, priests, rabbis, and youth leaders concerned about maintaining the continuity of their faith to younger generations. Third are scholars and researchers doing studies about youth, families, aging, and religion.

For families, these data provide suggestions about what parents could (or should not) do if they want to encourage children to follow them in their faith. These can also apply to nonreligious parents who are skeptical of organized religion but wish to give their children a foundation in moral and ethical principles the parents have found to be valuable. There is good news for concerned parents in the results from this study: *Families do matter* in determining the moral and religious outcomes of young adults, and they matter a great deal. Here are some take-away messages for parents from our research.

1. Parents have more religious influence than they think. It's easy to get the message that youth today are unresponsive to their parents' religious training. But the results of this study show that, even years later, parental religious socialization has been effective. In this the conclusions from our data are consistent with several other studies. Scott Myers analyzed data from a national sample of parents and offspring and concluded that "parents' religiosity is the primary influence on the religiosity of their adult offspring. Offspring's experiences in late adolescence and early adulthood have independent effects on religious behavior but do not diminish the effect of their family of origin."[7] John Wilson and Darren Sherkat say, "Those with strong ties to their family of origin...are less likely to drop out of church. There seems little question here that the family is a commitment mechanism for the church."[8] Mark Regnerus and Jeremy Uecker conclude that "Parent religiosity is typically the strongest predictor of both adolescent religious service attendance and religious salience . . . A high quality parent/child relationship leads to higher religiosity."[9] Or, as put most forcefully by Christian Smith and Melinda Denton:

> Contrary to popular misguided cultural stereotypes and frequent parental misperceptions, we believe that the evidence clearly shows that the single most important social influence on the religious and spiritual lives of adolescents is their parents.[10]

Thus, it may be something of a puzzle why, after all this evidence from social and behavioral science has been accumulating, hand-wringing continues about the family and its deficiencies in transmitting moral values.[11] But it may be an example of what Barry Glassner[12] calls the "Culture of Fear"—a tendency by would-be leaders to exaggerate problems, a sort of scare tactic used by those who wish to attract followers to their own position reflecting a political or religious agenda. For such alarmists, facts are of less importance than ideology.

2. *Fervent faith cannot compensate for a distant dad.* While most parents wanting to transmit their faith understand that their own examples and actions as parents are important in achieving success, some may not be aware that it is the nature and quality of the relationship they have with their child that is crucial—perhaps as much or more than what parents do or teach religiously. This might be difficult for highly religious parents to accept, since in high-boundary religious groups, such as Mormons, Evangelicals, and Orthodox Jews, living a devout life and teaching the sacred word to children is so important. However, our study indicates that relationships with parents that are felt to be close, warm, and affirming are associated with higher religious transmission than are relationships perceived as cold, distant, or authoritarian—regardless of the level of parental piety. Moreover, this is particularly true for relations with fathers.[13]

3. *Allowing children religious choice can encourage religious continuity.* This might be difficult for devoutly religious parents to accept: Encouraging freedom of choice in religion and being open to a child's religious experimentation can be effective in promoting religious continuity. Holding a

tight rein on one's children might work for some parents, at least in tight-knit religious communities where church and family activities are closely intertwined and the community is religiously homogenous. But in more open or diverse contexts with competing moral and cultural perspectives, parents who encouraged some degree of exploration while still providing a firm religious foundation have higher success rates, at least in our sample. This may seem puzzling, but we found that, in many of our high-continuity families, children who experienced freedom of choice were likely to follow their parents' religious example.

4. *Don't forget the grandparents.* Increasingly, family influences are extending beyond the nuclear family of mothers and fathers to involve grandparents and great-grandparents. Moving beyond the nuclear family in understanding sources of support and socialization is increasingly necessary.[14] For many children, grandparents are the de facto moral and religious models and teachers in lieu of parents who are too exhausted or too busy on weekends to go to church or temple. As longevity continues to expand, even great-grandparents are continuing to exert religious influence, as seen in several families in our study.

5. *Don't give up on Prodigals, because many do return.* Devout parents are often devastated to find that their children have become Religious Rebels, young adults who have rejected their parents' religious tradition and converted to another religion or dropped out altogether. But one implication of our study is this: Many Prodigals do return. In our sample, the Religious Rebels who returned to the fold had parents who waited, were open and accepting, and did not push. Many studies—including this one—have found that young adults zig and zag in their faith explorations, trying out several religious styles for size before settling into something comfortable.[15] Acceptance and affirmation, rather than judgment and preaching, are the keys.

Finally, the results of this study are also relevant to sociologists and social scientists studying the family. They suggest that most families are doing pretty well in their primary functions, which are, as American sociologist Ernest Burgess[16] said ninety years ago, to foster companionship and to raise children, providing them with the moral wherewithal to make the right decisions as adults. Intact families tend to have an easier time of this than parents who have divorced; religiously homogenous parents are more successful than parents in interfaith marriages; parents who are warm and affirming do better than those who are cold and distant; and families where grandparents reinforce the parents' religious socialization efforts succeed more than where they do not. But where any of these supports is lacking, other family mechanisms can compensate; *families are wonderfully resilient.*[17] This is one of the central messages of our study.

These findings also make contributions to family theory and the sociology of youth and religion. The model in Figure 10.1 depicts not only a summary of what we have found but also how the many religious influences that youth encounter come together to contribute to their religious identity, practices, and beliefs. We invite future researchers to expand and modify the theory with new data and new conceptualizations of family influences on religious development.

What Can Clergy and Religious Leaders Do?

The findings from this study are important not only to parents but also to religious leaders who work with families, children, and youth. Once we had results from our data, we saw they might have important implications for priests, ministers, rabbis, and other religious leaders. We were curious to find out about their own experiences in dealing with families and transmission, so we decided to conduct interviews with a number of religious leaders to get their views on family transmission of religion. We interviewed nineteen clergy and religious educators from several religious traditions: Roman Catholic, Jewish, Mainline Protestant, Evangelical and Conservative Protestant, Mormon, Unitarian, and Hindu.

It was interesting, and affirming, to hear how the interviews with these religious leaders supported what we had discovered in the analysis of our data. For example, clergy from diverse religious traditions mentioned that one characteristic of parents who successfully impart their religious beliefs to their children was *having a warm and affirming relationship* with a child. An Evangelical minister said, "They have a close relationship. The children admire the parents. They have a common emphasis on preserving family values." A Conservative rabbi said, "A supportive, nurturing relationship." A Catholic priest said:

> In my confessional I hear parents confessing about what they've done or haven't done to their teens. I hear teens confessing what they have done

or haven't done to their parents. It's a shame they can't talk to each other and confess. That's the best kind of transmission—a warm and open relationship.

Related to this was a second issue that our study showed was related to passing on the faith: *parental religious involvement* and being religious role models in church and in the home. Another Catholic priest advised, "You should take your children to church. Take them *inside* the church—not just *to* church. Say grace before meals. Say family prayers—a decade of the rosary or Bible reading as a family." One of the Mormon bishops described how the Latter-Day Saints (LDS) church encourages parental involvement: "Our church is built around parents and children being involved together in our activities. We demand a lot of time and involvement by parents, and if the parents don't do their part, the church can't do its part either."

A third theme mentioned in most of the clergy interviews was the importance of *parental consistency and warmth.* "The parents live their religious values in daily life, so there is consistency between what they do and what they believe," a Unitarian minister said. An Evangelical pastor repeated this theme: "Children won't adopt it if they see inconsistency in their parents' walk, if they [the parents] don't do as they say, if their religion is just for Sundays and not consistent through the week." Another Evangelical pastor called this "transparency": "They have a faith that holds during times of crisis and stress. If there's inconsistency, if there's hypocrisy, there's not going to be any faith transmission." A Catholic Priest said: "Dad can bring Junior to Mass every Sunday, but if Dad doesn't show Junior his love every other day of the week, he's not going to take Dad's church into his heart." So what we have seen in our research—that parents' role modeling and solidarity matter greatly—was reinforced by these priests and ministers.

Fourth, the religious leaders we talked with were very interested in our findings concerning the extent and nature of generational differences in religion. On the one hand, most of those we interviewed felt there were decided differences between contemporary younger people and those of yesterday, or between older and younger generations today. A Catholic priest noted that younger generations like to experiment more. An Evangelical pastor said youth expect to worship more informally and are much more focused on emotion. Another Evangelical talked about the "sound bite culture" of today's youth: "They have spiritual ADD. They don't sit still…They are like channel surfing, religiously." A Reform rabbi noted that young people "are all over the place. They can't settle down. But maybe I was that way too when I was nineteen?"

On the other hand, many clergy added that the similarities across generations are more significant than the differences among them. A Presbyterian minister described the differences among generations in his congregation as follows:

> They're different, but they're the same. The yearnings are the same—for meaning, for connectedness—but it's more difficult to fulfill them than it was for their parents or grandparents. Then they face such a fragmented culture—the multiple media, how they access religion, Facebook identities. Churches don't make sense to them. Then the committee structure of leadership [in churches] doesn't make sense to young people today. They form a group to get something done; they do it, then disband and regroup. So loyalty to a long-standing group doesn't make sense. But looking for meaning, purpose, relatedness—these don't change; they're just expressed differently across generations.

A Mormon bishop commented this way about generational differences and similarities and the role of the church in addressing needs of youth:

> Kids today have the same needs and hopes that kids have had for generations, and that's why the Church has set up its practices and traditions—to give structure and meaning to those needs of the spirit and body, and to channel them into holy expression. That's been the same [for generations].

Similarly, a rabbi remarked that the spiritual needs of younger generations are the same but the challenge is that they are suspicious of organized religion.

> It's not like they are different in needs. These are the same as what their parents were at their age. And it's not like God is different. He still speaks to those who follow His commandments of love and justice…But [youth] are disenchanted with organizations. They say, "I'm not into this congregation thing. I worship God by myself."

A Hindu religious leader put it this way:

> The message of peace, love, justice goes across nations and age groups. It resonates with college students and their elders. Youth want that and they'll work for it—they'll put other things on hold and work for it. And it will be the same tomorrow, [for generations] after that.

Finally, our results concerning the lack of religious transmission stimulated a number of reactions from those interviewed. They were, of course, most interested in what we found about the number of parents whose children were following them in their own religious tradition, and some appeared dismayed.

Expressing the most apprehension were some Evangelical pastors and youth leaders that we interviewed. When we reported our results showed that six in ten Evangelical parents in our sample had young adult children who also identified with an Evangelical group—a percentage higher than some other religious traditions—their focus, instead, was on the 40% of Evangelicals whose children who were *not* Evangelicals. This was unpleasant news. One pastor said, "It's sad. We aren't doing as well as we should in marketing to our youth. We can't let up." Said a youth minister: "They are the lost sheep. We have to go after them since the families haven't done the job and the churches haven't done the job." A pastor said:

> Parents are up against it. There's so much worldly influence out there. There's TV, social media, pornography. Everywhere they turn there's something that runs counter to what the parents teach. So we have got to stand up for them and be strong.

The Roman Catholic priests and Mainline Protestant ministers might have had the greatest cause for alarm; in our sample, only four in ten Catholic parents had young adult children indicating they were Catholic, and for Mainline Protestants the figure was just three in ten. Nevertheless, surprisingly few of the Mainline Protestant ministers expressed dismay, citing the desirability of "authenticity...finding a faith of one's own," as a Methodist pastor put it. In discussing our findings, an Episcopal priest said,

> You have a group of young people in your sample that you call the Prodigals. We have lots of them in our churches. They drift away in high school. After

they finish college and marry and have a baby, they return. Give them time. And maybe it's not good for people to just "inherit" religion unquestioningly. It's got to become theirs.

A Unitarian minister sounded a similar theme: "We expect [our young people] to go out. We want them to experiment and choose and find what's spiritually authentic for them. And we have a number of fourth-generation U-U's [Unitarian-Universalists] in our congregation, people who say, 'My great-grandparents in Iowa were U-U's.' They have returned." An Episcopal Priest said, "We're not in a popularity contest. Our church lost the 'Country Club Episcopalians' several decades ago. So those who are still here are really committed."

Reflecting on what we have found in our study, as well as these interviews with religious leaders, I think there are some practical implications for religious organizations—four ideas that ministers, priests, rabbis, and religious educators should consider as programs for enhancing intergenerational transmission of faith in their communities.

1. Focus on the family as a unit—much more than most congregations do today. If churches want to retain the next generation, they must not ignore families and strengthening connections across generations in their programming. Unfortunately, most churches ignore this, without even realizing it They may have programs they call "intergenerational," but these involve bringing together individuals of different ages—children, youth, adults, older adults—not parents and *their* children, grandparents and *their* grandchildren. Most churches have a vast array of religious education programs for groups segregated by age— Sunday school classes, youth groups, singles' gatherings, mothers' groups, couples' groups, seniors' groups—but very few focused on strengthening families across generations. Thus in a typical congregation there are many generation-segregated programs and few generation-integrated programs. The findings of our study suggest there is a need to focus on whole families and on strengthening intergenerational bonds, something that few of the Catholic, Mainline Protestant, and Evangelical ministers we interviewed mentioned being an objective in their congregational programming.

The most successful programs fostering intergenerational connections and the nurturing of families have been instituted by Mormons, of which a prime example is their Family Home Evening on Monday nights. The

LDS parents and bishops we spoke with attributed the success of their faith in religious transmission to activities such as this that integrate family and faith and emphasize family growth and development. They have certainly been successful—in our sample, for example, eight out of ten Mormon parents share with their young adult children affiliation with the Mormon faith.

2. *Take a long-range view.* A second message to religious communities concerned about youth is this: Don't panic. It's important to consider the generation effects we describe in chapters 1 and 2, and differences between age groups should be placed within the context of broader cultural trends that involve spirituality and religion over time. Clergy should be reminded that historically religious intensity has ebbed and flowed ant that this has been particularly evident among youth. The present era of a lower rate of church affiliation and participation may represent a temporary dip over time. Several decades ago, a similar drop in church attendance and religious observance occurred; this was in the 1960s, corresponding to the early Baby Boomers' entry into young adulthood. But this gave way to resurgence of religious observance in the following decades, composed in part by Boomers returning to church. This may well be the case in the future. The next decade or the decade after that may bring a resurgence of interest in organized religious groups and religious traditions, perhaps in an effort to regain the sense of community that may have been lost in today's highly individualized society.

3. *The younger generation does grow up.* Consider what gerontologists call aging, or life cycle, effects: Today's youth will not stay young for long. The seemingly diverse religious expressions seen among teens and twenty- to-thirty-somethings may change in the course of their lives as they grow up and grow older. For some young adults, a return to their religious tradition occurs when they marry; for others this happens with the birth of children or later on, with the onset of the empty nest, grandparenthood, or retirement or even later, with aging-related challenges concerning health or the death of a spouse.[18] If church seems irrelevant to a nineteen-year-old, that might change for her as she becomes a mother of school-age children or a seventy-three-year-old widow when the social support of a congregation may become increasingly important. Some Prodigals return, even if many years later.

4. Religious renewal has often been sparked by generational innovation. There is another way to view the story of "discontinuity" in religious transmission: the possibilities for religious revival or reform because of young adults' critiques and departures. Several clergy we interviewed did not seem troubled about the youth they saw switching from the religious tradition of their parents and grandparents. They reframed this behavior not as rejection but as religious "innovation." They described ways in which young adults are changing the practice and interpretation of religion through their attempts to find more meaningful forms of religious expression. As a Mainline Protestant minister we interviewed put it:

> Christianity today has lost its appeal for many [youth]. That's because Christian churches are too caught up in the past, in doctrinal wars about beliefs that few people except for the pastors and priests care about. All the kids are doing is trying to get us back to the real Christian message. They are calling us to return to the gospel *of* Christ, because the gospel *about* Christ that we've been preaching has too much emphasis on organizations and "right" beliefs.

At least for some religious leaders, the fact that some children do not inherit the same religious affiliation, practice, and belief of their parents can be a good and welcome thing. They see today's young people as searching. Traditional religious institutions need to adapt and change if they are to stay relevant and have meaning. Some religious groups are already responding to the calls for reform on generational lines. Within the Catholic community several unsponsored groups of youth have formed recently.[19] One is a liberalization movement to reform church doctrine and governance to give greater choice for individual conscience, to liberate women from what many consider to be second-class citizenship in the church, and to make church polity less authoritarian. Another, from an entirely different direction, has been named "dynamic Orthodoxy." These youth call themselves "hard-core Catholics" and call for a return to centuries-old Catholic traditions, preferring pre-Vatican II liturgy and music.

Among Protestant progressives, the plea for reform has been very public and sometimes divisive. Former Episcopal Bishop John Shelby Spong's 1998 book, *Why Christianity Must Change or Die,*[20] became a rallying cry for reforms involving the ordination of women as priests and bishops, the ordination of gays and lesbians, and the consecration of gay marriages. Not surprisingly, this led to a backlash by those opposed to these innovations, led primarily by older members of the Episcopal, Presbyterian, Methodist, and Lutheran communities who left and formed their own, more Evangelically oriented churches following in what they perceived as the true tradition of their faith.

Within the Evangelical Christian community as well there has been change led primarily by younger church leaders. The Emerging Church Movement developed rapidly during the last decade. Often called simply "Emergent," it is a voluntary, loosely organized, social network-dependent initiative whose mission is to revitalize Christianity for the contemporary world. It represents a sort of neoevangelical critique that, as noted by sociologist Gerardo Marti,[21] reflects three reformative concerns: (a) rescuing the church from bureaucracy, such as from CEO-type ministers; (b) rescuing the church from right-wing politics, such as opposition to environmental protections; and (c) rescuing the church from denominational barricades. Emergent Christianity appears to be growing rapidly, particularly among Millennials and Generation Xers. In 2010, 724 Emergent Church groups were active in forty-six states, linked together by websites and blogs. Emergence often takes an ecumenical approach, making overtures outside Protestantism to Catholics, Muslims, Jews, Buddhists, and Hindus. Leaders in the Emerging Christians Movement such as Brian McLaren have become well known for their media appearances and books.[22] Though the movement's foundations represented a critique of Evangelicalism, particularly the politicization of Evangelicals by the extreme right, it critiques Christianity for its simplistic views of gaining a heavenly salvation; oppressive anxieties about sexual morality; judgmental stance toward other Christians and to non-Christian religion; and apathy toward social justice issues such as gender inequality, race relations, and environmentalism. It should come as no surprise that the majority in the Emerging Church Movement are individuals between the ages of eighteen to thirty-five.

Continuity and Change

In conclusion, as we look back over the findings of our study, the message we see about religion across generations concerns both continuity and change. This should be taken as good news by religious families as well as religious leaders. There are important and enduring expressions of religion and spirituality that are carried from one generation to another, but there is also innovation and development. This is how religious expression changes and this is how it can remain vital through time.

It follows that clergy and families should recognize that young adults can be, and are, catalysts of religious reform and rejuvenation. Departing from the family religion may not be revolution or rebellion—it may be restoration, as was discussed by several of the ministers and rabbis quoted above. Then, in another round of the cycle of generations, these youthful reformers can teach their children about a more loving, just, and joyful faith, spirituality, and a religion that they will in turn transmit to their own children.

APPENDIX | Research Methods And Procedures Of The Study

T HIS APPENDIX PROVIDES a summary of the social science procedures used in this research. First is a description of the methods used in the quantitative study using data from thirty-five years of longitudinal surveys from 1970 to 2005. Then we discuss procedures in the qualitative study, in-depth interviews conducted in 2005–2008 that led to the family case studies summarized throughout the book.

The LSOG Survey Data, 1970 Through 2005

Overview

The Longitudinal Study of Generations (LSOG) began in 1970 as a cross-sectional study with 2,044 respondents, members of 358 three-generation families consisting of Generation (G) 1 grandparents, their G2 middle-aged adult children and spouses, and their G3 teenage or young adult children. The study design was unique because respondents were related to each other on the basis of family membership, so we could link parent–child, grandparent–grandchild, sibling, and spousal relationships.[1] Though it eventually became a thirty-five-year longitudinal study, the research initially was intended as a one-time survey of generational differences and similarities and their consequences for mental health. With a grant funded by the National Institute of Mental Health to Vern Bengtson (then a second-year assistant professor), data collection was carried out 1970–1971. Later, in 1985, a grant from the National Institute on Aging provided support to turn the cross-sectional study into a longitudinal panel, collecting data from these families at three-year intervals (though there was a five-year span between the 2000 and 2005 surveys). Beginning in 1991, the G4 great-grandchildren were enrolled in the study as they turned sixteen. Across the thirty-five years of the study, more than 3,500 family members have participated in the LSOG.

The LSOG has focused on issues pertinent to family development, particularly the consequences of intergenerational relationships for the physical and psychological health and well-being of family members. The surveys also contain a wide array of questions related to attitudes, beliefs, and values, as well as work, occupational status, and economic well-being—questions that have been repeated at each wave of data collection. The resulting longitudinal and grandparent–parent–grandchild-great-grandchild data enable the study of individual and family lives in the context of the profound social and historical changes occurring over the past several decades.

The Baseline (1970) LSOG Sample and Response Rates

The sampling frame was identified via a multistage stratified random sampling procedure from the population of 840,000 individuals enrolled in southern California's largest health maintenance organization (HMO). Our objective was to locate a sample of three-generation family members in which a grandchild was between sixteen and twenty-six years old. From the HMO's 1965–1968 membership rolls we were able to identify 59,000 male HMO members age fifty-five or older with a spouse enrolled, as these were the most likely to be potential grandfathers. From these we randomly selected one in six names. We sent these individuals a letter inviting them to be part of our multigenerational family study and asking if they had grandchildren between the ages of fifteen and twenty-six; if so, we requested their names and addresses, as well as those of their parents. This was in the days before computerized medical records, and many of the HMO's files were years out of date. More than 3,500 of our mailings were returned by the U.S. Post Office indicating that no one by that name was at this address or returned by relatives saying the respondent had died or was incapacitated. Almost the same number did return the inquiry survey but said they had no grandchildren in the sixteen- to twenty-six-year-old age range. We did not hear back from another large group of individuals, though we sent up to four letters to nonrespondents before giving up. The pool of eligible responses that resulted, after tabulating the information received from grandfathers about their spouses, children, and grandchildren, was composed of 3,168 individuals in three generations. Of the 2,044 who returned the survey, 73% lived in southern California: almost all of the grandparents, 65% of the middle-aged parents, and 62% of the adolescent or young adult grandchildren. Four percent of the total lived outside of the United States.

Why didn't we design the study to be based on a nationally representative sample? Today, almost all surveys involve samples designed to represent the population of the United States of America. Such surveys are conducted by telephone using computer-assisted, random-digit long-distance dialing with tens of thousands of survey marketing professionals trained to carry out interviews. But in the late 1960s, when we started the LSOG, this approach was a long way off in the future. It was before computerized random-digit long-distance dialing technology was available, so nationally representative samples were rare in sociological research because of the extremely high cost of recruiting participants by door-to-door canvassing of potential respondents. The strategy we took—that of sampling from a known population such as a large health plan and collecting data with mail-out/mail-back questionnaires—was the accepted method for conducting sociological survey research at the time. The LSOG surveys were sent out in waves, by generation. The response rate for the first wave was 65% (2,044 out of 3,168). This is comparable to similar surveys conducted today: The National Survey of Youth and Religion response rate was 57% for the first wave[2]; the first wave of the Faith Matters survey was 53%[3]; and the National Survey of Families and Households had a response rate of 74%.[4] While response rates for mail-back surveys like the LSOG are generally lower than for face-to-face or telephone interviews, telephone data collection methods have become less reliable today with the higher rates of cell phone use and declining use of landline telephones, which makes determining the sample base more difficult. For these reasons, the response rate and reliability of the LSOG surveys are reasonable in comparison with comparable surveys.

Initial Sampling Frame and Representativeness

How far can we generalize the results of the LSOG surveys? Because the original sample was drawn in 1969 from the membership of a large health plan serving the southern California region, other social scientists have raised concerns about how representative it is of the regional population and how generalizable the results might be to the American population as a whole. The issue has arisen particularly with regard to minority representation, since there are so many more nonwhites in southern California today compared with the late 1960s. Because we have stayed with the same families over the thirty-five years and have not altered our sample (aside from adding new spouses and the great-grandchildren in these families), these population changes in ethnic composition do not show up in our tables and figures. We have taken the issue of nonrepresentativeness bias seriously. In a recent reanalysis of the original sampling frame conducted by Merril Silverstein, we detected some selection bias, but less than anticipated. In 1970 African Americans were about the same proportion in the LSOG as in the U.S. Census (5.2% vs. 7.3%). Hispanics were underrepresented by about half (7.2% in the 1970 LSOG sample vs. 14.7% in the relevant regional census data in 1970). The LSOG sample was somewhat better educated than the census population in 1970, with a larger proportion having completed high school and a year or two in college, and it also contained fewer individuals at the lowest level of education (none to 8th grade) than the regional 1970 census data. There was a higher proportion of males in the LSOG sample (49.6% males vs. 47.6% in the region), reflecting the study's oversampling of grandfathers.

The demographic differences between the LSOG and the regional census data in 1970 reflect the high representation of labor union members in the health plan population. Health plan membership was one of the major benefits that had been negotiated by labor unions in the 1950s. Many of these men were retirees from the region's large steel plants that opened during World War II, while others were union members in the entertainment industry. Unfortunately, few people of color had been members of craft labor unions in southern California before the 1970s, so blacks and particularly Hispanics were under-represented in the LSOG. Thus the resulting sample consisted mostly of white, working-class and middle-class individuals and their families. Nevertheless, levels of income and levels of educational attainment in the sample turned out to be relatively consistent with 1970 regional census statistics.[5]

Over time, the demographics of southern California have changed substantially, primarily because of immigration from Mexico, Central America, and Asia. But because the focus of the LSOG was on multigenerational *families* as they changed or remained stable over time, and new families were not added to the original sample, the racial and ethnic composition of the LSOG has remained more or less the same, with a 7% minority, as what it was in 1970. This is because the purpose of a longitudinal study is to start with a certain group of individuals (or families) at one point of time and follow them to see change or stability in characteristics over time. One cannot add new groups into the study and achieve exact longitudinal time for comparison. Although the LSOG has been criticized for not having enough minority families represented, we have completed studies on the intergenerational connections in minority families in our sample; in another publication we discuss how race and ethnicity affect religious transmission in the African American, Hispanic, Asian, and white ethnic families in our study.[6]

Longitudinal Sample and Response Rates

In 1985 the study became a longitudinal panel study of aging families when funding became available from the National Institute on Aging. Data were then collected every three years. The numbers and ages of participants in each wave of the LSOG cross-classified by generation and gender are presented in Table A.1.

The eligible sample in subsequent waves of the LSOG has included all family members who were eligible at baseline (even if they did not respond at Wave 1), with the following adjustments. Over the eight waves, participants were lost through death or dementia ($n = 783$), if they had divorced a G3 lineage member and had no G4 children ($n = 33$), or if they could not be located after the fourteen years between Wave 1 and Wave 2 ($n = 423$). There also have been family additions to the original eligible sample, including new spouses (e.g., when young adult G3s married); in order to collect data from both parents of the G4s; and, most significantly with Wave 4 in 1991, to add the great-grandchildren (G4s, $n = 610$) of the original grandparents as they reached sixteen years of age. When G4s marry, we also include their spouses, potential parents of G5s, whom we hope to include in the longitudinal study sometime in the future.

The LSOG has had high longitudinal participation rates since 1970, considering the age of the original respondents, the duration of the study, the use of self-administered surveys, and the gap between Wave 1 and Wave 2. The longitudinal response rate has averaged 74% between survey waves since 1985. This is comparable to other recent panel studies. For example, in the second wave of the National Survey of Youth and Religion, the retention rate was 77%, making the combined overall response rate for Waves 1 and

TABLE A.1 Cross-Sectional LSOG Sample Sizes by Generation and Gender, Wave 1 (1970) to Wave 8 (2005)

		Wave 1 (1971)		Wave 2 (1985)		Wave 3 (1988)		Wave 4 (1991)		Wave 5 (1994)		Wave 6 (1997)		Wave 7 (2000)		Wave 8 (2005)	
		n	Age	n	Age	n	Age	n	Age	n	Age	n	Age	n	Age	n	Age
G1:	M	266	68	91	80	64	81	44	83	28	85	16	88	8	89	6	94
	F	250	66	130	77	111	80	93	83	75	85	45	87	32	89	20	92
G2:	M	322	46	243	60	239	62	250	65	216	68	198	70	187	73	164	77
	F	379	42	313	56	329	59	307	62	318	65	308	68	278	71	255	74
G3:	M	385	20	226	33	315	37	406	40	300	43	303	46	304	49	315	53
	F	442	19	328	33	425	36	461	39	408	42	389	45	410	48	396	52
G4:	M	—	—	—	—	—	—	82	20	139	21	206	24	324	24	280	28
	F	—	—	—	—	—	—	116	20	198	21	259	24	356	24	330	28
Total		2044		1331		1483		1759		1682		1724		1899		1766	

2 over 45%[7]; for Wave 3 it was 77%, with a combined Wave 1–Wave 3 response rates of 44%.[8] In the Putnam and Campbell Faith Matters survey, the response rate for the second wave was 62%.[9] We think it is remarkable how many respondents have continued to fill out and return the twenty-six-page surveys over the thirty-five years of the study. Relevant to study, the number of G2s who returned surveys in 1970 and 2005 is 343, over 66% of the original Wave 1 participants after one subtracts those who are known to have died. For the G3s the number is even higher: $n = 418$, or 79% of Wave 1 participants net of those who have died. Incidentally, for the 2005 survey we initiated an online survey for G3s and G4s, which increased response rates for young adult males.

Attrition Bias over Longitudinal Waves and Methods for Correction.

The LSOG has collected data over a long period of time, and, as in any longitudinal study, there have been losses in the sample over time (attrition) due to deaths, individuals dropping out of the study or moving away without providing forwarding addresses, and so on. This creates problems for longitudinal studies of missing data. We have employed a variety of statistical techniques to quantify potential distortions in the dataset that might be created by sample attrition. These have been reported in detail elsewhere.[10] To summarize, we examined reasons that surveys were not completed and estimated a series of logistic regressions to determine which factors predicted attrition from one wave to the next. Results suggested that there was a tendency for older respondents, males, ethnic minorities, and those with lower education to exit the study. We then examined attrition causes and consequences using Maximum Likelihood Estimation (MLE), with the assumption that data were "missing at random" (MAR).[11] The MLE approach offers a practical way to use all information collected, account for every family configuration, and increase the power of model comparisons.[12] The results of the analyses indicate that any attrition bias effects that could be detected were small.

We analyzed data from all respondents, including those who provided partial data, and used this procedure to impute full information from them.[13] This produced considerably better growth estimates than analyzing only information from respondents with complete data. In addition to the MLE approach described above, we have employed the Heckman two-stage method to correct for sample selection bias over time by first estimating the probability of attrition for members of the baseline sample and then weighting the participating sample by this probability.[14]

Generalizability of LSOG Results

As noted above, the fact that the LSOG is based on a regional sample has led to questions concerning the generalizability of findings. Thus a central concern of the study has been to examine its external validity—that is, the degree to which it is possible to generalize findings beyond the regional sample. We have examined this is by comparing LSOG responses to national norms on key family measures developed by the LSOG (e.g., data reflecting the family solidarity model) when used with nationally representative samples and examining the degree to which they are the same. For example, we compared our sample distributions on the solidarity variables to those from the National Survey of American Life (NSAL) at the University of Michigan.[15] The NSAL is a large, nationally representative study of more than 6,000 individuals whose purpose is to examine psychological distress, coping, help-seeking, and social resources among African Americans, white non-Hispanic Americans, and African Caribbeans. The NSAL survey includes questions on family solidarity replicated from the LSOG. To assess generalizability through comparing response distributions, we extracted the white non-Hispanic portion of the sample to match the ethnic profile of the LSOG and compared measurement properties of short versions of the solidarity–conflict scales, which are historically the most analyzed constructs developed by the LSOG. For example, parents were asked about their feelings toward a target child, and the child's feelings toward mother and father, on two constructs: affectual solidarity and intergenerational conflict. Each is represented by a scale with high internal reliability. The affectual solidarity scale is comprised of five items directed toward parents: how well you understand this child, how well this child understands you, how well you get along with this child, how the communication is between you and your child, and "in general, how close do you feel toward this child?"

As shown in Table A.2, in both the LSOG and the NSAL the five items of the solidarity–conflict scale loaded on two factors representing the positive or affectual aspect of the parent–child relationship (feeling close, getting along, understanding) and the negative or conflictual aspect (disagreeing, arguing, criticizing). This held true for all combinations, including parent–child, child–mother, and child–father reports. Cronbach's alpha coefficients show that in both the LSOG and the NSAL the two scales are similarly reliable, supporting the measurement adequacy of these LSOG items on a nationally representative sample. For example, the alpha reliability coefficient for the solidarity report of the parent toward the child is .913 in the 2000 LSOG and .922 in the 2002 NASL.

TABLE A.2 Cronbach's Alpha Reliability for Affectual Solidarity and Conflict Scales*, Parents Asked About Child and Child Asked About Parents

	LSOG[a]	NSAL[b]
Affectual Items		
Parent → Child	0.913	0.922
Child → Mother	0.908	0.918
Child → Father	0.901	0.908
Conflict Items		
Parent → Child	0.776	0.893
Child → Mother	0.744	0.836
Child → Father	0.794	0.884

*Shorter versions
[a]Longitudinal Study of Generations
[b]National Survey of American Life

Replication is another important indicator of the generalizability of findings from any given survey. Relationships between variables identified in the LSOG have been replicated in studies using other datasets. For example, the "intergenerational stake" phenomenon—that parents, compared to their children, tend to view their joint relationship more positively and report higher levels of intergenerational solidarity[16]—has been found using the LSOG measures in a U.S. national sample,[17] a U.S. regional sample,[18] and a Canadian sample, with similar results.[19] The constructs comprising intergenerational solidarity have been used in a Japanese sample,[20] a Welsh sample,[21] a five-nation European study,[22] and a Chinese sample.[23] Similarly, patterns and consequences of intergenerational solidarity have been replicated in studies based on regional samples in the United States, including in urban Boston,[24] rural Iowa,[25] the rural southeast,[26] and three additional nationally representative samples.[27] Thus these data indicate that conclusions concerning family relations and processes based on data from the LSOG appear to be robust across a variety of diverse samples, geographically and ethnically, as well as for nationally representative U.S. samples. One can therefore have considerable confidence that the results reported from the LSOG are general, not unique to this particular sample, and thereby applicable to broader populations.

The LSOG provides researchers a unique dataset in studying families. Not only does it include data from members in linked family generations over time, but it also reflects a "whole family" design, including lateral family members (siblings, spouses, and in-laws). It has been continually replenished with younger generation family members. This feature allows for a "generation-sequential"[28] longitudinal design, such that individuals of the same chronological age but of different birth cohorts, born a generation apart, can be compared to parcel out age, period, and cohort effects.

The Qualitative Study of Families and Religious Transmission

The three-year surveys of the LSOG provided much information over the years about the religious orientations and practices of respondents and the degree to which they are shared by other family members. However, survey data provide only limited understanding of *how* and *why* intergenerational relationships are maintained or not maintained over time. We were interested in knowing how religious traditions, beliefs, and practices are maintained across generations in some families while limited to a single generation in others. We designed an in-depth qualitative study of individuals and families across generations to examine these issues. Below we describe the qualitative methods and procedures.

The Family Interview Sample

For the qualitative study, our research team conducted interviews with 156 family members from 25 of the multigenerational families represented in the LSOG. We

TABLE A.3. Characteristics of the Qualitative Interview Sample

GENERATION	NUMBER	YEAR OF BIRTH (RANGE)	AVERAGE AGE AT INTERVIEW	PERCENT FEMALE
G1 (Great-grandparents)	6	1909–1915	95.3	100
G2 (Grandparents)	32	1919–1935	77.7	53
G3 (Parents)	57	1945–1964	54.5	59
G4 (Grandchildren)	62	1967–1988	29.3	54

selected these families and the individuals within them so as to reflect a wide spectrum of family characteristics and religious backgrounds. Our criteria for selecting the sample of families from the LSOG panel included religious affiliation (we wanted to include a variety of religious traditions), their degree of religious involvement (from highly religious to religiously indifferent), degree of family solidarity (families with high conflict as well as high cohesion), and race/ethnicity. (We wanted the sample to be as diverse as possible.) We started sampling by choosing those families in which a member of the oldest generation (grandparents [G1s] in the original 1970 LSOG survey) was still alive and able to be interviewed. Ultimately, we were able to interview only six of these G1s, all born between 1909 and 1915, all great- or great-great grandparents. All of these G1s have died since we interviewed them, so we are fortunate to have their perspectives included in the study. We interviewed descendants of these six G1s family heads, and four generations of an additional nineteen families we selected from the LSOG. Table A.3 displays the average age at the time of interview and birth years for each generation in the interview sample.

We attempted to represent a range of religious affiliations in the interview sample. This did not result in the selection of uniformly "Catholic" or "Evangelical" multi-generational families, because of religious "switching" across generations, but it did help us achieve our goal of religious diversity. Based on what individuals reported in their interviews, and using the religious tradition classification system developed by Steensland et al. (2000), the religious tradition profile of the interview sample compared to the most recent LSOG survey (2005) resulted in the distribution shown in Figure A-1.

Although purposive in its sampling design, the interview sample is by and large representative of the LSOG sample as a whole in terms of religious traditions, although some religious minority groups are intentionally overrepresented. In comparing the interview and LSOG survey samples, we see that 17% of the interview sample affiliates with the Evangelical Protestant tradition, which is close to the 20% in the 2005 survey sample. The interview sample has about the same representation of Mainline Protestants and Catholics as the LSOG sample (both between 12% and 14%). In order to enhance religious diversity, we oversampled Mormon and Jewish families. Mormons ended up comprising 14% of the interview sample compared to 6% of the LSOG. (They represent

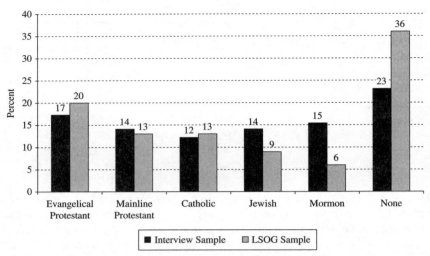

FIGURE A-I Religious Traditions Represented in the Interview Sample and the LSOG 2005 Survey Sample

Excludes "other" religious traditions

about 2% of the national population.) Jews made up 13% of the interview sample and 9% of the LSOG (2% nationally). The "nones" comprised a somewhat lower proportion of the interview families (23%) compared to the LSOG survey sample (36%, with about 19% in the American population).

The Interview

The research team developed and refined the interview schedule over the course of two years, conducting pilot interviews to test multiple iterations of interview questions. The interview guide covered the following areas:

1. Individual/demographic characteristics
2. Family relationships and traditions
    a. Family background
    b. Family traditions
    c. Family ethnic heritage
3. Values and religion
    a. Grandparental influences on religion
    b. Parental influences on religion
    c. Perceptions of value similarities/differences across generations
    d. The role of religion in one's childhood
    e. Role of religion and spirituality in one's life today
4. Concluding questions

The interviews were semistructured, allowing the interviewer to probe for details and ask for clarification about each individual's recollection of his or her family history. Interviews were conducted between November 2005 and January 2009, with the majority occurring between January 2007 and August 2008. The interviews varied in length from 45 minutes to almost 3 hours; they averaged 90 minutes.

Analytical Strategies

The team of researchers coded transcribed interviews using a detailed line-by-line approach to identify themes or concepts embedded in each sentence. This painstaking process helped to identify common themes and subthemes across individual interviews and families and resulted in a codebook that was grounded in the data. The primary coding categories focused on (a) family roles and relationships; (b) traditions, practices, and experiences; (c) values and beliefs; (d) transmission; and (e) challenges, crises, and turning points. We used Atlas.ti, qualitative data analysis software, to assist in the coding process. Unlike many qualitative studies, in which individuals are connected primarily by a shared experience or issue (e.g., a study of Mormon converts or of young adults who had switched from childhood religious affiliations), this project was complicated by the fact that individuals in the study were related to each other. This created complex coding challenges, since a daughter's recollections of her father's efforts to pass on his religious beliefs had to be linked to the father's interview account of the same. Furthermore, we were analyzing "whole" families, not just groups of discrete individuals, each of whom represented a family.

From an initial review of the data we developed an overview of the major themes we found to be related to the transmission of religious values. We used these themes as lenses through which to view the data from each of the twenty-five families in our sample as we developed family "case studies." Creating the family case studies required a shift in focus away from the individual respondent's data and the individual level of analysis to the data from the person's family members and thus the family as the level of analysis. As we compared and synthesized the interview data from all members in a given family, we focused on family's experiences with the following issues: (a) intergenerational solidarity or conflict (including parenting style and the role of grandparents); (b) the impact of marriage, divorce, and remarriage on religious transmission; (c) religious education; (d) cohort similarities and differences; (e) siblings and within-family variation; (f) race, ethnicity, and culture; (g) high-boundary religious communities such as Mormons, Jews, and Evangelical Christians; (h) nonreligion, the nones (unaffiliated, atheists, agnostics, secularists); (i) Religious Rebels, Zealots, and Prodigals; and (j) personal situations such as health, illness, addiction, family disruption, and the religious consequences or antecedents. These major analytic themes turned out to be so useful that they became the topics of chapters in this book.

The family case studies relied primarily on analyses of the transcribed interviews and field notes, but we also took advantage of our access to the LSOG surveys collected over thirty-five years, which included data from family members we were not able to interview. The written responses to open-ended questions in the survey (e.g., about disagreements or disappointments experienced with a child, parent[s], grandparent[s], and a grandchild) provided useful additional information about the connections between extended family members. Reviewing surveys from several time waves and from many relatives helped us to better understand continuity and changes in the family over time.

Statistical Procedures.

The procedures used for the data analyses in this volume are intentionally descriptive and nontechnical, because we wanted to keep the presentation of data accessible to all types of readers. We have assessed religious similarity between parents and their children (or grandparents and their grandchildren) by testing the significance of inter-generational differences in religiosity using cross-tabulations (percentages) and correlations. These allow results to be easily communicated to the nontechnical reader through familiar bar graphs.

TABLE A.4. Factors Associated with Parents' Influence on Young Adult's Composite Religiosity Measure, 1970 and 2005

	1970 G2-G3			2005 G3-G4		
	1	2	3	1	2	3
Parent's composite religiosity score	0.62***	0.63***	0.62***	0.60***	0.55***	0.54***
Parent's age		0.07	0.07		−0.07	−0.07
Parent's gender (1=female)		0.03	0.01		0.05	0.05
Parent's education		−0.06	−0.05		−0.004	−0.01
Child's age		−0.08	−0.07		0.08	0.10
Child's gender (1=female)		0.13***	0.13***		0.04	0.03
Child's education		−0.004	−0.02		−0.08	−0.08
Child married		0.07	0.06		0.22***	0.22***
Closeness to Parent			0.11**			0.08
Adjusted R^2	0.39***	0.41***	0.42***	0.36***	0.42***	0.42***
R^2 Change		0.03**	0.01**		0.07***	0.005

Note: Standardized coefficients
*p<.05. **p<.01. ***p<.001.

One research question was whether parent–child similarity in religiosity had changed between 1970 and 2005. Another was whether there had been a significant change in grandparent–grandchild similarity in religiosity between 1970 and 2005. To conduct statistical tests of difference, we created a database linking data collected from parents and their young adult children in both 1970 and 2005. The 1970 data was from G2 parents and their G3 children; the 2005 data was from the same G3s, now middle-aged parents, and their G4 children. We constructed a similar database for examining grandparent–grandchild religious similarity in 1970 and 2005.

In structuring the parent–child dyadic databases, we paired parents with "unique children." This means that if children have more than one sibling in the sample, one or more could be paired with a common parent in the sample. This creates an overrepresentation of some parents in dyads when there are multiple children who are respondents in the study (as occurred in slightly over one-third of the cases), resulting in a "multiple parent" used in more than one dyad which presents the potential for statistical attenuation.

TABLE A. 5. Factors Associated with Grandparents' Influence on Young Adult's Religiosity Using a Composite Measure, 1970 and 2005

	1970 G2-G3 (n = 474)			2005 G3-G4 (n= 167)		
	I	2	3	I	2	3
Grandparent's composite religiosity score	0.30***	0.32***	0.31***	0.29***	0.25**	0.25**
Grandparent's age		-0.04	-0.02		0.04	0.05
Grandparent's gender (1=female)		-0.02	-0.01		0.09	0.08
Grandparent's education		0.01	0.02		-0.005	-0.02
Child's age		-0.04	-0.02		-0.15†	-0.14
Child's gender (1=female)		0.12**	0.12**		0.14†	0.13†
Child's education		-0.04	-0.04		-0.13	-0.12
Child married		0.02	0.01		0.20*	0.20*
Closeness to Grandparent			0.15***			0.07
Adjusted R^2	0.09	0.10	0.12	0.08	0.12	0.12
R^2 Change		0.02	0.02***		0.08*	0.005

Note: Standardized coefficients
† $p <.10$, *$p<.05$. **$p<.01$. ***$p<.001$.

However, we tested this extensively in earlier research with the same data using a similar sampling procedure and found no significant increase or decrease in predictability.[29] In this study we replicated all the analyses of religious similarity reported in this volume with "unique parent and unique child" dyads—that is, only one child per parent, and, if there was more than one or two children per family in the study (or only one parent), the remaining child/children or parent was deleted from the analysis. We found no significant difference in the results, so we used the "unique dyad" approach, which was an advantage because it increased statistical power. The same strategy was followed in constructing the grandparent–grandchild dyads.

In the initial analyses comparing parent–child or grandparent–grandchild similarity in religiosity we used correlations as a measure of similarity or transmission. For parent-child and grandparent-grandchild similarity in religious tradition, we used cross-tabulation procedures and chi-square statistics. To describe significant differences in the degree of parent–child and grandparent–grandchild congruency in religiosity between 1970 and 2005, two statistical tests were employed: Fisher test of difference between two independent samples and Pearson's chi-square tests.

For correlational analyses of change in religiosity between 1970 and 2005, we calculated Fisher's z statistics based on the difference between the two correlations and the size of each of the samples. The resulting z-score indicates whether the difference in correlations between the parents and children, or grandparents and grandparents, between 1970 and 2005 is significant. Also calculated were the Fisher's z statistics and p values for the differences between close and not close parent–child correlations. To assess differences in parent-child and grandparent-grandchild similarity in religious tradition between 1970 and 2005, we used Pearson's chi-square tests of differences. We use these tests primarily in chapters 3, 4 and 5.

In addition, we used,[30] hierarchical regression procedures to assess intergenerational influence, using the young adult's religiosity scores as the outcome variable, while controlling for possible covariates. Regression analyses were run in Mplus 4.0, using full information maximum likelihood (FIML) to adjust for missing data. We used robust standard errors to adjust for the family-level dependency among cases. The coefficients, reflecting parent–child and grandparent–grandchild influence on young adults' religiosity, controlling for a variety of demographic controls, produced the same results as reported in the figures in chapters 3, 4, and 5. We reproduce the regression tables here. Table A.4 shows factors associated with parents' influences on young adult children's composite religiosity scores, 1970 to 2005. Table A.5 summarizes factors associated with grandparents' influence on grandchildren's religiosity.

In Table A.4 we assess the degree to which the parents' religiosity predicted the young adult's religiosity, controlling for variables such as the parents' age, gender, and education, as well as the child's age, education, and marital status. Here we have combined the four religiosity measures that have been reported separately throughout this book into a composite religiosity score, analyzing 1970 and 2005 survey data. As can be seen, at both time points the parents' religion was a significant predictor (in 1970 standardized coefficients = 0.62, p<.001; in 2005 = .054, p<.001). This provides support for presenting the unstandardized coefficients in the figures depicting intergenerational effects in chapters

3 and 4: even after controlling for other factors, there is significant parental influence on young adults' religiosity. Moreover, the degree of such influence is much the same in 2005 as it was in 1970. One thing should be noted concerning the effect of parental warmth (solidarity) on intergenerational religious influence, as discussed in chapter 4. According to Table A.4 this was not significant in 2005. However, this table as a composite analysis combines both mothers and fathers. When analyzed separately, the effect of fathers' warmth (as perceived by the young adult) is highly significant though that of mothers' is not. This provides additional support to the conclusions in chapter 4 about "parental piety does not compensate for a distant dad."

Table A.5 summarizes whether the grandparents' religiosity score predicts the young adult's religiosity score, controlling for variables such as the grandparents' age, gender, and education, as well as the grandchild's age, gender, education, and marital status. At both time points the grandparents' religion was a significant predictor (1970 standardized coefficients = 0.31, p<.001; 2005 = .025, p<.01). Thus, after controlling for other factors, there appears to be a significant grandparental influence effect on young adults' religiosity, and that the degree of such influence was much the same in 2005 as it was in 1970—as reported in chapter 5.

NOTES

Preface

1. A retrospective review of these research themes and a personal reflection on a long and happy academic career can be viewed in Bengtson (2011).

2. So far in this preface I have been using the first-person singular pronoun. This may be misleading, since this project has been a collaborative research effort with Dr. Norella Putney and Dr. Susan Harris, along with a team of students and colleagues. Thus, elsewhere in the book I use the plural "we." At the same time, this has been a very personal project—and book—for me, and when giving opinions of interpretations, as in the preface and the conclusion, I use the first-person singular to make this clear.

3. Lewis (1955).

Chapter 1

FAMILIES OF FAITH: CHALLENGES TO CONTINUITY

1. In the 1960s the idea of a "generation gap" became not only a preoccupation of the mass media but also the subject of much scholarly debate as youthful Baby Boomers marched at the forefront of cultural, political, and religious movements involving civil rights, student rights, the war in Vietnam, and the sex-and-drug "counterculture." Each was viewed with alarm by most of the adult establishment; in the last book published before her death, one focusing on culture and religion, anthropologist Margaret Mead said, "Youth today are not rebelling against their parents. They're abandoning them." (Mead, 1970, p. 12). For a discussion and review of the empirical literature on generational differences in the 1960s' "Decade of Protest" see Bengtson (1970), Bengtson, Furlong & Laufer (1974).

2. Bellah, Madsen, Sullivan, Swindler & Tipton (1985).

3. Putnam (2000). The phrase Putnam coined, "bowling alone," had to do with a small town in which the center of community life and social interaction since the 1950s had been a bowling alley in which local bowling leagues engaged in friendly competition

each night of the week. However, by the late 1990s when Putnam studied the town, the bowling leagues and the flurry of social contact they generated had gone out of fashion, the victims, Putnam argued, of an increasing tide of individualism. Instead, Putnam encountered a solitary individual who was, in place of the groups that had populated the bowling alley in earlier years, "bowling alone."

4. For data cited here on changes in family structure since World War II see Casper & Bianchi (2002), Cherlin (2010).

5. For a review of the scholarly debate about "family decline" in American society see Bengtson (2001).

6. Popenoe (1993). A family demographer, Popenoe became affiliated with the Family Research Council, a conservative Christian group promoting traditional family forms, and an articulate spokesperson in the "family values" debates of the 1990s. He is particularly well known for his writings on absent fathers and the role they play in family problems (Popenoe, 1996).

7. Arnett (2004), p. 174.

8. Vitz (1998), p. 1.

9. Coontz (1992).

10. Myers (1996), p. 864.

11. Smith & Denton (2005), p. 261.

12. For useful reviews of trends in American church membership and participation see Chavez (2011), Wuthnow (1988, 2007), Putnam & Campbell (2010), and Warner (2005).

13. Chavez (2011, pp. 86–87). Data based on self-reported denominational affiliation by General Social Survey respondents, 1972–2008.

14. See Stack (2012b). However, see also Stack (2012a), which places the rate of Mormon growth closer to 18% in the United States from 2000 to 2010, rather than the 45.5% often reported based on Church records. That is, LDS Church growth rates are lower based on nationally representative surveys of individuals, than they are from Church records.

15. Pew Forum on Religion & Public Life (2012).

16. Roof (1999).

17. For excellent overviews of religious trends during the latter decades of the twentieth century see Roof (1993, 1999), Wuthnow (1999, 2007), and Putnam & Campbell (2010). Warner (2005) provides an excellent analysis of what he calls "disestablishment and diversity" in American religion. For a discussion of post–World War II developments in the Evangelical and conservative Christian traditions see Hunter (1987), Barna (1994).

18. Roof (1999).

19. Wuthnow (1998, 2007).

20. Fuller (2001); Heelas, Woodhead, Seel, Szerszynski & Tusting (2004); Greer & Roof (1992).

21. Arnett & Jensen (2002), p. 467.

22. The term "emerging adults" is used increasingly in the social sciences to describe the age period from the late teens through the mid- to late-twenties. This was introduced by adolescent psychologist Jeffery Arnett (2004). He argues that this term is preferable

to others such as "late adolescence," "young adulthood," "transition to adulthood," or even "youth." Smith & Snell (2010) endorse the "emerging adult" label in reporting the third wave of Smith's monumental National Survey of Youth and Religion (when their respondents were age eighteen to twenty-three): "That is because, rather than viewing these years as simply the last hurrah of adolescence or an early stage of real adulthood, it recognizes the very unique characteristics of this new and particular phase of life. The features marking this stage are intense identity exploration, instability, a focus on self, feeling in limbo or in transition or in between, and a sense of possibilities, opportunities, and unparalleled home. These are often accompanied...by large doses of transience, confusion, anxiety, self-obsession, melodrama, conflict, disappointment, and sometimes emotional devastation" (p. 6). In this volume we use the terms "emerging adults" and "young adulthood" interchangeably when we refer to the G4s (great-grandchildren) in our four-generation study. These range in age from nineteen to thirty-five with an average age of about twenty-eight.

23. Cherlin (2010), p. 65.
24. U.S. Census Bureau (2008).
25. Raley & Bumpass (2003).
26. Martin (2006).
27. Martin et al. (2009).
28. U.S. Census Bureau (2008).
29. The terms "youth movements" and "generational consciousness" were often mentioned in the 1960s and 1970s (Bengtson, 1970), whereas they are absent in today's media. Emerging adults today are certainly less visible politically than youth were then. During the 1960s' "decade of protest", "the political activism of college students and twenty-somethings' political activities changed the course of their lives, with consequences seen for several decades afterward" (Dunham & Bengtson, 1992). We see little that is similar in the way of youth movements today, either in culture or in politics. Today's emerging adults have not challenged existing cultural forms—music, dance, lifestyle, education—in the same way as the Early Boomers did forty and fifty years ago.
30. See Beaudoin (1998), Rabey (2001), Barna (1994).
31. Fuller (2001), Wuthnow (1998), Greer & Roof (1992). For the nonreligious see Zuckerman (2011).
32. For a discussion of Moral Therapeutic Deism as an emerging religious orientation among American teenagers see Smith & Denton (2005), Heft (2006). For observations about the moralistic, practical, and doctrine-lacking religious views of young adults see Hersh (1998), Carrol (2002), Flory & Miller (2000).
33. For an examination of religious participation in early adulthood, with a focus on age and family life cycle effect on church involvement see Stolzenberg, Blair-Loy & Waite (1995).
34. Wuthnow (2005), p. 110.
35. Dean (2010b). For a thoughtful journalistic account of the background of the OMG generation see Zernike (2009).
36. Dean (2010a), p. 24. Dean's term, "worshiping at the church of benign whateverism," is wonderfully evocative of the theological innocence shown by young adults in several current studies, such as Smith and Denton (2005).

37. Dyck (2010).

38. Kinnaman & Lyons (2007).

39. Flory & Miller (2008).

40. Merritt (2007).

41. Hayes (2007).

42. Roof (1993).

43. Roof (1999).

44. Wuthnow (2007).

45. Wuthnow (2007), p. xvii.

46. Putnam & Campbell (2010), p 137.

47. Dornan (2004), p. 137.

48. Arnett (2004), p. 187.

49. Bourdon (2000), Mellaart (1967).

50. This has been conceptualized as the "contract between generations" (Bengtson, 1993): The older generation gives birth to, nurtures, and brings up the younger generation, who in turn takes care of the older generation in its declining years. Such a generational contract seemed to have worked at the family level, when life expectancy was forty, fifty, perhaps sixty-five years; but today, when in industrial societies life expectancies exceed eighty years and economic responsibility for elders has been transferred from families to societies, can such a contract be maintained? This is a concern that sufaced relatively recently, in the late 1980s. It quickly became a highly partisan political issue that involves a "generational equity" debate. While it may be, as Bengtson argues, a phantom issue raised by some politicians to attack government welfare spending, it will continue to resonate with those who feel old people are receiving too much in the way of government "entitlements" to the expense of younger age groups. That the younger age groups will inevitably grow older and therefore be entitled to receive similar benefits--unltess the level of such benefits is consideralbly reduced–seems to be reasoning that is lost on such partisans.

51. See Edgell (2006) for a review of religion and family in the context of changes in American society recently.

52. The life course theoretical perspective is economically summarized in Elder, Johnson & Crosnoe (2003). For an application of the life course perspective to families and the life course see Bengtson, Elder & Putney (2006).

53. The classic example is sociologist Glen Elder's (1975) groundbreaking study of "Children of the Great Depression" where he used data from the Berkeley and Oakland longitudinal studies of child development. Begun in the late 1920s by the University of California-Berkeley's Institute for Human Development and continued into the 1990s, these studies documented that historical (period) effects had an impact on individuals' development (aging effects) that lasted long into their adult life and made those born before the Great Depression different from those born at its beginning (cohort effects).

54. "Longer years of linked lives" is increasingly important because delayed elder mortality has resulted in significant benefits to families, including a greater "safety net" of support, more grandparental help and financial assistance for grandchildren, and a higher degree of stability, security, and continuity for grandchildren (see Bengtson, 2001).

55. An exception is the superb analysis of life course trajectories in religion using the longitudinal Berkeley study data by Dillon & Wink (2007).

56. To be valid, any study of religious transmission should be based on data from at least two generations—that is, with information collected from both parents and children. Prior to the present study, however, there have been few investigations that have done this; in the vast research literature on parent–child relationships almost all rely on reports from one generation, either the parent or the child, about the quality of their relationship or the style or frequency of their interaction. One exception is a study by Myers (1996), who used a 1980–1992 longitudinal dataset to provide an interactive model of religious inheritance. He found that three sets of variables aid the transmission of religiosity: parental religiosity, quality of the family relationship, and traditional family structure. Another study reporting data from both adolescents and parents in a nationwide sample is by Bader & Desmond (2006) using 1995 and 1996 Adolescent Health data. They conclude that parents who model religious behavior by attending church frequently and who ascribe high importance to religion have more highly religious children.Several older studies used parent–child dyads or triads but the sample were taken from particular religious groups and their sizes were small (Clark, Worthington & Danser, 1988; Dudley & Dudley, 1986; Hoge, Petrillio & Smith, 1982; Pearce & Thorton, 2007). Nevertheless, these studies (from the days before social research enjoyed as generous funding as today) offer important insights about the role of parent-child relationships in religious transmission.

57. Throughout this book, names and other identifying details have been altered in order to maintain the confidentiality and anonymity that we promised our respondents.

Chapter 2:

RELIGION AND SPIRITUALITY ACROSS GENERATIONS

1. Using "generation" to mean an age group located in history has its problems, since the most common use of the term is to identifying family structural relationships: grandparents, parents, and grandchildren are distinct generations in a lineage. However, in the 19th century social historians began using the term to identify age groups involved in social change--the "new generation" fomenting the 1872 revolution, for example. Recently religious scholars have used generational terms to identify changes in American religious life. Several decades ago Roof (1993) suggested that Baby Boomers' generation was leading a trend away from religious institutions toward a more fluid and personal spirituality. Wuthnow (2007) brought the generations-as-religiously -unique argument forward by contrasting the religious "patchworks" characterizing in Generation X with the religious orientations of their Baby Boomer predecessors. In this book we will try to be clear when we mean "generations" in the sense of an age grouping (as in this chapter) or as a position in a family's lineage (G1, G2, G3, G4).

2. In the interview component of our study, based on the 25 families who were selected from the 350 or so families in the larger longitudinal sample of families, the number of interviews in each of the seven age groups is as follows. The World War I (WWI) generational cohort ($N = 6$) consists of the Generations (Gs) in the LSOG survey. G2s are members of the Depression Era ($N = 21$) and silent generation ($N = 14$). The G3s are the older and younger Baby Boomers ($Ns = 39$ and 15, respectively); G4s are Gen

Xers ($N = 41$) and Millennials ($N = 21$). The G1s/WWI cohort in the Longitudinal Study of Generations (LSOG) spans from 1890 to 1915; those in the interview subsample were born between 1909 and 1915. Due to the sampling parameters of the LSOG—participants must be at least sixteen to participate—the Millennials in the LSOG and interview samples were born between 1980 and 1988. Other attempts to define the age range of the millennial generation vary, extending the end to those born in 1991 (Pew Research on Social & Demographic Trends, 2010) or even 2000 (Howe & Strauss, 2000). For more details about the sampling procedures and religious affiliations represented in the twenty-five families see the Appendix.

3. Smith & Denton (2005).

4. One possible explanation for the similarity between these two cohorts (Depression Era and Later Boomers) in calling themselves "spiritual but not religious" is that of intergenerational transmission. This may be the case. One-half of the Later Boomers in the interview sample have parents who were born during the Depression Era; the parents of the remaining half were members of the silent generation.

5. Smith & Denton (2005).

6. The Pew Forum on Religion & Public Life (2008) reports much higher rates of "religious unaffiliated" and "other Christian" among thirty- to forty-nine-year-olds, who bridge the Gen X and Later Boomer generations.

7. Smith & Denton (2005).

8. Smith & Denton (2005).

9. Wuthnow (2007), p. 14.

Chapter 3

HAS FAMILY INFLUENCE DECLINED?

1. We appreciate the assistance of Merril Silverstein, Gary Horlacher, and Jessica Lendon in the data analyses reported in this chapter.

2. Pew Forum on Religion & Public Life (2008).

3. In this figure we report unstandardized correlations between parents' and young adult children's responses; all are statistically significant at the $p < .001$ level. In other analyses, we also used hierarchical regression to predict whether the parents' religiosity score predicted the young adult's religiosity score, controlling for variables such as the parents' age, gender, and education, as well as the child's age, education, and marital status. We combined the four religiosity measures into a composite religiosity score and compared the 1970 and 2005 data. We found that at both time points the parents' religion was a significant predictor (in 1970 standardized coefficients = 0.62, $p < .001$; 2005 = .054, $p < .001$). We can be confident, then, that even after controlling for other factors, there is a significant parental influence effect on young adults' religiosity, and that the degree of such influence is much the same in 2005 as it was in 1970. The regression model results are presented in Table A-4 in the Appendix.

4. For each dimension, Fisher statistical tests of differences between 1970 and 2005 in the parent–child correlations (z-transformed values) were not statistically significant ($t < 1.96$). Another test involved examining overlap of 95% confidence intervals

(CIs) for both the unstandardized and standardized coefficients; these provided the same results: Unstandardized 95% CI = 1970 (0.59, 0.74); 2005 (0.51, 0.73). Standardized 95% CI = 1970 (0.54, 0.68), 2005 (0.46, 0.66).

5. See Wuthnow (2007) and Putnam & Campbell (2010).

6. Smith & Denton (2005).

7. Chavez, (2011)

8. We grouped the over 100 specific denominations reported by our respondents into these general religious traditions following a well-known procedure used in survey research developed by Steensland et al. (2000). However, we separated out Mormons, Jews and nones are part of Steensland et al.'s categorization because of their importance in some of our analyses.

9. Pew Forum on Religion & Public Life (2008) and Chavez (2011).

10. It should be noted further that the similarity or dissimilarity between parents and children who identify themselves as "Jewish" often does not reflect religious beliefs or practices. Jewish identity is expressed as religious Judaism, cultural Judaism, or both, as is discussed in chapter 10. Some highly religious parents have children who have rejected their Jewish religion, though they keep rituals like bar mitzvahs that celebrate Jewish culture and identity and despite not being religious they reply they are Jewish when asked "What is your religion?"

11. Pew Forum on Religion & Public Life (2008).

12. For comments on the growth of atheist organizations on college campuses, see Zuckerman (2011).

13. See Pew Forum on Religion and Public Life (2008).

14. Wuthnow (2007).

15. For data on the decline in church attendance over time, see Hout & Fischer (2002), Wuthnow (2007), Putnam & Campbell (2010), Chavez (2011).

16. The scale reliability (Cronbach's alpha) of two items measuring a literal interpretation of the Bible is .88 in 2005 and .87 in 1970, indicating that they are measuring the same underlying concept.

17. The scale reliability (Cronbach's alpha) of the two items measuring civic religiosity is .82 in 2005 and .72 in 1970.

Chapter 4

THE IMPORTANCE OF WARMTH: PARENTAL PIETY AND THE DISTANT DAD

1. Thanks to Petrice Oyama for her contributions to this chapter and to Dr. Gary Horlacher for his assistance in analyzing the data.

2. Smith & Denton (2005); Hoge, Petrillo & Smith (1982).

3. Acock & Bengtson (1978), Putney & Bengtson (2002).

4. For the model of intergenerational value socialization used as the basis for a theory of religious transmission developed in chapter 10, see Bengtson, Biblarz & Roberts (2002). For the attachment theory that is one basis for the intergenerational solidarity model, see Bowlby (1988).

5. Bengtson, Biblarz & Roberts (2002).

6. The original conceptualization and measurement of the intergenerational solidarity model is described in Bengtson, Olander & Haddad (1976); Bengtson & Schrader (1982). For an updated version of the model, including the addition of conflict as a dimension, see Bengtson, Giarrusso, Mabry & Silverstein (2002). The theoretical and conceptual base of intergenerational solidarity is most fully discussed in Roberts, Richards & Bengtson, 1991. The solidarity model has been criticized by Connidis & McMullin (2002) and the concept of "intergenerational ambivalence" has been proposed as an alternative conceptualization. However, subsequent empirical analyses have demonstrated that the solidarity and ambivalence are not opposite constructs; rather, intergenerational ambivalence can be seen as the intersection of solidarity *and* conflict (Bengtson, Giarrusso, Mabry & Silverstein, 2002; Silverstein, Gans, Lowenstein, Giarrusso & Bengtson, 2010).

7. For an analysis of parent–child similarity in values such as individualism–collectivism and their intergenerational similarities, see Bengtson (1975). This examination is based on the Wave 1 (1970) survey and examines parent–child as well as grandparent–grandchild value similarity.

8. For examples of how parent–child closeness is related to intergenerational influence on educational and occupational achievement values see Bengtson, Biblarz & Roberts (2002). Acock & Bengtson (1980) examine how the similarity *perceived,* or attributed, by parents to children or children to parents compares to the actual similarity between parents and found considerable variance. This suggests that asking parents to rate their similarity in values and opinions to their children, or vice versa, as has been done in most survey research, probably leads to a biased estimate. The "intergenerational stake" hypothesis indicates that parents consistently overestimate the similarity of their mutual relationship, while their children consistently underestimate this similarity (Giarrusso, Stallings & Bengtson, 1995). Thus there is often a bias on the part of one generation compared to another in describing their joint relationship.

9. For each dimension of religiosity in 2005, Fisher tests of difference in similarity (correlations, transformed to z values) between parents perceived as close versus not close were statistically significant (Z score). For religious intensity, $z = 3.86$ ($p < .001$); for religious participation, $z = 5.65$ ($p < .001$); for Biblical literalist beliefs, $z = 2.99$ ($p < .01$); and for civic religiosity, $z = 4.56$ ($p < .001$).

10. The "intergenerational stake" hypothesis was presented in the first empirical paper published using Longitudinal Study of Generations data. The term that was used in the literature at that time was the "developmental stake" (Bengtson & Kuypers, 1971).

11. For data supporting the intergenerational stake hypothesis—that parents tend to overestimate and their children tend to underestimate the closeness of their mutual relationship, even when measured across a twenty-year time period—see Giarrusso, Stallings & Bengtson (1995). Support for the intergenerational stake hypothesis has been consistent throughout the thirty-five years of survey data collection in this study, as well as in studies by other investigators, for example Ward & Spite (1996), Thompson et al. (1985), Marshall (1995),

12. For religious traditions overall, there is a significant difference in parent–child congruence (similarity) between parents perceived as close versus not close. Where the

relationship is reported as close, 65% of parents have children who share their religious tradition, while for relationships that are not close, 52% of parents have children with the same religious tradition (chi square = 10.8 [$df = 1$], $p < .01$).

13. Fathers and children who have a close relationship are significantly more similar in their religious tradition than fathers and children whose relationship is not close (chi square = 9.7 [$df = 1$], $p < .01$); for mothers and their children, there is not a significant difference between a close and not close relationship in the similarity of their religious tradition (chi square = 2.5 [$df = 1$]. $p = .11$). For religious participation, fathers and children with a close relationship are significantly more similar than fathers and children whose relationship is not close (chi square = 8.7 [$df = 1$], $p < .01$). For mothers and children, there is not a significant difference between a close and not close relationship in the degree of parent–child similarity (chi square = .8 [$df = 1$], $p = .11$). We find the same patterns for Biblical literalist beliefs. Fathers and children who have a close relationship are significantly more similar in Biblical literalism than fathers and children whose relationship is not close; while for mothers and their children, there is not a significant difference between a close and not close relationship in the similarity of their Biblical literalist beliefs. Mothers and children who have a close relationship are significantly more similar in their religious intensity than mothers and children whose relationship is not close (chi square = 6.6 [$df = 1$], $p < .05$), while for fathers and children, there is not a significant difference between close and not close relationship in their religious intensity (chi square = 1.3 [$df = 1$], $p = .248$).

14. This may reflect a finding from *How Families Still Matter* (noted above) that absent fathers have less influence on their children's values. In the earlier study, "absence" referred specifically to divorced fathers who had less contact with their children (Bengtson, Biblarz & Roberts, 2002). In this case, it may reflect the perceived quality of the relationship between an adult child and an emotionally absent father, who is less likely to transmit religious values and traditions than an emotionally close father.

15. This may be related to the notion that Jewish identity is passed down through the mother, especially within more Orthodox Jewish traditions. In other words, in order for a child to be considered Jewish, his or her mother must be Jewish. Therefore, the mother–child relationship may play a greater role for Jews than for other religious groups.

16. We want to remind readers throughout the volume of the limits on generalizing from these findings, since the survey is based on a southern California sample of three-generation families drawn in 1969 and it simply is not known how similar or different it would be to a nationally representative sample of three-generation families drawn in 2010. See chapters 1 and 2 and the Appendix for a discussion of characteristics of the Longitudinal Study of Generations longitudinal study procedures and the sample.

17. "Ideal types" in sociological terms do not imply a normative valuation; one type is not "better" than another. Furthermore, each ideal type necessarily reduces complexity in order to make sense of extraordinarily complex relationships. That is, "warm" and "affirming" parents certainly experience conflicts with their children, and "strained" parents can be loving and affirming, though preoccupied or ineffectual. We use the ideal

type as a conceptual tool to identify and understand the key dimensions of parent–child relationships that affect religious transmission.

Chapter 5

THE UNEXPECTED IMPORTANCE OF GRANDPARENTS (AND GREAT-GRANDPARENTS)

1. We are grateful to Merril Silverstein, Jessica Lendon, Petrice Oyama, and Frances Nejat-Heim for their contributions to this analysis. In other analyses, we used hierarchical regression procedures to identify factors associated with grandparents' influence on young adult grandchildren's religiosity (Bengtson, Lendon, Putney, Harris & Silverstein, 2012). A summary of this analysis is presented in Table A-5 of the Appendix.

2. For more extensive documentation of the argument that grandparents play a more important role in the lives of more grandchildren than in earlier periods of American history see Bengtson (2001), King & Elder (1999), Mueller & Elder (2003), Uhlenberg (2005).

3. Uhlenberg (2005); Silverstein, Giarrusso & Bengtson (2003).

4. Silverstein, Giarrusso & Bengtson (2003); King & Elder (1999). It is important to note that the relationship between grandparent and grandchild develops and changes over time, as empirically documented with LSOG data by Silverstein & Long (1998).

5. Swartz (2009), Szinovacz (1998).

6. American Association of Retired Persons (2012).

7. Pratt & Fiese (2004); Silverstein, Giarrusso & Bengtson (2003).

8. King & Elder (1999).

9. U.S. Census Bureau (2009).

10. Erickson (1950).

11. U.S. Census Bureau (2009), Pew Forum on Religion & Public Life (2009), Pew Research on Social & Demographic Trends (2010).

12. The first collection of research-based articles on grandparenthood was published only a little over two decades ago, in Bengtson and Robertson (1985).

13. For each dimension of religiosity, Fisher tests of difference in grandparent–grandchild similarity (correlations, transformed to z values) in 1970 compared to 2005 were not statistically significant. For religious intensity, $z = -0.6$ ($p > .10$); for religious participation, $z = 1.1$ ($p > .10$); for Biblical literalist beliefs, $z = -.09$ ($p > .10$); and for civic religiosity, $z = -0.5$ ($p > .10$). In addition, we used hierarchical regression to assess whether the grandparents' religiosity score predicted the young adult's religiosity score, controlling for variables such as the grandparents' age, gender, and education, as well as the grandchld's age, gender, education, and marital status. We found that at both time points the grandparents' religion was a significant predictor (1970 standardized coefficients = 0.31, $p < .001$; 2005 = .025, $p < .01$). We can be confident, then, that even after controlling for other factors, there is a significant grandparental influence effect on young adults' religiosity, and that the degree of such influence is much the same in 2005 as it was in 1970. The results of the regression model data are presented in Table A-5 in the Appendix.

Chapter 6

1. Thanks to Joy Lam who assisted in the research for this chapter.
2. Data reported are from the Pew Forum on Religion & Public Life (2008).
3. Regarding the data shown on the bars of these tables regarding interfaith marriage by religious tradition the percentage reflects an averaged sum of father–child and mother–child similarity rates.
4. Xu, Hudspeth & Bartkowski (2005).
5. Pew Forum on Religion & Public Life (2008).

Chapter 7

INTERRUPTIONS IN RELIGIOUS CONTININUITY: RELIGIOUS REBELS, ZEALOTS, AND PRODIGALS

1. Thanks to Frances Nedjat-Haiem, Thien-Huong Ninh, and Gary Horlacher for their contributions to this chapter.
2. The parable of the prodigal son is found in Luke 15: 11–32.
3. Wilson & Sherkat (1994).
4. Smith & Sikkink (2003).
5. Smith & Sikkink (2003).
6. Regnerus & Uecker (2006).
7. Sandomirsky & Wilson (1990).
8. Several studies show that a warm and close relationship toward parents is both a buffer against rebellion and a catalyst for returning to the fold. Wilson & Sherkat (1994) say that "Children who were close to their parents while in high school not only are less likely to rebel, but are more likely to return if they do so" (p. 158). Regnerus & Uecker (2006) concur: "Parents' religiosity [is a] consistent predictor of religious transformation" and is "protective against rapid religious decline" (p. 232).

Chapter 8

THE "NONES": FAMILIES OF NONRELIGIOUS YOUTH

1. See, for example, the recent surveys of the "unchurched" or "nonreligious" in the Pew Forum on Religion & Public Life (2008), in Wuthnow (2007), in Putnam & Campbell (2010), and by Baker & Smith (2009a, 2009b). For a superb review of rates and patterns of atheism, agnosticism, and belief in God across the world today see Zuckerman (2007); for an analysis of apostasy, why people who once were religious have rejected religion, see Zuckerman (2011).
2. Baker & Smith (2009a), Hout & Fischer (2002).
3. Pew Forum on Religion & Public Life (2008).
4. Pew Forum on Religion & Public Life (2008).
5. Bainbridge (2009a), p. 320.
6. Pruyser (1992), p.186.
7. For a slightly different categorization and a thoughtful commentary on the varieties of nonbelievers and "unchurched believers" see Baker & Smith (2009a, 2009b)

and Manning (2009). Cimino and Smith (2007) provide a useful examination of secular humanism, atheism, and progressive secularism in American society.

8. Vargas (2012).

9. Chavez (2011). The observation that 92% of Americans believe in God is based on General Social Survey (GSS) data from a 2008 nationally representative sample. The GSS has conducted such surveys at least every other year since 1972, and Chavez notes that, over the past twenty years, the percentage of those who say they believe in God has remained essentially constant. However, it was significantly higher in the 1950s, when 99% of Americans said they believed in God.

10. Zuckerman (2007), Chavez (2011). As Chavez notes, tracking church attendance is easier said than done, because people do not always tell the literal truth when they answer survey questions about their behavior. While the General Social Survey results indicate that 38% of Americans claimed weekly church attendance, the 2005 American Time Use Survey found that only 26% reported attending church that week.

11. Chavez (2004), Hout & Fischer (2002), Inglehart & Baker (2000).

12. There is great variation in religious beliefs around the world, according to statistics assembled by Zuckerman (2011). The percentage of nonbelievers in God varies from less than 1% in such nations as Kenya, Nigeria, Syria, and Iran to more than 40% in Finland, Germany, Norway, France, Japan, and Israel. Norris & Inglehart (2004) advance a controversial thesis to explain this variation. They argue that in societies characterized by plentiful food distribution, excellent public health care, and widely accessible housing—that is, in modernized societies—religiosity wanes. Conversely, in societies where food and shelter are scarce and life is less secure, religious belief is strong. "[L]evels of societal and individual security in any society seem to provide the most persuasive and parsimonious explanation" for belief in God (Norris & Inglehart, 2004, p. 109).

13. Wuthnow (1988).

14. Zuckerman (2011).

15. Sherkat (2010).

16. Pew Forum on Religion & Public Life (2010).

17. Edgell, Gertis & Hartmann (2006).

18. Hout & Fischer (2002).

19. Hout & Fischer (2002). Putnam & Campbell (2010) and the Pew Forum on Religion & Public Life (2008) show similar results.

20. Sherkat (2010).

21. Zuckerman (2011), p. 2.

22. Pasquale (2010).

23. Manning (2009), p. 21.

24. Caplo & Sherrow (1977), p. 300.

25. Leavy (1988), p. 201.

26. Hunsberger (1983).

27. Pasquale (2010), Bainbridge (2009b), Ben-Hallahmi (2007), Hunsberger & Brown (1984).

28. Zuckerman (2011), p. 200. Italics added.

29. Zuckerman (2011), p. 202.

30. Edgell, Gertis & Hartmann (2006).

Chapter 9

THE POWER OF COMMUNITY: FAMILIES OF MORMONS, JEWS, AND EVANGELICALS

1. Frances Nedjat-Haiem and Ernest Horstmanshoff contributed to this chapter.

2. The Church of Jesus Christ of the Latter-Day Saints (LDS) capitalizes the first letter in "Church," as in "the teachings of the Church." The same is true of many Mormon practices and rituals such as Family Home Evening and a Temple marriage. We follow that practice throughout the volume.

3. Melton (2009), Joyce (2009). For 2011 figures, see Church of Jesus Christ of Latter-Day Saints (2011). It should be noted that statistics collected by the LDS church are private and not accessible to outside investigators. This has proven frustrating to social scientists wishing to examine their reliability and validity. Some critics suggest that membership statistics, forwarded to the Salt Lake City headquarters by individual stakes and wards, are unreliable because their accuracy varies from district to district, country to country, with little regulation.

4. Today the LDS "Mutual" is known as "Young Men and Young Women."

5. Neusner (1988), p. 371.

6. Neusner (1988), p. 372.

7. Joyce (2009).

8. Mead & Hill (1990).

9. Dashefsky, Lazerwitz & Tabory (2003).

10. Marsden (1987), Smith (1998).

11. For an excellent discussion of Evangelicals and their faith see Kinnaman & Lyons (2007).

12. For statistics about the growth of Evangelicals over time and comparisons to other religious groups see Altemeyer & Hunsberger (2005), Chavez (2011), Pew Forum on Religion & Public Life (2008), Wuthnow (2007).

13. Kinnaman & Lyons (2007).

Chapter 10

CONCLUSION: WHAT WE HAVE LEARNED AND HOW IT MIGHT BE USEFUL

1. For insightful comments from Evangelicals and other religious leaders who have voiced concern about youth drifting away from their religious traditional religion, and suggestions about how to counter this trend, see Barna (1994, 1995), Dean (2010a, 2010b), Dyck (2010), Hayes (2007), Kinnaman & Lyons (2007).

2. Bengtson & Laufer (1974).

3. Bainbridge (2009a), Ben-Hallahmi (2007), Hunsberger & Brown (1984).

4. Pasquale (2010).

5. For a discussion of generations and trends in religion see Roof (1999).

6. Bengtson, Copen, Putney & Silverstein (2009).

7. Myers (1996), p. 865.

8. Wilson & Sherkat (1994), p. 158.

9. Regnerus & Uecker (2006), p. 592.

10. Smith & Denton (2005), p. 261. This comment is based on the first wave of the National Survey of Youth and Religion with data from teenagers ages fourteen to eighteen. In the second book from the project, reporting on the third wave of data collection when the respondents were four years older, Smith & Snell (2010) report the same result—that parental influence is one of the strongest predictors of emerging adults' religious beliefs and practices.

11. Arnett (2004), Vitz (1998), Senator Rick Perry quoted in *Atlantic Monthly* (2012).

12. Glassner (1999).

13. This finding is consistent with a large body of socialization theory, ranging from Freud's identification theory to John Bowlby's (1988) attachment theory and Diane Baumrind's typology of parenting styles. See Baumrind (1966).

14. Bengtson (2001).

15. Smith & Snell (2010), Pearce & Denton (2011), Arnett (2004).

16. Burgess (1911), quoted in Bengtson (2001).

17. For discussions of family resilience see Bengtson, Biblarz & Roberts (2002); Putney, Bengtson & Wakeman (2007).

18. See "Does religiosity increase with age?" (Bengtson, Silverstein, Harris, Putney & Min, 2012)

19. Garces-Foley (2010).

20. Marti (2010).

21. McLaren (2009, 2011).

Appendix

1. The first analysis using the three-generation dataset—matched parent–child and grandparent–grandchild dyads, using structural equation modeling—is reported in Bengtson (1975). This compared value orientations of individualism–collectivism and materialism–humanism across generational dyads. The results indicated very few generational differences. It should be noted that there was an earlier three-generation study in the 1960s by the pioneering family sociologist Reuben Hill (1960). Hill studied a group of families in the Minneapolis area to examine consumer behavior, family roles, and intergenerational relationships. Hill was the developer of the "family life cycle" perspective, which guided family research and theory for more than two decades.

2. Smith & Denton (2005), p. 295.

3. Putnam & Campbell (2010), p. 558.

4. Sweet & Bumpass (1996).

5. See Bengtson, Biblarz & Roberts (2002).

6. Putney, Lam, Nedjat-Haiem, Ninh, Oyama & Harris (2013).

7. Pearce & Denton (2011), p. 188.

8. Smith and Snell (2010), p. 310.

9. Putnam & Campbell (2010), p. 560.

10. See Feng, Silverstein, Giarrusso, McArdle & Bengtson (2006).

11. McArdle, 1994.

12. McArdle & Bell (2000).

13. Feng, Silverstein, Giarrusso, McArdle & Bengtson (2006).

14. Silverstein et. al. (2002).

15. Jackson et al. (2004).

16. As originally reported from Wave 1 Longitudinal Study of Generations data in Bengtson & Kuypers (1971), the "generational stake" finding has been replicated in data over twenty years later (see Giarrusso, Stallings & Bengtson, 1995).

17. Ward & Spitze (1996).

18. Thompson et al. (1985).

19. Marshall (1995).

20. Morioka et al. (1985).

21. Burholt, Wenger & Silverstein (1996).

22. Lowenstein, Katz & Daatland (2005); Silverstein, Gans, Lowenstein, Giarrusso & Bengtson (2010).

23. Silverstein, Cong & Li (2006).

24. Rossi & Rossi (1990).

25. Whitbeck et al. (1991).

26. Atkinson et al. (1986).

27. Bengtson & Harootyan (1994); Krause et al. (1992); Umberson (1992).

28. Silverstein & Conroy (2009).

29. Acock & Bengtson (1980); Bengtson, Biblarz & Roberts (2002); Glass, Bengtson & Dunham (1986).

30. For analyses using hierarchical linear regression in analyzing these data see Bengtson, Lendon, Putney, Harris & Silverstein (2012); Bengtson, Hayward & Krause (2013).

REFERENCES

Acock, A.C., & Bengtson, V.L. (1978). On the relative influence of mothers and fathers: A covariance analysis of political and religious socialization. *Journal of Marriage and the Family*, 40(3), 519–530.

Acock, A.C., & Bengtson, V.L. (1980). Socialization and attribution processes: Actual versus perceived similarity among parents and youth. *Journal of Marriage and the Family*, 42(3), 501–515.

Altemeyer, B., & Hunsberger, B. (2005). Fundamentalism and authoritarianism. In R. Paloutzian & C. Park (Eds.), *Handbook of the psychology of religion* (pp. 377–386). New York: Guilford.

American Association of Retired Persons. (2012). *Insights and spending habits of modern grandparents*. Washington, DC: AARP Research & Strategic Analysis. Retrieved November 18, 2012, http://www.aarp.org/grandparentresearch/fullreport.

Arnett, J. (2004). *Emerging adulthood: The winding road from the late teens through the twenties*. New York: Oxford University Press.

Arnett, J., & Jensen, L. (2002). A congregation of one: Individualized religious beliefs among emerging adults. *Journal of Adolescent Research,* 17(5), 451–467.

Atkinson, M.P., Kivett, V.R., & Campbell, R.T. (1986). Intergenerational solidarity: an examination of a theoretical model. *Journal of Gerontology, 41*, 408–416.

Bader, J.O., & Desmond, S.A. (2006). Do as I say and I do: The effects of consistent parental beliefs and behaviors upon religious transmission. *Sociology of Religion,* 67(3), 313–329.

Bainbridge, W.S. (2009a). Atheism. In P.B. Clarke (Ed.), *The Oxford handbook of the sociology of religion* (pp. 319–335). Oxford: Oxford University Press.

Bainbridge, W.S. (2009b). Atheism. *Interdisciplinary Journal of Research on Religion,* 1, 1–26.

Baker, J.O., & Smith, B. (2009a). None too simple: Examining issues of religious nonbelief and nonbelonging in the United States. *Journal for the Scientific Study of Religion*, 48(4), 719–733.

Baker, J.O., & Smith, B. (2009b). Studying nones: Some characteristics of the religiously unaffiliated. *Social Forces,* 87(3), 1251–1264.

Barna, G. (1994). *Baby busters: The disillusioned generation.* Chicago: Northfield.

Barna, G. (1995). *Generation next: What you need to know about today's youth.* Ventura, CA: Regal Books.

Baumrind, D. (1966). Effects of authoritative parental control on child behavior. *Child Development,* 37, 887–907.

Beaudoin, T. (1998). *Virtual faith: The irreverent spiritual quest of Generation X.* San Francisco, CA: Jossey-Bass.

Bellah, R., Madsen, R., Sullivan, W., Swidler, A., & Tipton, S. (1985). *Habits of the heart: Individualism and commitment in American life.* New York: Harper & Row.

Bengtson, V.L. (1970). The "generation gap:" A review and typology of social-psychological perspectives. *Youth and Society,* 2(2), 7–32.

Bengtson, V.L. (1975). Generation and family effects in value socialization. *American Sociological Review,* 40(3), 358–371.

Bengtson, V.L. (1993). Is the "contract across generations" changing? Effects of population aging on obligations and expectations actress age groups. In V.L. Bengtson and W.A. Achenbaum (Eds.), *The changing contract across generations* (pp. 3–24). New York: Aldine.

Bengtson, V.L. (2001). Beyond the nuclear family: The increasing importance of multi-generational bonds. *Journal of Marriage and Family,* 63, 1–16.

Bengtson, V.L. (2011). Gerontology with a "J": Personal reflections on theory-building in the sociology of aging. In R.J. Settersten & J. Angell (Eds.), *Handbook of sociology of aging* (619–626). New York: Springer.

Bengtson, V.L., Biblarz, T.J., & Roberts, R.E.L. (2002). *How families still matter: A longitudinal study of youth in two generations.* New York: Cambridge University Press.

Bengtson, V.L., Copen, C.E., Putney, N.M., & Silverstein, M. (2009). Religion and intergenerational transmission over time. In K.W. Schaie & R.P. Abeles (Eds.), *Social structures and aging individuals: Continuities and challenges* (pp. 376–408). New York: Springer.

Bengtson, V.L., Elder, G.H. Jr., & Putney, N.M. (2006). The life course perspective on ageing: Linked lives, timing and history. In M.L. Johnson, V.L. Bengtson, P.G. Coleman, & T.B.L. Kirkwood (Eds.), *The Cambridge handbook of age and ageing* (pp. 493–501). Cambridge, UK: Cambridge University Press.

Bengtson, V.L., Furlong, M.J., & Laufer, R.S. (1974). Time, aging, and the continuity of the social structure: Themes and issues in generational analysis. *Journal of Social Issues,* 30(2), 1–30.

Bengtson, V.L., Giarrusso, R., Mabry, J.B., & Silverstein, M. (2002). Solidarity, conflict, and ambivalence: Complementary or competing perspectives on intergenerational relationships? *Journal of Marriage and Family,* 64, 568–576.

Bengtson, V.L., & Harootyan, R. (Eds.). (1994). *Intergenerational linkages: Hidden connections in American society.* New York: Springer.

Bengtson, V. L, Hayward, R.D., & Krause, N.M. (2013). Parents and the transmission of religion: Variations by age, solidarity with parents, and religious tradition. Paper presented at the American Sociological Association, New York.

Bengtson, V.L., & Kuypers, J.A. (1971). Generational difference and the "developmental stake." *Aging and Human Development*, 2(1), 249–260.

Bengtson, V.L., & Laufer, R.S. (Eds.). (1974). *Special Issue: Youth, Generations, and Social Change. Journal of Social Issues*, 30(2, 3).

Bengtson, V.L., Lendon, J., Putney, N.M., Harris, S.C., & Silverstein, M. (2012). Transmission across generations: The religious influence of grandparents on young adults. 2012.

Bengtson, V.L., Olander, E.B., & Haddad, A.A. (1976). The "generation gap" and aging family members: Toward a conceptual model. In J.E. Gubrium (Ed.), *Time, roles and self in old age* (pp. 237–263). New York: Human Sciences Press.

Bengtson, V.L., & Robertson, J. (Eds.). (1985). *Grandparenthood*. Beverly Hills, CA: SAGE.

Bengtson, V.L., & Schrader, S.S. (1982). Parent–child relations. In D. Mangen & W. Peterson (Eds.), *Handbook of research instruments in social gerontology*, Vol. 2 (pp. 115–185). Minneapolis: University of Minnesota Press.

Bengtson, V.L., Silverstein, M., Harris, S.C., Putney, N., & Min, J. (forthcoming). Does religiosity increase with age? Age changes and age differences in religiosity over 35 years. *Journal of the Scientific Study of Religion*.

Ben-Hallahmi, A. (2007). Atheists: A psychological profile. In Michael Martin (Ed.), *The Cambridge companion to atheism* (pp. 300–313). New York: Cambridge University Press.

Bourdon, F. (2000). *Petra: Jordan's extraordinary ancient city*. New York: Barnes & Noble.

Bowlby, J.A. (1988). *A secure base: Parent–child attachment and healthy human development*. London: Routledge.

Burgess, E.W. (1911). *The Function of Socialization in Social Evolution*. Chicago: University of Chicago Press.

Burholt, V., Wenger, G.C., & Silverstein, M. (1996). The structure of parent-child relations among very old parents in Wales and the United States: A cross-national comparison. Paper presented at the annual meeting of the Gerontological Society of America, Washington, DC.

Caplovitz, D., & Sherrow, F. (1977). *The religious drop-outs: Apostasy among college graduates*. Beverly Hills, CA: SAGE.

Carrol, C. (2002). *The new faithful: Why young Americans are embracing Christian orthodoxy*. Chicago: Loyola Press.

Casper, L., & Bianchi, S.M. (2002). *Continuity and change in the American family*. Thousand Oaks, CA: SAGE.

Chavez, M. (2004). *Congregations in America*. Cambridge, MA: Harvard University Press.

Chavez, M. (2011). *American religion: Contemporary trends*. Princeton, NJ: Princeton University Press.

Cherlin, A. (2010). *Public and private families*. New York: McGraw-Hill.

Cherry, C., DeBerg, B., & Porterfield, A. (2001). *Religion on campus: What religion really means to today's undergraduates*. Chapel Hill: University of North Carolina Press.

Church of Jesus Christ of Latter-Day Saints. (2011). Facts and statistics. Salt Lake City, UT: Church of Jesus Christ of Latter-Day Saints, December 31. Retrieved August 10, 2012, http://www.mormonnewsroom.org/facts-and-statistics/country/united-states/.

Cimino, R., & Smith, C. (2007). Secular humanism and atheism beyond progressive secularism. *Sociology of Religion*, 68(4), 407–424.

Clark, C.A., Worthington, E.I., & Danser, D.B. (1988). The transmission of religious beliefs and practices to firstborn early adolescent sons. *Journal of Marriage and the Family,* 50(2), 463–472.

Connidis, I.A., & McMullin, J.A. (2002). Sociological ambivalence and family ties: A critical perspective. *Journal of Marriage and Family*, 64(3), 558–567.

Coontz, S. (1992). *The way we never were: The American family and the nostalgia trip.* New York: Basic Books.

Copen, C.E., & Silverstein, M. (2008). Intergenerational transmission of religious beliefs to young adults: Do grandmothers matter? *Journal of Contemporary Family Studies*, 38, 497–510.

Davey, F.A. (1994). *Believing and belonging: Religion in Great Britain since 1945.* Oxford: Blackwell.

Dashefsky, A., Lazerwitz, B., & Tebory, E, (2003). The journeys of the "straight way" or the "roundabout path:" Jewish identity in the U.S. and Israel. In M. Dillon (Ed.), Handbook of the Sociology of Religion (pp 240–260). New York: Cambridge University Press.

Dean, K.C. (2010a). *Almost Christian: What the faith of our teenagers is telling the American church.* New York: Oxford University Press.

Dean, K.C. (Ed). (2010b). *OMG: A youth ministry handbook.* Nashville, TN: Abington Press.

Dillon, M., & Wink, P. (2007). *In the course of a lifetime: Tracing religious beliefs, practice, and change.* Berkeley: University of California Press.

Dornan, P. (2004). Youth and faith in the postmodern world. In Donaldson, E.C. (Ed), *Catholic Youth at the Crossroads* (pp. 116–139). Milwaukee, WI: Paulist Press.

Dudley, R.I., & Dudley, M.G. (1986). Transmission of religious values from parents to adolescents. *Review of Religious Research,* 28(1), 3–16.

Dunham, C.C., & Bengtson, V.L. (1992). Long-term effects of political activism on inter-generational relations. *Youth and Society*, 24(1), 31–51.

Dyck, D. (2010). *Generation Ex-Christian: Why young adults are leaving the faith… and how to bring them back.* Chicago: Moody.

Edgell, P. (2006). *Religion and family in a changing society.* Princeton, NJ: Princeton University Press.

Edgell, P., Gertis, J., & Hartmann, D. (2006). Atheists as "other": Moral boundaries and cultural membership in American society. *American Sociological Review*, 71, 211–234.

Elder, G. (1974). *Children of the Great Depression.* Chicago: University of Chicago Press.

Elder, G.H., Johnson, M.K., & Crosnoe, R. (2003). The emergence and development of life course theory. In J.T. Mortimer & M.J. Shanahan (Eds.), *Handbook of the life course* (pp. 3–19). New York: Kluwer Academic-Plenum.

Erickson, E. (1950). *Childhood and society.* New York: Norton.

Feng, D., Silverstein, M., Giarrusso, R., McArdle, J., & Bengtson, V.L. (2006). Attrition of older parents in a three-decade study of multigenerational families. *Journals of Gerontology: Social Science*, 61, S323–S328.

Flory, R.W., & Miller, D.E. (2000). *Gen X religion*. New York: Routledge.

Flory, R.W., & Miller, D.E. (2008). *Finding faith: The spiritual quest of the Post-Boomer generation*. New Brunswick, NJ: Rutgers University Press.

Fuller, R. (2001). *Spiritual but not religious*. New York: Oxford University Press.

Garces-Foley, K. (2010). Finding engaged young adult Catholics. Paper presented at the annual meeting of the Society for the Study of Social Problems, Baltimore, MD, October.

Giarrusso, R., Stallings, M., & Bengtson, V.L. (1995). The "intergenerational stake" hypothesis revisited: Parent–child differences in perceptions of relationships 20 years later. In V.L. Bengtson, K.W. Schaie, & L.M. Burton (Eds.), *Adult intergenerational relations: Effects of societal change* (pp. 227–263). New York: Springer.

Gilgoff, D. (2009). Americans say no to religion but not to faith. *U.S. News & World Report*, May 6, 2009. http://www.usnews.com/news/relition/articles/2009/05/06/many-americans-are-saying-goodbye-to-religion-but-not-faith.

Glass, J., Bengtson, V.L., & Dunham, C. (1986). Attitude similarity in three-generation families: Socialization, status inheritance or reciprocal influence? *American Sociological Review*, 51, 685–698.

Glasner, B. (1999). *The culture of fear*. New York: Basic Books.

Greer, B., & Roof, W.C. (1992). Desperately seeking Sheila: Locating religious privatism in American society. *Journal for the Scientific Study of Religion*, 31(3), 356–352.

Hayes, M. (2007). *Googling God: The religious landscape of people in their 20s and 30s*. New York: Paulist Press.

Heelas, P., Woodhead, L., Seel, B., Szerszynski, B., & Tusting, K. (2004). *The spiritual revolution: Why religion is giving way to spirituality*. Malden, MA: Blackwell.

Heft, J.L. (2006). *Passing on the faith*. New York: Fordham University Press.

Hersh, P. (1998). *A tribe apart: A journey into the heart of American adolescence*. New York: Ballantine Books.

Hill, R.E. (1970). *Family development in three generations*. New York: Basic Books.

Hoge, D.R., Petrillo, G.H., & Smith, E.I. (1982). Transmission of religious and social values from parents to teenage children. *Journal of Marriage and the Family*, 44(3), 569–580.

Hout, M., & Fischer, C.S. (2002). Why more Americans have no religious preference: Politics and generations. *American Sociological Review*, 65, 165–190.

Howe, N., & Strauss, W. (2000). *Millennials rising: The next great generation*. New York: Vintage Books.

Hunsberger, B.E. (1983). Apostasy: A social learning perspective. *Review of Religious Research*, 25, 21–38.

Hunsberger, B., & Altemeyer, B. (2006). *Atheists: A groundbreaking study of America's nonbelievers*. Amherst, NY: Prometheus Press.

Hunsberger, B.E., & Brown, L.B. (1984). Religious socialization, apostasy, and the impact of family background. *Journal for the Scientific Study of Religion*, 23, 239–251.

Hunter, J.D. (1987). *Evangelicalism: The coming generation*. Chicago: University of Chicago Press.

Inglehart, R., & Baker, W. (2000). Modernization, cultural change, and the persistence of traditional values. *American Sociological Review*, 65, 19–51.

Jackson, J.S., Neighbors, H.W., Nesse, R.M., Trierweiler, S.J., & Torres, M. (2004). Methodological innovations in the National Survey of American Life. *International Journal of Methods in Psychiatric Research*, 13(4), 289–298.

Joyce, C.A. (Ed.). (2009). *The world book almanac and book of facts for 2008*. Pleasantville, NY: Readers' Digest.

King, V., & Elder, G.H. Jr. (1999). Are religious grandparents more involved grandparents? *Journal of Gerontology: Social Sciences*, 54, S317–S328.

Kinnaman, D., & Lyons, G. (2007). *Un-Christian: What a new generation really thinks about Christianity… and why it matters*. Grand Rapids, MI: Baker Books.

Krause, N., Herzog, R.A., & Baker, E. (1992). Providing support to others and well-being in later life. *Journal of Gerontology: Psychological Sciences*, 47(5), 300–311.

Leavy, S. (1988). *In the image of God: A psychoanalyst's view*. New Haven: Yale University Press.

Lewis, C.S. (1955). *Surprised by joy*. London: Routledge Kegan-Paul.

Lowenstein, A., Katz, R., & Daatland, S.O. (2005). Filial norms and intergenerational support in Europe and Israel: A comparative perspective. In M. Silverstein (Ed.), *Intergenerational relations across time and place. Annual Review of Gerontology and Geriatrics* (Vol. 24, pp. 200–223). New York: Springer.

Manning, C. (2009). Atheism, secularity, the family, and children. In P. Zuckerman (Ed.), *Atheism and secularity*. Vol. 1, *Issues, concepts, and definitions* (pp. 165–179). Santa Barbara, CA: Praeger.

Marsden, G.M. (1987). Evangelical and fundamental Christianity. In M. Eliade (Ed.), *The encyclopedia of religion*. (pp. 190–197). New York: Macmillan.

Marshall, V.W. (1995). Commentary: A finding in search of an interpretation: Discussion of the intergenerational stake hypothesis revisited. In V.L. Bengtson, K.W. Schaie, & L.M. Burton (Eds.), *Adult intergenerational relations: Effects of societal change*. New York: Springer.

Marti, G. (2010). The emerging church movement: All your questions answered (and a few more besides). Presentation at Society for the Scientific Study of Religion annual meeting, Baltimore, MD.

Martin, J., Hamilton, B.E., Sutton, P.D., Ventura, S.J., Menacker, F., Kirmeyer, S., et al. (2009). Births: Final data for 2006. *National Vital Statistics Reports*, 57(7). Retrieved May 11, 2011, http://www.cdc.gov/nchs/data/nvsr/nvsr57/nvsr57_07.pdf.

Martin, S.P. (2006). Trends in marital dissolution by women's' education in the United States. *Demographic Research*, 15, 537–560.

McArdle, J.J. (1994). Structural factor analysis experiments with incomplete data. *Multivariate Behavioral Research*, 29(4), 409, 454.

McArdle, J.J., & Bell, R.Q. (2000). Recent trends in modeling longitudinal data by latent growth curve methods. In T.D. Little, K.U. Schnabel, & J. Baumert (Eds.), *Modeling longitudinal and multiple-group data: practical issues, applied approaches, and scientific examples* (pp. 69–107). Mahwah, NJ: Erlbaum.

McLaren, B.D. (2008). *Everything Must Change: Jesus, Global Crisis, and a Revolution of Hope*. New York: Nelson.

McLaren, B.D. (2010). *Reinventing Your Church*. Grand Rapids, MI: Zondervan.

Mead, M. (1970). *Culture and commitment: A study of the "generation gap."* New York: Doubleday.

Mead, F.S., & Hill, S. (1990). *Handbook of denominations.* Nashville, TN: Abingdon Press.

Mellaart, J. (1967). *Catal Huyuk: A neolithic town in Anatolia.* London: Thames & Hudson.

Melton, J.G. (1996). *The encyclopedia of American religions* (5th ed.). Detroit: Gale/Cengage Learning.

Melton, J.G. (2009). *Melton's encyclopedia of American religions* (8th ed.). Detroit: Gale/Cengage Learning.

Merritt, C.H. (2007). *Tribal church: Ministering to the missing generation.* Herndon, VA: Alban Institute.

Morioka, K., Sugaya, Y., Okuma, M., Nagayama, A., & Funjii, H. (1985). Intergenerational relations: Generational differences and changes. In K. Morioka (Ed.), *Family and life course of middle-aged men.* Osaka, Japan: Osaka University.

Mueller, M.M., & Elder, G.H. Jr. (2003). Family contingencies across the generations: Grandparent–grandchild relationships in holistic perspective. *Journal of Marriage and Family*, 65(2), 404–417.

Myers, S.M. (1996). An interactive model of religiosity inheritance: The importance of family context. *American Sociological Review*, 61, 858–866.

Neusner, J. (1988). Judaism in contemporary America. In C.H. Lippy & P.W. Williams (Eds.), *Encyclopedia of American religious experience* (pp. 372–386). New York: Scribner's.

Norris, P., & Inglehart, R. (2004). *Sacred and secular: Religion and politics worldwide.* New York: Cambridge University Press.

Pasquale, F. (2010). A portrait of secular group affiliates. In P. Zuckerman (Ed.), *Atheism and secularity,* Vol. 1, *Issues, concepts, and definitions* (pp. 69–82). Santa Barbara, CA: Praeger.

Pearce, L.D. & Denton, M.L. (2011). *A faith of their own: Stability and change in the religiosity of America's adolescents.* New York: Oxford University Press.

Pearce, L.D., & Thornton, A. (2007). Religious identity and family ideologies in the transition to adulthood. *Journal of Marriage and Family*, 69, 1227–1243.

Pew Forum on Religion & Public Life. (2008). *U.S. religion landscape survey.* Washington, DC: Pew Forum on Religion & Public Life. http://religions.pewforum.org/pdf/report2-religious-landscape-study-full.pdf.

Pew Forum on Religion & Public Life. (2009). *Faith in flux: Changes in religious affiliation in the U.S.* Washington, DC: Pew Forum on Religion & Public Life. http://www.pewforum.org/Faith-in-Flux.aspx.

Pew Forum on Religion & Public Life. (2010). *Religion among the Millennials.* Washington, DC: Pew Forum on Religion & Public Life. http://www.pewforum.org/age/religion-among-the-millennials.aspx.

Pew Forum on Religion & Public Life. (2012). "'Nones' on the rise." Washington, DC: Pew Forum on Religion & Public Life, October 9. http://www.pewforum.org/Unaffiliated/nones-on-the-rise.aspx.

Pew Research on Social & Demographic Trends. (2010). *The return of the multi-generational family household.* Washington, DC: Pew Research on Social & Demographic

Trends. http://www.pewsocialtrends.org/2010/03/18/the-return-of-the-multi-generational-family-household/.

Popenoe, D. (1993). American family decline, 1960–1990: A review and appraisal. *Journal of Marriage and the Family*, 55, 527–555.

Popenoe, D. (1996). *Life without father*. Glencoe, IL: Free Press.

Pratt, M.W., & Fiese, B.H. (Eds.). (2004). *Family stories and the life course: Across time and generations.* Mahwah, NJ: Erlbaum.

Pruyser, P.W. (1992). Problems of definition and conceptualization in the psychological study of religious unbelief. In A.W. Eister (Ed.), *Changing perspectives in the scientific study of religion* (pp. 185–200). New York: Wiley.

Putnam, R. (2000). *Bowling alone: America's declining social capital.* New York: Simon & Schuster.

Putnam, R., & Campbell, D. (2010). *American grace: How religion divides and unites us.* New York: Simon & Schuster.

Putney, N., & Bengtson, V.L. (2002). Socialization and the family: A broader perspective. In R.A. Settersten, Jr., & T.J. Owens (Eds.), *Advances in life-course research: New frontiers in socialization* (pp. 165–194). London: Elsevier.

Putney, N.M., & Bengtson, V.L. (2006). Family change and social change: The far-reaching consequences of population aging and globalization. In C. Gomes (Ed.), *Social development and family change* (pp. 131–149). New York: Cambridge Scholar Press.

Putney, N.M., Bengtson, V.L., & Wakeman, M.A. (2007). The family and the future: Challenges, prospects, and resilience. In R. Pruschno (Ed.), *Challenges of an aging society: Ethical dilemmas, political issues* (pp. 117–155). Baltimore, MD: Johns Hopkins University Press.

Putney, N.M., Lam, J.Y., Nedjat-Haiem, F., Ninh, T.-H., Oyama, P., & Harris, S.C. (2013). The transmission of religion across generations: How ethnicity matters. In M. Silverstein & R. Giarrusso (Eds.), *Solidarity and beyond: Continuity and discontinuity between generations in an aging society* (pp. 291–313). Baltimore, MD: John Hopkins University Press.

Rabey, S. (2001). *In search of authentic faith: How emerging generations are transforming the church.* Colorado Springs, CO: Waterbrook Press.

Raley, R.K., & Bumpass, L.L. (2003). The topography of the divorce plateau: Levels and trends in union stability in the United States after 1980. *Demographic Research*, 8, 245–259.

Regnerus, M.D., & Uecker, J.E. (2006). Finding faith, losing faith: The prevalence and context of religious transformations during adolescence. *Review of Religious Research,* 47, 217–237.

Roberts, R.E.L., Richards, L.N., & Bengtson, V.L. (1991). Intergenerational solidarity in families: Untangling the ties that bind. *Marriage & Family Review*, 16(1–2), 11–46.

Roof, W.C. (1989). Multiple religious switching: A research note. *Journal for the Scientific Study of Religion*, 28(4), 530–535.

Roof, W.C. (1993). *A generation of seekers: The spiritual journeys of the Baby Boom generation.* San Francisco, CA: HarperCollins.

Roof, W.C. (1999*). Spiritual marketplace: Baby Boomers and the remaking of American religion.* Princeton, NJ: Princeton University Press.

Rossi, A.S., & Rossi, P.H. (1990). *Of human bonding: Parent–child relations across the life course*. New York: Aldine de Gruyter.

Sandomirsky, S., & Wilson, J. (1990). Processes of disaffiliation: Religious mobility among men and women. *Social Forces*, 68(2), 1211–1229.

Sherkat, D.E. (2010). Review: *What Americans really believe: New findings from the Baylor Surveys of Religion. Journal for the Scientific Study of Religion* (Rodney Stark), 49, 194–196.

Silverstein, M., Cong, Z., & Li, S. (2006). Intergenerational transfers and living arrangements of older people in rural China: Consequences for psychological well-being. *Journal of Gerontology: Social Sciences*, 61, S256–S266.

Silverstein, M., & Conroy, S. (2009). Intergenerational transmission of moral capital across the family life course. In U. Schönpflug (Ed.), *Cultural transmission: Psychological, developmental, social, and methodological aspects* (pp. 317–333). New York: Cambridge University Press.

Silverstein, M., Conroy, S., Wang, H., Giarrusso, R., & Bengtson, V.L. (2002). Reciprocity in parent-child relations over the adult life course. *Journal of Gerontology: Social Sciences, 57*, S3–S13.

Silverstein, M., Gans, D., Lowenstein, A., Giarrusso, R., & Bengtson, V.L. (2010). Older parent–child relationships in six developed nations: Comparisons at the intersection of affection and conflict. *Journal of Marriage and Family*, 72(4), 1006–1021.

Silverstein, M., Giarrusso, R., & Bengtson, V.L. (2003). Grandparents and grandchildren in family systems. A socio-developmental perspective. In V.L. Bengtson & A. Lowenstein (Eds.), *Global aging and its challenges to families* (pp. 75–102). New York: Aldine de Gruyter.

Silverstein, M., & Long, J. (1998). Trajectories of solidarity in adult grandchild–grandparent relationships: A growth curve analysis over 23 years. *Journal of Marriage and the Family*, 60(4), 912–923.

Six, B., Geppert, K., & Schönpflug, U. (2009). The intergenerational transmission of xenophobia and rightism in Germany. In U. Schönpflug (Ed.), *Cultural transmission: Psychological, developmental, social, and methodological aspects* (pp. 370–390). New York: Cambridge University Press.

Smith, C., & Denton, M. (2005). *Soul searching: The religious and spiritual lives of American teenagers*. New York: Oxford University Press.

Smith, C., & Sikkink, D. (2003). Social predictors of retention in and switching from the religious faith of family origin: Another look using religious tradition self-identification. *Review of Religious Research*, 45, 188–206.

Smith, C., & Snell, P. (2010). *Souls in transition: The religious and spiritual lives of emerging adults*. New York: Oxford University Press.

Spong, J.S. (1998). *Why Christianity must change or die: A bishop speaks to believers in exile*. New York: HarperCollins.

Spong, J.S. (2001). *A new Christianity for a new world: Why traditional faith is dying and how a new faith is being born*. New York: HarperCollins.

Stack, P.F. (2012a). Mormonism leading the way in U.S. religious growth. *The Salt Lake Tribune*, May 2. http://www.sltrib.com/sltrib/news/54026798-78/lds-religious-church-largest.html.csp.

Stack, P.F. (2012b). Change lowers Mormonism's growth rate. *The Salt Lake Tribune*, May 18. http://www.sltrib.com/sltrib/news/54036926-78/church-lds-membership-growth.html.csp.

Steensland, B., Park, J., Regnerus, M., Robinson, L., Wilcox, W.B., & Woodberry, R. (2000). The measure of American religion: Toward improving the state of the art. *Social Forces*, 79, 291–318.

Stolzenberg, R., Blair-Loy, M., & Waite, L.J. (1995). Religious participation in early adulthood: Age and family life cycle effects on church membership. *American Sociological Review*, 60, 84–103.

Swartz, P. (2009). Intergenerational family relationships in adulthood: Patterns, variations, and implications in the United States. *Annual Review of Sociology*, 35, 191–212.

Sweet, J.A., and Bumpass, L.L. (1996). *The National Survey of Families and Households—Waves 1 and 2: Data description and documentation.* Madison: Center for Demography and Ecology, University of Wisconsin-Madison.

Szinovacz, M.E. (Ed.). (1998). *Handbook on grandparenthood.* Westport, CT: Greenwood Press.

ter Bogt, T., Meeus, W., Raaijmakers, Q., van Wel, F., & Vollebergh, W. (2009). "Don't trust anyone over 25": Youth centrism, intergenerational transmission of political orientations, and cultural change. In U. Schönpflug (Ed.), *Cultural transmission: Psychological, developmental, social, and methodological aspects* (pp. 419–440). New York: Cambridge University Press.

Thompson, L., Clark, K., & Gunn, W. (1985). Developmental stage and perceptions of intergenerational continuity. *Journal of Marriage and the Family*, 47, 913–920.

Uhlenberg, P.R. (2005). Historical forces shaping grandparent–grandchild relationships: Demography and beyond. In M. Silverstein (Ed.), *Intergeneration relations across time and place* (pp. 77–97). New York: Springer.

Umberson, D. (1992). Relationships between adult children and their parents: Psychological consequences for both generations. *Journal of Marriage and the Family*, 54, 1002–1003.

U.S. Census Bureau. (2008). Table MS-2: Estimated median age at first marriage, by sex: 1890 to present. Washington, DC: U.S. Census Bureau. Retrieved May 11, 2011, http://www.census.gov/.

U.S. Census Bureau. (2009). Grandparents Day 2009: Sept. 13. Washington, DC: U.S. Census Bureau. Retrieved May 10, 2011, http://www.census.gov/newsroom/releases/archives/facts_for_features_special_editions/cb09-ff16.html.

Vargas, N. (2012). Retrospective accounts of religious disaffiliation in the United States. *Sociology of Religion*, 73, 200–223.

Vitz, P.C. (1998). Family decline: The findings of social science. In P.C. Vitz and S.M. Krason, (Ed), *Defending the family: A sourcebook* (pp. 1–17.). Steubenville, OH: Catholic Social Science Press.

Ward, R.A., & Spitze, G. (1996). Consistency of reports by coresident children and parents. Paper presented at the annual meeting of the Gerontological Society of America, November.

Warner, R.S. (2005). *A church of our own. Disestablishment and diversity in American religion.* New Brunswick, NJ: Rutgers University Press.

Whitbeck, L.B., Simons, R.L., & Conger, R.D. (1991). The effects of early family relationships on contemporary relationships and assistance patterns between adult children and their parents. *Journal of Gerontology: Social Sciences, 46,* S301–S337.

Wilson, J., & Sherkat, D.E. (1994). Returning to the fold. *Journal for the Scientific Study of Religion,* 33(2), 148–161.

Wuthnow, R. (1988). *The restructuring of American religion: Society and faith since World War II.* Princeton, NJ: Princeton University Press.

Wuthnow, R. (1998). *After heaven: Spirituality in America since the 1950s.* Berkeley: University of California Press.

Wuthnow, R. (1999). *Growing up religious: Christians and Jews and their journeys of faith.* Boston: Beacon Press.

Wuthnow, R. (2005). *America and the challenge of religious diversity.* Princeton, NJ: Princeton University Press.

Wuthnow, R. (2007). *After the Baby Boomers: How twenty- and thirty-somethings are shaping the future of American religion.* Princeton, NJ: Princeton University Press.

Xu, X., Hudspeth, C.D., & Bartkowski, J.P. (2005). The timing of first marriage: Are there religious variations? *Journal of Family Issues,* 26, 584–618.

Zernike, K. (2009). *Generation OMG. The New York Times,* March 8. http://www.nytimes.com.

Zuckerman, P. (2007). Atheism: Contemporary numbers and patterns. In M. Martin (Ed.), *The Cambridge companion to atheism* (pp. 47–65). Cambridge, UK: Cambridge University Press.

Zuckerman, P. (2011). *Faith no more: Why people reject religion.* New York: Oxford University Press. Bengtson, V.L., & Schrader

INDEX

Note: page numbers in italics refer to figures.

Christians, nondenominational, case studies, 23, 27, 37, 39, 42, 49
Christian Scientists, case studies, *14*, 15–16
church attendance. *See* religious participation
church membership. *See* religious affiliation
Church of Christ, case studies, 23
Church of Jesus Christ of the Latter-Day Saints. *See* Mormons
Church of Religious Science, case studies, 32
civic religiosity
    grandparent-child similarity, change over time, 102, *102*
    measures of, 65
    parent-child similarity, *55*, 55–56, 64–65, *65*, 66, 74, *74*, 77
clergy. *See* religious leaders
cohorts, in life course theory, 12. *See also* generations
cohorts effects, *vs.* aging effects, 191–92, 214
college
    campus atheist groups, increase in, 60
    and church attendance, 81
    Evangelical student groups, 178
    questioning of faith in, 3, 136, 148
community
    decline of, 5
    and family religious continuity, 165, 169, 171, 174, 181, 182, 190
    Millennial Generation on, 45
    as support for religious socialization, 82, 84
    World War I Generation on, 24
conservative Christians
    and Biblical literalism, transmission of, 63
    identification with political right, 149, 205
Conservative Jews
    beliefs of, 172
    movement toward Orthodoxy, 175–77
    as percentage of U.S. Jews, 172

continuity across generations . *See also* transmission; *specific affiliations*
    church programs to encourage, 202–3
    perceived decline in, 5, 6, 11, 54, 56, 185–86, 195–96
    sources of, 166–67, 167–68, 171, 172, 177–78, 181–82, 190
    strategies for encouraging, 195–98
    and transmission, influence on, *193*, 193–94
continuity across generations, failure of
    case studies, 168–71, 173–75
    causes of, 182, 190
    clergy's views on significance of, 201–2, 204
Coontz, Stephanie, 6
coping mechanism, religious faith as
    in Depression Era Generation, 25–26
    in Early Baby Boomers, 33–34
cultural boundaries, and transmission across generations, 16, 121, 166, 181, 190
cultural change. *See* social change
cultural influences, and transmission, 193, *193*
Culture of Fear, and perceived decline of transmission, 196

Dean, Kenda Creasy, 10
death of loved one, impact on faith, 35
decline of the family, perception of, 6, 184–85
denominational loyalty. *See* religious affiliation
denominations, quasi-ethnic, 142
Denton, Melinda, 7, 48, 50, 196
Depression, impact on religious beliefs, 27–28
Depression Era Generation
    definition of, 22
    historical events affecting, 28
    religious beliefs of, 25–28, 51, *52*, 191
disaffiliation. *See* Rebels, Religious
diversity, of emerging adults, 9
diversity, religious
    in emerging adults, 9–10
    Millennials' embrace of, 49–51

as refuge in times of social change, 5
and religion, connection between, 11
resilience of, 198
and transmission, success in, 184–85
families' religious continuity. *See also*
    transmission; *specific affiliations*
church programs to encourage, 202–3
perceived decline in, 5, 6, 11, 54, 56,
    185–86, 195–96
sources of, 166–67, 167–68, 171, 172,
    177–78, 181–82, 190
strategies for encouraging, 195–98
and transmission, influence on, *193*,
    193–94
families' religious continuity, failure of
case studies, 168–71, 173–75
causes of, 182, 190
clergy's views on significance of,
    201–2, 204
family closeness. *See* intergenerational
    solidarity
family interaction. *See* family solidarity
family solidarity, and successful
    transmission, 171, 179, 181, 190. *See
    also* intergenerational solidarity
family structure. *See* divorce; remarriage,
    impact on transmission; single-
    parent households
fathers. *See also* family solidarity;
    intergenerational solidarity;
    parenting style and transmission
child's preference for religion of, *116*,
    116–17
in G3, religion by affiliation, 116–17
and transmission of faith, 71, 76–79,
    77, *78*, 194
and transmission of nonreligious
    affiliation, 152
Fischer, Claude, 148–49
Flory, Richard, 10
France, religious belief in, 148
free will, Generation Xers' focus on,
    42–43

Garcia, Bernardo, 89–90, 91
Garcia, Eduardo, 40, 90–91
Garcia, Estella, 54, 89–90, 91

Garcia, Ignacio, 89
Garcia, Luis, 32, 89–90, 91, 98
Garcia, Manuel, 54, 89
Garcia, Marisol, 41–42,
Garcia family, 89–91, 97–98
gay rights, as issue, 56, 149, 177, 178,
    204–5
gender. *See also* fathers; grandfathers;
    grandmothers; mothers
    grandparental, and grandparent-child
        religious similarity, 103–4, *104*, *105*,
        219
    parental, and transmission, 76–79, *77*,
        218
    and religious affiliation, 148
    and transmission of nonreligious
        affiliation, 152
generational consciousness, 9
Generation Ex-Christian (Dyck), 10
generation gap, 1960s' decade of protest
    and, 5, 185
generations, 21–22. *See also* age cohorts;
    religious beliefs; *specific generations*
    differences and similarities in, clergy's
        views on, 199–201
    differences in, and transmission, 193, *193*
    and religious trends, 190–91
Generation X
    and church reform movements, 205
    definition of, 22
    Early Boomers as parents of, 4
    faith in science, 43–45
    and grandparents, influence of, 100
    heterogeneity of, 38–39, 44
    independent thinking in, 41–43
    nonbelievers, beliefs of, 42–45
    pragmatism of, 44
    religious believers, beliefs of, 39–42,
        44, *52*, 191
Generation Y. *See* Millennial Generation
Glasner, Barry, 196
God
    believers in, as percentage of U.S.
        population, 147
    internalization of, in Silent Generation,
        28, 29
    rejection of, in Generation X, 43–45

Millennial Generation (*Cont.*)
  definition of, 22
  and grandparents, influence of, 100
  heterogeneity of, 46, 50
  Moralistic Therapeutic Deism in, 34,
    48
  religious affiliation, decline in, 148,
    191
  religious beliefs of, 45–53, *52*
  and religious diversity, embrace of,
    49–51
  and religious education, 48–49, 50
  religious skepticism in, 46–49
  tentative, nonjudgmental perspective of,
    46–47, 49–51
  transmission failure in, 4
Miller, Don, 10
moral behavior
  family as transmitter of, 11
  religion as transmitter of, 11
  role models and, 72, 92, 143, 160, 162,
    164, 171, 181, 182, 190, *193*, 194,
    199
Moralistic Therapeutic Deism
  in Early Baby Boomers, 34
  in Millennial Generation, 34, 48
  Smith on, 34, 48
Moralistic Therapeutic Deism, 9
Mormon affiliation
  conversion to, 119, 131, 140
  transmission of, relative success in,
    152–53
Mormon Church, growth of, 167
Mormon communities, support of
    religious continuity in, 165, 171
Mormon families, interconnection of
    family and religious practices in,
    166, 167–68, 169, 171, 202–3
Mormon families' religious continuity
  case study, 168–71
  cultural boundaries and, 121, 166, 181,
    190
  relative success of, 152–53
  sources of, 165, 167–68, 181–82, 190
Mormon grandparent-child similarity,
    change over time, 103, *103*

Mormon parent-child similarity
  change over time, *58*, 59, 65
  intergenerational solidarity and, *75*, 76,
    78, *78*, 84–86, 97
  same-faith marriage and, 113
  unhappy marriage and, 122
Mormons
  age of marriage in, 122
  case studies, 16–17, 18, 31–32, 34–35,
    39–40, 41, 49, 50, 63, 71, 168–71
  conception of religion in, 26–27
  cultural *vs.* religious identification in,
    59
  Family Home Evening, 166, 167, 169,
    202
  as high tension affiliation, 133
  interfaith marriage among, 114
  intergenerational bonds, programs to
    encourage, 202–3
  membership, changes in, 7
  missions of, 84, 167, 169
  as parents of nonreligious persons, 152,
    152
  Prodigals, 141–42, 143
  as relatively isolated minority group,
    165, 181
  religious education, emphasis on, 167
  Religious Rebels from, 134–35, 167
  and same-faith marriage, 119–20,
    128
  small sample size, 59, 65, 103
  sociological characteristics, 165, 190
  Zealots, 131, 133–35
mothers. *See also* intergenerational
    solidarity; parenting style and
    transmission
  child's preference for religion of, *116*,
    116–17
  in G3, religion of, by affiliation, 116
  and transmission of faith, 71, 76–79,
    77, *78*
  and transmission of nonreligious
    affiliation, 152
  working, and grandparents' influence,
    100
Myers, Scott, 6, 195

National Study of Youth and Religion, 7, 50
National Survey of American Life (NSAL), *213*, 213–14
nature and God, World War I Generation on, 23–24, *52*
New Age spirituality, in subjects, 29
Nones (nonreligious persons)
case studies, 3, *14*, 15, 16, 17, 29, 153–62, 171
as category, interpretation of, 59
distribution of by generation, 1970 *vs.* 2005, 149–50, *150*
diversity of views within, 7, 59–60, 145–46, 146–47
parents' religious tradition, 1970 *vs.* 2005, 151–52, *152*
rate of interfaith marriage among, 114
Rebels from, 133
religious intensity, parent-child similarity over time, 60
stigma attached to, 148
types of, 147
values of, *vs.* religious values, 163
Nones, increase in, 7
during 1960s-70s, 59
distribution of by generation, 149–50, *150*
research on, 150–51
sources and causes of, 103, 148–49, 151–52, *152*, 162–63
Nones affiliation, prevalence of in interfaith marriages, 116–17
Nones affiliation, transmission of, 60, 149, 152, *152*, 163, 189. *See also* Nones grandparent-childsimilarity, change over time; Nones parent-child similarity
case studies, 153–62, 171
and free choice, as issue, 163–64
and institutions, lack of, 163
Nones grandparent-child similarity, change over time, 103, *103*
Nones parent-child similarity, 189
change over time, *58*, 59–60, 151
divorce and, 117, *117*

grandparents and, 108–9
for interfaith marriages, 115, *115*, *116*
intergenerational solidarity and, *75*, 76, *78*
for same-faith marriages, 115, *115*
nonjudgmental attitude, of Millennial Generation, 49–50
NSAL. *See* National Survey of American Life

OMG: A Youth Ministry Handbook (Dean), 10
Orthodox Jews, 172

parent-child closeness. *See* intergenerational solidarity
parent-child similarity, change over time, 65–67, 185
in Biblical literalism, *55*, 55–56, 63–64, *64*, 66
in civic religiosity, *55*, 55–56, 64–65, *65*, 66
presumed decline in, 54
in religious affiliation, *55*, 56, 57–60, *58*, 66
in religious intensity, *55*, 55–56, 60–61, *61*, 66
in religious participation, *55*, 55–56, *62*, 62–63, 66
statistical procedures in measurement of, *218*, 219–20
parenthood, increased age of, 8
parenting style and transmission
ambivalent (mixed-message) parenting, 79, 88–94, 97–98, 186
cold, distant, authoritarian parents, 78–79, 84–88, 97, 186, 190, 194, 196
effective, clergy's views on, 198–99
effective strategies, 96–98, 186, 190, 194, 196, 197–98, 198–99
in Intergenerational Religious Momentum model, *193*, 194
strained or preoccupied parenting, 79, 94–96, 98, 186
types of parenting styles, 79

parenting style and transmission (*Cont.*)
  warm, affirming parenting, 96–98, 186,
    190, 194, 196, 197–98, 198–99
  warm, affirming parents, 79, 80–84,
    140–41, 186
parents
  bonds with, lifetime impact of, 71
  concerns about religious transmission,
    vii, ix, 55, 144, 189, 192
  and transmission, importance of
    understanding, 4, 13, 195
parents, religious influence of. *See also*
    parent-child similarity, change over
    time; transmission
  in Intergenerational Religious
    Momentum model, *193*, 193–94
  ongoing effectiveness of, 185–86,
    195–96
  perceived decline of, 5, 6, 11, 54, 56,
    185–86, 195–96
Pasquale, Frank, 150
peers, influence of, and transmission, 193,
    193
period, in life course theory, 12
Pew Forum report (2008), 59
polarization, increase in
  in Biblical literalism, 64, *64*
  in civic religiosity, 65, *65*
  in religious intensity, 61, *61*
  in religious participation, *62*, 62–63
politicization of religion, increase in,
    148–49
Poole, Adam, *14*, 15, 18
Poole, Anne, *14*, 17, 41
Poole, Barbara, *14*, 15
Poole, Ben G1, 13–14, *14*
Poole, Bruce, 14, *14*, 16, 17
Poole, Dave, *14*, 18
Poole, Edith G1, 13–15, *14*, 24
Poole, Jerry, *14*, 18
Poole, Judy, *14*, 15–16
Poole, Julius ("Jules"), *14*, 15
Poole, Marta, *14*, 16, 38
Poole, Mary, *14*, 16–17, 18
Poole, Michael, *14*, 18
Poole, Nick, *14*, 17–18

Poole, Pat, *14*, 15
Poole family, 13–18, *14*, 19
Popenoe, David, 6
pragmatism, in Generation X, 44
prayer
  by Depression Era Generation, 26
  by Millennials, 47
  by parents for children, 3, 18
  by rejectors of formal religion, 35–36,
    38
  Silent Generation on, 29–30
  by World War I Generation, 24
pressure, religious
  and family religious continuity, 182
  in Mormon church, 167
  and Religious Rebels, 131, 134–35,
    137–38, 142–43, 160–62, 162–63,
    170, 171, 173, 188, 190
Prodigals, Religious
  case studies, 134, 141–42, 143
  definition of, 133, 142, 188
  factors affecting, 143
  life cycle effects and, 203
  Mainline Protestant clergy on, 201–2
  research on, 133
  return, methods of encouraging, 186,
    189, 197
Protestantism
  cultural boundaries surrounding, 121
  reform movements in, 204–5
Pruyser, Paul, 146–47
public life, importance of religion in. *See*
    civic religiosity
Putnam, Robert, 5, 11

quasi-ethnic denominations, 142

Rebels, Religious
  affiliation and, 133
  case studies, 18, 131, 133–35, 135–38,
    138–40, 160–62
  clergy's views on significance of,
    201–2, 204
  definition of, 132, 142, 188
  emotional withdrawal of, 137, 144
  Mormon, high cost incurred by, 167

parenting styles and, 186
percentage contemplating disaffiliation,
vs. actual Rebels, 147
religious pressure and, 131, 134–35,
142–43, 160–62, 162–63, 170, 173,
188, 190
religious revival through, 204–6
research on, 133
terms for, 132
as Zealots, 132–33
Reform Jews, 172
Regnerus, Mark, 196
religion. *See also* religious beliefs;
spirituality *vs.* religion
changes in, 7–8
Early Baby Boomers' definition of,
32–33
and families, connections between, 11
increased politicization of, 148–49
perception of, in Generation X, 43
as refuge in times of social change, 5
vs. spirituality, separation of, 8
religion of place, decline of, 8, 16
religious, as term, Depression Era
Generation on, 26–27
religious affiliation. *See also particular
affiliations*
changes, increasing number of, 54–55
changes, motivation for, 78–79
declining importance of, 56, 128, 148,
185
factors affecting, 56
historical fluctuations in, 203
Later Baby Boomers's willingness to
change, 36, 38
low *vs.* high tension affiliations, 133
as measure of religiosity, 56
and religious rebellion, rate of, 133
religious affiliation, grandparent-child
similarity over time, 102–3, *103*
religious affiliation, parent-child
similarity
change over time, 55, 56, 57–60, *58*,
66
intergenerational solidarity and, *75*,
75–76, *77*, 77–78, *78*

religious beliefs. *See also* articulation of
religious beliefs
aging (life cycle) effects and, 191–92,
203
of Depression Era Generation, 25–28,
51, *52*, 191
of Early Baby Boomers, 31–36, *52*
of Generation X, 39–42, 44, *52*, 191
historical events affecting, 53
of Later Baby Boomers, 36–38, *52*
of Millennial Generation, 45–53, *52*, 191
of Silent Generation, 28–31, *52*, 191
of World War I Generation, 22–24, 51,
52, 191
religious education
cross-generational, 202–3
and family religious continuity, 166,
173, 174, 176, 177–78, 180, 182,
202–3
impact of, 48–49
Millennial Generation and, 48–49, 50
Mormons and, 167
and transmission, 13, 143, 193, *193*
religious identities, linked lives and, 12
religious intensity
definition of, 60
as measure of religiosity, 56
religious intensity, grandparent-child
similarity, 102, *102*, 104, *105*
religious intensity, parent-child similarity,
55, 55–56, 60–61, *61*, 66, 74 *74*, 77
religious leaders
experience of, as confirmation
of Intergenerational Religious
Momentum model, 198–99
on generations, similarities and
differences between, 199–201
need to adapt to changes, 204–5
religious leaders and transmission
importance of understanding, 4, 192,
195, 202–3
influence on, 193, *193*
interest in understanding, 192, 195–98
on significance of transmission rates,
201–2
strategies for, 198–205, 202–4